CAMUS:
THE CHALLENGE OF DOSTOEVSKY

CAMUS:
THE CHALLENGE
OF DOSTOEVSKY

Ray Davison

UNIVERSITY
of
EXETER
PRESS

First published in 1997 by
University of Exeter Press
Reed Hall, Streatham Drive
Exeter, Devon EX4 4QR
UK

British Library Cataloguing in Publication Data
A catalogue record of this book is available
from the British Library

Hardback ISBN 0 85989 531 9
Paperback ISBN 0 85989 532 7

Typeset in 10/12pt Monotype Plantin
by Kestrel Data, Exeter

Printed and bound in Great Britain
by Short Run Press Ltd, Exeter

To Laura, Eleanor and Lydia

Contents

Acknowledgements

A book is always a social product, even though its defects belong entirely to its author. I thus owe a special expression of thanks to Sue Mills who, with care and infinite invention, transformed several hundred pages of opaque manuscript into elegant computer files. In a very real sense, this book would not have reached its final form without her assistance. I can also say that without her perduring interest in the subject, her support and encouragement during the compositional struggles which most authors are not spared, the goal of completion would not have been reached so readily. I am also indebted to Professor Keith Cameron of Exeter University for advice and help with formatting the disk for publication. He gave generously of his time, energy and patience. I am unlikely to be able to reciprocate these favours except by acknowledging them here. I must also thank my sister Sylvia and Professor Robert Niklaus for reading the book in its final stages and for giving me the benefit of their attention and experience. To all my colleagues at Exeter University including Dr David Cowling, who helped me with the bibliography, I also record my debt, for I do not think any of them has been spared my solicitations. I also express appreciation to Professor John Flower of Kent University whose friendship and encouragement have helped to produce this book. Finally, I pay tribute to Professor Philip Thody whose fine inspirational teaching played an important part in my interest in the literature of ideas and to Dr Roger Pensom of Hertford College, Oxford, whose intellectual power and warmth have provided me with so much benefit and illumination over very many years.

Ray Davison
Exeter University, 1997

Introduction

This work is not intended to be an essay in comparative literature, if one means by that the juxtaposition of two writers with the declared objective of exploring and identifying areas of affinity and divergence; nor does it aim to substantiate any intellectually impoverished claim of direct 'influence' of Dostoevsky on Camus. The notion of influence appears curiously outmoded in these days of intertextuality and almost everybody is familiar with the argument that even close resemblance does not necessarily prove influence. Rather, taking as its point of departure Camus's own statements about the impact of reading Dostoevsky upon his intellectual formation and development, the purpose of the book is to describe and demonstrate the ways in which Dostoevsky's thought and fiction, whether Camus agreed or disagreed with its range of ideas and arguments, served to stimulate and crystallize his own thought in several important respects. Indeed, Camus's work appears to be conceived in a profound spirit of debate and dialogue with the Russian writer and the terms of the debate focus on two major issues. First, Dostoevsky believed deeply, like Pascal before him, that without Christian faith and the conviction that the soul is immortal, love of life and real attachment to the world are impossible. Despair, suicide and abulia are, for Dostoevsky, the certain lot of the atheist and the 'unembarked'. He also believed absolutely that, without faith in God, ethical imperatives lose their authority and legitimacy and collapse into nihilism. For this reason, any attempt to build Western socialism or the Kingdom of Man outside authentic Christian parameters was doomed to failure and would degenerate into violence, murder and political tyranny.

Camus was completely fascinated by Dostoevsky's world and likened his encounter with it to a revelation, meaning that it possessed the power to teach us something we already know but are reluctant to acknowledge. First, like Nietzsche and Gide before him, he admired Dostoevsky for his psychological depth. This admiration soon developed into a pervasive preoccupation with the Russian writer as a penetrating analyst and prophet of twentieth-century 'absurd' sensibility. Subsequently, he claimed that Dostoevsky, not Marx or Hegel, was the real prophet of our times, for he had correctly predicted the political future of socialist revolution and had foreseen the dangers of nihilism, Caesarian paternalism, totalitarianism, and *Realpolitik*. However, whatever the depth of his interest in the Russian writer, whether Camus is looking at Dostoevsky as the analyst of the absurd or the prophet of political nihilism, his own thought ultimately challenges Dostoevsky's central theses. Thus, the whole of Camus's early work is designed to demonstrate that absurdity and love of life are not in any way exclusive but are logically interdependent, that a new, positive absurd hero is conceivable and that it is, on the contrary, faith that is the true obstacle to passionate experience of the world. Later, he tried to prove that values can be sustained and legitimized in a world without faith and that a new Hellenic, humanist politics of freedom and justice could rescue politically progressive thought from nihilism and tyranny. This Hellenic humanism is formulated as a lay alternative which is morally superior to Christian-based humanism. These central tenets of Camus's philosophy appear to be articulated as replies to the challenge of Dostoevsky. It is in this sense that Dostoevsky was, for Camus, a critical encounter, a privileged focus and epicentre of dialogue for the exploration and exposition of his own thought and political views which were, simultaneously, so dramatically similar to and, ultimately, so markedly different from those of the Russian writer.

1

Camus and Dostoevsky
An Encounter in Profile

Ever since his appearance, in tandem with Tolstoy, on the French literary scene in the late 1880s,[1] Dostoevsky has held considerable sway over French intellectuals. Writers with such different views as Proust, Gide, Sartre and Nathalie Sarraute,[2] have all found, in Dostoevsky, matters for comment and reflection. Nina Gourfinkel, one of Dostoevsky's prominent French critics, neatly encapsulates this widespread preoccupation with Dostoevsky, in France and elsewhere, when she remarks: 'Dostoïevski est entré dans la circulation sanguine de la société moderne' ['Dostoevsky has entered the blood-stream of modern society'].[3]* Among the names of those expressing an interest in Dostoevsky and claiming his radical importance to the literature of France, is to be found that of Albert Camus, who once observed: 'sans Dostoïevski la littérature française du xxème siècle ne serait pas ce qu'elle est' ['without Dostoevsky, twentieth-century French literature would not be what it is'].[4]

The details of Camus's interest in Dostoevsky make it clear that this was in no sense a passing enthusiasm of his youth or any other particular phase of his existence but a life-long and profound preoccupation. According to Roger Quilliot, his *Pléiade* editor, and Jean Grenier, his philosophy teacher at the *Lycée d'Alger*,[5] Camus began reading Dostoevsky in the early 1930s, a point reinforced by Camus himself who dates the encounter, precisely, in 1933.[6] In March 1938, this interest took a more concrete form when Camus staged Copeau's adaptation of *Les Frères Karamazov* for the *Théâtre de l'Equipe*. Camus not only directed the play but took the part of

*All translations are my own, with communication of meaning rather than stylistic sophistication as my basic aim.

3

Ivan, a character destined to haunt his thinking throughout his life. Looking back at the whole period of his theatrical activity in Algeria and recalling the various parts he had played, Camus could say:

> J'ai aimé par-dessus tout Ivan Karamazov. Je le jouais peut-être mal, mais il me semblait le comprendre parfaitement. Je m'exprimais directement en le jouant.[7]

> [Above all else, I loved Ivan Karamazov. I didn't perhaps play him well but it seemed to me that I understood him perfectly. I was expressing myself directly when playing him.]

In 1942, Camus devoted a substantial section of his first major philosophical essay, *Le Mythe de Sisyphe*, to a study of Dostoevsky.[8] The Russian writer also finds, if anything, a more prominent place in Camus's second philosophical text, *L'Homme révolté*, of 1951. In fact, Dostoevsky is the only writer, among those most often cited by Camus, to figure largely in both philosophical essays. In 1955, when Radio Europe was organizing a tribute to Dostoevsky, Camus wrote a short but revealing article, which he called 'Pour Dostoïevski',[9] where he mentioned that portraits of both Tolstoy and Dostoevsky hung on the walls of his study to indicate his admiration of their genius. In the same article, he refers to his discovery of Dostoevsky in his youth and to his continuing preoccupation with him:

> J'ai rencontré cette œuvre à vingt ans et l'ébranlement que j'en ai reçu dure encore, après vingt autres années.[10]

> [I encountered Dostoevsky's work when I was twenty and its reverberating impact upon me still continues a further twenty years later.]

Later, in 1958, Camus answered a questionnaire, for the first issue of the review, *Spectacles*, concerning his view of Dostoevsky, in which he argues that Dostoevsky's works are of the greatest relevance to the problems of twentieth-century man and that it is Dostoevsky, not Marx, who is the true political prophet of our times.[11] Finally, on 30 January 1959, Camus's own adaptation of Dostoevsky's *Les Possédés* opened at the *Théâtre Antoine* in Paris. The theatre programme contained an important *prière d'insérer* from Camus in which he, once again, refers to the seminal role played by Dostoevsky and, in particular, by *Les Possédés* in his intellectual formation and development:

4

Les Possédés sont une des quatre ou cinq œuvres que je mets au-dessus de toutes les autres. A plus d'un titre, je peux dire que je m'en suis nourri et que je m'y suis formé.[12]

[*Les Possédés* is one of the four or five works that I rank above all others. In more ways than one, I can say that it has enriched and shaped me.]

As is the case of *Les Frères Karamazov*, Camus directed the play but he took no part in the acting. The adaptation had moved to the *Théâtre de Tourcoing* by January 1960 and a special performance was given on the night of Camus's death.[13]

Whilst the above details clearly indicate the continuity of preoccupation with Dostoevsky in Camus's life (Dostoevsky inspires a play at the beginning and end of Camus's career and occupies a key position in both major philosophical texts), they still do not do justice to the depth and range of reference to Dostoevsky in Camus's work. Allusions to Dostoevsky first appear in the *Carnets* in August and December 1938[14] and are a regular feature of Camus's work, capable of appearing in any area of his writing. Thus, references to Dostoevsky occur in Camus's Nobel Prize speech, where he refers to our century's 'grands inquisiteurs'[15] and also in the later 'Conférence du 14 décembre', given at the University of Upsala. Here, Camus argues that Stephan Trophimovitch's desire, in *Les Possédés*, to be 'un reproche incarné' ['a reproach incarnate'] is an inadequate liberal response to the troubles of both his and our own times.[16] Dostoevsky finds his way also into Camus's political journalism, with references in both *Actuelles* I[17] and II,[18] and into his essay on Roger Martin du Gard, where several allusions occur.[19] The collection of essays, *L'Été*, has, at its centre, the fine piece of writing called 'L'Exil d'Hélène', in which Camus voices his nostalgia for the realm of natural beauty in a world of letters increasingly colonized by political preoccupations. Two major references to Dostoevsky occur in the text, one to how 'les paysages' ['landscapes'] are disappearing from Western literature since Dostoevsky, the second to 'les bouffons de Dostoïevski' with their self-absorption and public self-confession.[20] Elsewhere, *La Chute* reveals that Camus has a good knowledge of Dostoevsky's biography,[21] whilst *Carnets* III, composed of material written between 1951 and 1959, contains a whole range of references to the Russian writer. This text reveals a Camus capable of calling Mauriac a 'Dostoïevski de la Gironde' (a kind of inferior, provincial Dostoevsky),[22] and displaying an impressive knowledge of and involvement in many different dimensions of Dostoevsky's work, including details about his membership of the Petrashevski circle[23] and of his celebrated speech about Pushkin which Camus found 'admirable'.[24]

However, explicit and conscious references do not account for all the manifestations of Camus's interest in Dostoevsky. Indeed, Camus's work contains countless echoes and intertextual traces of Dostoevsky, giving the impression, as Germaine Brée has pointed out,[25] that Camus's mind is so impregnated with Dostoevsky's world, that Dostoevsky's universe has so thoroughly penetrated Camus's own, that he spontaneously and perhaps unconsciously reproduces echoes of Dostoevsky in his own books. It will be a central aim of this study to demonstrate how Camus's life and art are marked indelibly by Dostoevsky. However, this claim is not advanced, in any sense, on the basis that Camus was Dostoevsky's 'créature'. On the contrary, the point has to be made that one of the reasons for Camus's interest in Dostoevsky, in both *Le Mythe de Sisyphe* and *L'Homme révolté*, is the fairly technical one that Camus can illustrate his own thought by opposition and contrast. In this sense, Camus is distancing himself from the world of Dostoevsky in both of his major philosophical essays, despite their common preoccupations.

Illustration by contrast is, admittedly, a favoured strategy of Camus in his response to other writers: he frequently uses their works, less perhaps for their autonomous or inherent interest, but more for the particular moments when they either significantly coincide or enter into conflict with his own, sometimes ignoring the specific meanings of various details within the individual author's worlds and, consequently, laying himself open to the charge of distortion. Certainly, Dostoevsky interested him for the purposes of illustration by contrast and, certainly also, there are elements of possible distortion in Camus's presentation of Dostoevsky's world.[26] At the same time, however, the relationship between Camus and Dostoevsky goes far deeper than any such 'technical' considerations, (it is doubtful that the same claim could be made about Camus's interest in, let us say, Jaspers or Husserl who are also both used for the purposes of illustration by contrast in *Le Mythe de Sisyphe*). Distancing and definition by contrast there may well have been from Camus in response to Dostoevsky, but Camus also found, in the Russian writer, a world full of familiar passions and strongly felt affinities. Camus reveals this in two highly significant statements: first, in the course of his study of Dostoevsky in *Le Mythe de Sisyphe*, he says of Dostoevsky's fiction:

Mais quelle prodigieuse création que celle où ces êtres de feu et de glace nous semblent si familiers! Le monde passionné de l'indifférence qui gronde en leur cœur ne nous semble en rien monstrueux. Nous y retrouvons nos angoisses quotidiennes. Et personne sans doute comme Dostoïevski n'a su donner au monde absurde des prestiges si proches et si torturants.[27]

[But what an extraordinary creation is this one, where beings of fire and ice seem so familiar to us. The passionate world of indifference which rumbles in their hearts does not seem in any way monstrous to us. We rediscover there our daily anxieties and, to be sure, nobody, like Dostoevsky, has managed to give the world of absurdity such close and tormented brilliance.]

Some sixteen years later, in the 'Prière d'insérer des *Possédés*', he echoes the point:

Les créatures de Dostoïevski, nous le savons bien maintenant, ne sont ni étranges ni absurdes. Elles nous ressemblent, nous avons le même cœur.[28]

[The creatures of Dostoevsky, we now know well, are neither strange nor absurd. They are like us, we have the same heart.]

These two statements, taken together with the allusion to the 'ébranlement' ['reverberating impact'—literally the term means disorienting jolt, thorough shake-up or upheaval] which he experienced when first reading Dostoevsky,[29] clearly indicate that Camus identified very powerfully with certain aspects of Dostoevsky's world. They fascinate him, throughout his life, as a revelation and exploration of his own preoccupations, problems and anxieties. They provide him with a startling and magnetic exposition of the world of absurdity and moral insecurity. The persuasive force of these consciously felt affinities create a gravitational centre in Dostoevsky's world, which engages Camus in a dialogue that serves to stimulate, crystallize, feed and shape his emerging thought.[30]

This sense of affinity and identity in Camus's encounter with Dostoevsky has, at the same time, an equally powerful and paradoxical antithetical movement which challenges Camus to formulate a reply to Dostoevsky's world. Dostoevsky believed in Christ and the Tzar. His Slavic proclivities alienated him from Western rationalism and he thrived on turbulent ambiguities and contradictions, expressed in a fictional world of compelling half-light and mystery. Camus, on the other hand, was an agnostic Cartesian and

Mediterranean, a consistent supporter of liberal and democratic values, an advocate of mesura and stoical self-possession before fate. The full extent of the paradoxical and contrastive[31] nature of Camus's interest in Dostoevsky is never really explicitly recognized by Camus himself but it is worth noting now to provide a context for the view that Camus's work is informed and fuelled by a spirit of debate and dialogue engendered by his crucial encounter with the challenging world of Dostoevsky. What Camus does have to recognize is that the writer who so perfectly well understood, and transposed into great fiction, the absurd in all its psychological, moral and political complexities, was a Christian with a conviction that life is impossible without faith, and political justice and morality impossible without the absolute authority of God. This, to our way of thinking, is the epicentre of Camus's interest in Dostoevsky, dynamizing him into formulating replies to Dostoevsky's central challenges. Camus knows Dostoevsky's 'underground', as it were, but aspires to lead the Western atheist and agnostic intellectual out of the underground, first towards a positive hedonistic individualism and then towards the community of humanist revolt: *l'homme absurde*, Meursault, and the Hellenic *pensée de midi* will be Camus's replies to Dostoevsky's world of grace and Christian humanism.

Camus's preoccupation with Dostoevsky is conveniently explored in two phases, which follow the pattern of development of Camus's own thought, from *L'Absurde to La Révolte*, between 1942 and 1950. In the first phase, Camus is more concerned with Dostoevsky as the analyst and novelist of the absurd. In the latter phase, it is Dostoevsky the prophet of nihilism and political murder who arouses his interest. The point can be briefly illustrated by Camus's changing perspectives on *Les Possédés* and *Les Frères Karamazov* between 1942 and 1959. In *Le Mythe de Sisyphe*, Camus refers to both novels but he is not at all concerned with their political implications. He is interested in the metaphysical aspects of the characters. He is anxious, for example, to claim Kirilov as a positive absurd hero, Stavroguine as a tzar of indifference and Ivan as a champion of absurd innocence and freedom in a world without God. The political perspectives of both texts are ignored. However, both in *L'Homme révolté* in 1951, and in 1959, at the time of the adaptation of *Les Possédés*, Camus returns to the novels but they are now seen as works of great political prophecy, containing prefigurations of totalitarianism through Chigalev and Ivan's legend of the Grand Inquisitor. Kirilov loses some importance in these new perspectives but Ivan Karamazov and Piotr Verkhovensky of *Les Possédés* become pivotal figures, for Camus, in the history of Western European metaphysical revolt and its perversion into political tyranny. This is not to claim that Camus's interest in Dostoevsky's ideas about the absurdity of life is wholly replaced by a concern with the social and political significance of his works, for both writers approach politics and ethics from a meta-physical standpoint (as distinct from an economic one) and thus the changing optics of Camus's preoccupations are very much com-plementary to each other. However, these distinctions do provide a suitable framework for this study.

The first chapters of this book will, accordingly, concentrate on the relationship between the Camus of *Le Mythe de Sisyphe* and Dostoevsky, the novelist and analyst of the absurd. It begins (Chapter 2) with a detailed consideration of Camus's treatment of Dostoevsky in *Le Mythe de Sisyphe*, noting particularly how Camus uses the Russian writer to illustrate his own ideas or define them by contrast. Chapter 3 explains why two Dostoevskian texts in particular, 'Jugement' ['The Verdict'] and 'Moralité un peu tardive' [Somewhat Belated Morality'], both known to Camus from Dostoevsky's *Journal d'un écrivain*, and both referred to in *Le Mythe de Sisyphe*, should be afforded a special status in the formulation of Camus's understanding of the notion of the absurd. The three subsequent chapters (4 to 6) attempt to assess the impact of Dostoevsky, generally, on Camus's early work. This part of the study is not approached thematically but via an analysis of Camus's interest in those Dostoevskian heroes who seem to attract his attention most in the early years, (Kirilov, Stavroguine and Ivan). This approach can be claimed to be both more interesting and more logical than a thematic approach, for Camus found, in Dostoevsky, not an abstract system of ideas or a particular thematic but a number of flesh and blood characters whose persuasions and attitudes haunted him throughout his existence. In the course of these chapters, echoes of Dostoevsky's presence in Camus's early work are identified or suggested in order to give a sense of the wide-ranging importance of Dostoevsky to the young Camus and to demonstrate how the discursive terms of the suggested debate and dialogue between the two writers find expression and resonance in Camus's fiction and theatre, helping to provide them with their characteristically compelling intellectual and philosophical texture.

A similar approach is used for the latter parts of the study. Chapter 7 uses Ivan and *Les Frères Karamazov* to examine the significance of the role of Dostoevsky in *L'Homme révolté* and, more precisely, in the elaboration of Camus's analysis of the history of metaphysical revolt. Chapter 8 deals with the importance of *Les Possédés* and, in particular, of Chigalev and the younger Verkhovensky's 'droit au

9

déshonneur' ['right to infamy'] in the formulation of Camus's view of nihilism, the will to power and *Realpolitik*. This chapter also attempts to assess the impact of what Camus described as Dostoevsky's prophetic political insight on his own view of Western political life. Camus's dramatization of *Les Possédés* and critical responses to it are also conveniently analysed in this context. Both Chapter 7 and 8 also try to show how *Les Frères Karamazov* and *Les Possédés* were instrumental in providing Camus with a conceptual framework for understanding the relationship between philosophical ideas and their historical and political incarnations. The final chapter throws into an abrupt contrast what most critics legitimately claim to be Camus's most Dostoevskian text, *La Chute*, and what is, arguably, his least Dostoevskian creation, the posthumous *Le Premier Homme*. Here, the intention is, first, to place the guilt-obsessed pronouncements of Clamence within the terms of the debate between Camusian revolt-based humanism and Dostoevsky's world of Christian grace. It poses the question: is Camus's humanism losing its negative/positive equilibrium and moving inexorably towards the very 'underground' of tormented self-doubt and cynicism which Dostoevsky believed would be the lot of all non-believing philanthropists and social reformers? It tries to answer this question in a number of ways and ends by interpreting *Le Premier Homme* as an attempt, by Camus, to extricate himself from Dostoevsky and embrace the world of Tolstoy. Already, in 1955, in his preface to the works of Roger Martin du Gard, Camus had expressed the wish that French literature, in general, should go beyond Dostoevsky, and he dreams of a novel that would combine the French sobriety and classical elegance of Martin du Gard with the density and form of Tolstoy.[32] *Le Premier Homme* can be seen as the partial fulfilment of such a wish and the hesitant beginning of a new, but tragically terminated, emotional cycle in Camus's creative life. The chapter thus distances itself from the line of argument developed in the first major study of *Le Premier Homme* by Jean Sarocchi who uses a comparison with Dostoevsky's *L'Adolescent* to claim that: 'la "Recherche du père", c'est-à-dire la meilleure part du *Premier Homme*, passe par les chemins de Dostoïevski' ['the "Quest for the father", that is to say the greater part of *Le Premier homme* follows a route through the pathways of Dostoevsky'].[33]

This is the first full-length study in English of Camus's interest in Dostoevsky. The earlier works of Irene Kirk[34] and Ernest Sturm[35] are concerned with *La Chute* and *Le Sous-Sol* and take the form of conventional comparative literature in large measure. Garret Green's[36] Stanford Honors essay on Dostoevsky, Berdyaev and

Camus, is a comparative analysis of ideas. There is a body of scholarly work devoted to Camus and Dostoevsky and this is listed in the bibliography and acknowledged as appropriate. This book was nearing completion when Peter Dunwoodie's full-length study in French appeared, *Une Histoire ambivalente: le dialogue Camus-Dostoïevski* (Paris, Nizet, 1996). Beginning with a similar expression of dissatisfaction as my own with the more traditional approaches of comparative literature and convinced that they have nothing further to add to our understanding of Camus's response to Dostoevsky, Dunwoodie opts for a fully-fledged intertextual approach based on the critical work and poetics of Bakhtin. Such an approach conceptualizes the notions of dialogue and debate in more specialized and flexible terms than the ones adopted here. Both Dostoevsky's and Camus's works are identified, by Dunwoodie, as strongly characterized by the twin concepts of 'inachèvement' and 'aporie' (open-endedness and aporia or uncertainty).[37] They thus become Bakhtinian centres of polyphonic discourse which intertextually relate to each other, sometimes explicitly, sometimes implicitly, sometimes consciously, sometime unconsciously. Such a notion of dialogue provides Dunwoodie with the freedom to pursue and capture what he calls:

> la lecture en filigrane de l'intertexte dostoïevskien (parmi d'autres) qui travaille les textes de Camus [and to describe] la dynamique des rapports entre ces œuvres afin de cerner la stratégie de reprise, d'appropriation et de réponses critiques à laquelle l'œuvre de Camus soumet le discours dostoïevskien.[38]

> [the study of the traces of the Dostoevskian intertext (among others) at work in Camus's texts [and to describe] the dynamic system of relationships between the works of both writers with a view to charting the strategy of reiteration, appropriation and critical response to which Camus's work subjects Dostoevsky's discourse.]

The totality of Camus's discourse is examined by Dunwoodie to explore its 'interférences textuelles' ['textual interferences'] with Dostoevsky's and these interferences constitute, in a variety of modes, the 'dialogisme' or 'l'expression d'un jeu d'intertextes' ['the expression of intertextual interplay'] at the heart of Camus's response to the Russian writer. Dunwoodie's work is designed for a more restrictive readership than my own and is also considerably less focused on the world of ideas and politics, although these do figure as part of *'le rapport dialogique'* [*'the dialogical relationship'*—his italics] linking the two writers. Inevitably, there are overlaps between the two books but these are very much outweighed by the differences emanating from the Bakhtinian approach. Wherever possible, I have integrated Dunwoodie's conclusions, if not his methodology, into the body of arguments developed here.

Finally, one further point should be made from the outset: I neither speak nor read Russian, any more than Camus did, who read Dostoevsky in French. I have read Dostoevsky both in English and in French, endeavouring to use the same translations as Camus, when they can be identified. French titles and names are used for Dostoevsky's work throughout the study, except, of course, when they are contained in quotations from English-speaking critics.

2

Dostoevsky and the Absurd Novel

It was stated, in the introduction, that Camus's interest in other writers was frequently governed by the technical idea that he could use their works as a means of illustrating, or defining by contrast, the general lines of his own thought. Intertextual self-definition was, for Camus, as it was for Montaigne, an essential element of his own compositional method: 'On reconnaît sa voie en découvrant les chemins qui s'en éloignent' ['You recognize your own pathway by discovering the ones which lead away from it'].[1] In both of his major philosophical works, Camus selects, to develop his thoughts, writers and thinkers who have meditated on the problems which he is discussing, whose point of departure he feels to be the same as his own but whose conclusions are different. He then tries to show that his own conclusions follow more logically from the common departure point and offers them in opposition to those which he rejects. His interest in Dostoevsky in *Le Mythe de Sisyphe*, in one sense, is no exception to this and a principal aim of this chapter will be to study the precise way in which Camus uses Dostoevsky to advance certain parts of the argument in *Le Mythe de Sisyphe*. At the same time, since Camus's study of Dostoevsky is the chief source of information about his love of the Russian writer during the early period, the chapter will also be used to shed light on those areas of Dostoevsky's thought which most preoccupied Camus at this stage, to provide an overall picture of Camus's attitude and responses to Dostoevsky in the early 1940s and to identify the works with which he was most familiar.

Camus's study of Dostoevsky is incorporated in the third section of *Le Mythe de Sisyphe* which deals with artistic creation within the context of absurd awareness. Here, Camus poses the problem of the relationship between philosophy and art and, more specifically, conceptualizes his notion of the absurd artist and the absurd novel. He indicates the way he intends to use Dostoevsky's works as a fruitful point of reference when he says, as a preface to his study:

> Jusqu'ici ce sont les échecs de l'exigence absurde qui nous ont mieux renseignés sur ce qu'elle est.[2]

> [Until now, it is the failures to satisfy the demands of the absurd that have best illuminated for us what these demands are.]

In other words, Dostoevsky's novels deal with absurd themes but not in a way which is in conformity with Camus's own criteria. Their failure to do so means they can be used in an exemplary way for the purposes of illustration by contrast and can serve as a salutory warning, to absurd novelists of the future, of the dangers of falling into the contradictions which threaten them when attempting to structure absurd themes in art. Such is Camus's preference for illustration of his argument by contrast and by reference to Dostoevsky's 'failure' that he tells us that although he could have used, to exemplify his view of the absurd novel, the work of a writer who had successfully complied with the requisites of absurd art (he claims that Melville's *Moby Dick* could be used in this respect, describing it as one of the 'œuvres vraiment absurdes' ['truly absurd works'] of world literature),[3] his objectives are more productively pursued by using the work of a writer who does not fulfil the precise idea of the truly absurd work of art.

One might expect, from Camus's positioning of the Dostoevsky study in the artistic section of *Le Mythe de Sisyphe* and from the general remarks that Camus makes to introduce the study, that a discussion would follow centred principally on aesthetic matters. However, this is certainly not the case, for the Dostoevsky study is almost totally concerned with philosophical analysis and, for this reason, would not really be out of place in the ideas section of the essay, alongside the remarks about Kierkegaard and Jaspers. Camus certainly does not discuss Dostoevsky's novels in terms of possible aesthetic departures from the principles which he defines as essential to the absurd work of art. For example, he does not examine Dostoevsky's descriptions of the material world to see whether they satisfy 'l'exigence absurde' ['the absurd's demands'] by concerning themselves with the irreducible nature of experience to reason or by concentrating on the proliferation of mime and mirror-images of life to demonstrate the failure of reason to explain existence. Rather, Camus uses Dostoevsky as a novelist who betrays the absurd philosophically in terms of ideas, in precisely the same way as did the Christian existentialist thinkers like Jaspers and Kierkegaard, by making the leap into faith.

It may be that the reason why Camus's arguments, in the Dostoevsky study, focus on philosophical rather than the aesthetic issues which the reader expects, is linked to historical circumstances. It is well known that, in the original, planned edition of *Le Mythe de Sisyphe*, the Dostoevsky study did not figure and an essay on Kafka, which is now an appendix to the main text, was to occupy the pages devoted in the final edition to Dostoevsky. Certainly, the Kafka essay, ruled out because of its possible controversial nature in Nazi-occupied France,[4] is much more concerned with aesthetics than the replacement study. For example, Camus analyses Kafka's symbolism and use of 'le quotidien' ['everyday details'] to see whether they operate in conformity with his absurd novelistic conditions[5] and the whole drift of argument, in the Kafka essay, is much more appropriate to the general context of artistic problems posed in this section of the essay. If historical circumstances account for the change[6] and the possible *non sequitur* in the switch from aesthetic to philosophical matters in the Dostoevsky study, it is, nonetheless, evident that Camus is completely fascinated by Dostoevsky's fictional universe because it embodies a vivid and dramatic exploration of the metaphysics of absurdity and the possible consequences of life without God. In addition, it must be said that if philosophical rather than aesthetic argument dominates Camus's Dostoevsky study in *Le Mythe de Sisyphe*, Camus never forgets that Dostoevsky is a novelist and not a philosopher—he is always sensitive to the existential vitality and dynamism of the characters and events which generate debate in Dostoevsky's novels.

Camus introduces Dostoevsky's work into the framework of *Le Mythe de Sisyphe* by describing it as 'une œuvre où tout soit réuni qui marque la conscience de l'absurde, dont le départ soit clair et le climat lucide' ['a work where everything combines to demonstrate awareness of the absurd, whose point of departure is clear, whose climate is one of lucidity'].[7] In the first part of the study, Camus sets about justifying this assertion by examining Dostoevsky's works to demonstrate that they satisfy the preliminary criteria of absurd works of art. He cannot make Dostoevsky serve an exemplary purpose as 'a failure' without first showing that he starts off on the right lines! He does this by referring to two of Dostoevsky's characters who commit suicide. First, he analyses Dostoevsky's treatment of suicide in the imaginary suicide letter called 'Jugement' which Dostoevsky wrote for the October (Camus says December) 1876 issue of *Journal d'un écrivain.* The letter is unsigned but is written by an imaginary individual who decides to commit suicide because he considers life futile.[8] This is followed by a much longer analysis of the motives which provoke the suicide of the engineer, Kirilov, in *Les Possédés,* and Camus decides that Kirilov's act, like that of the writer of 'Jugement', is rooted in lucid awareness of the absurd. He concludes: 'le thème du suicide chez Dostoïevski est donc bien un thème absurde' ['the theme of suicide in Dostoevsky is thus clearly an absurd theme'].[9] Whilst analysing Kirilov, Camus refers in passing to Stavroguine of *Les Possédés* and to Ivan Karamazov, and satisfies himself that their behaviour too is related to awareness of absurdity and that Dostoevsky is a novelist of the absurd in this preliminary sense: 'Ainsi les romans, comme le *Journal,* posent la question absurde' ['Thus the novels, like the *Journal,* pose the question of the absurd'].[10]

The second part of the study provides a key to the twin polarities of convergence and divergence which characterize Camus's early response to Dostoevsky. He begins by accusing Dostoevsky of a 'renversement métaphysique complet' ['complete metaphysical u-turn'],[11] of a total betrayal of his primary belief in the absurdity of life. He justifies this accusation with two references from Dostoevsky's texts. He quotes an extract from the *Journal,* taken from the entry of December 1876, entitled 'Moralité un peu tardive', where Dostoevsky comments on the lessons to be drawn from his analysis of suicide in 'Jugement'. Here, Dostoevsky explains that several people felt 'Jugement' to be such an overwhelmingly persuasive legitimization of suicide that it could actually augment the number of real suicides. For this reason, Dostoevsky says, it is vital for him to make his intentions clear and he adds:

> Pour moi, ce but [his intentions] était d'une telle évidence qu'involontairement je supposais que cette évidence éclaterait à tous les yeux. Il paraît que je me suis trompé . . . Mon article intitulé 'Jugement' touche à l'idée fondamentale et capitale de l'être humain: la nécessité absolue de croire à l'immortalité de l'âme. Le dessous de cette confession d'un homme qui se tue "par suicide logique", c'est la nécessité d'arriver tout droit à cette conclusion: sans la foi en son âme et l'immortalité de son âme, l'existence humaine est quelque chose de contre-nature, un intolérable non-sens.[12]

> [To me, this intention was so self-evident that unthinkingly I assumed that everybody would see it. It seems that I was mistaken. My article entitled 'The Verdict' deals with the most important

and fundamental idea of human reality: the absolute necessity of believing in the immortality of the soul. The underside of this confession of a man who kills himself "through logical suicide" is the necessity of moving directly to this conclusion: without faith in the existence of one's soul and in the immortality of one's soul, human existence is something unnatural, an unbearable nonsense.]

Dostoevsky concludes this explanation with the following, well-known affirmation, ruefully quoted by a Camus almost painfully averse to acknowledging that this dazzling analyst of the absurd could actually believe in God:

Si la foi en l'immortalité est aussi nécessaire à l'être humain, c'est donc qu'elle est l'état normal de l'humanité. Puisqu'il en est ainsi, l'immortalité de l'âme humaine existe sans aucun doute.[13]

[If faith in immortality is so unecessary to human beings, this is because it is the normal state of humanity. Because this is so, the immortality of the soul exists without any doubt whatsoever.]

Camus has to assert that Dostoevsky's use of this pragmatic argument (since faith in God is necessary, God must exist) means that he is dealing here not with an absurd novelist but with a Christian existentialist one. He confirms this view with a reference to the ending of *Les Frères Karamazov* where Aliocha, Ivan's Christian brother, standing at the grave of Ilioucha, the young boy who dies of consumption, lays the foundation stone of future human solidarity and communal happiness based on a belief in universal resurrection. Kolia, one of Ilioucha's school friends, asks Aliocha:

est-ce vrai ce qui dit la religion, que nous ressusciterons d'entre les morts, que nous nous reverrons les uns les autres, et tous et Ilioucha? [Aliocha replies] Certes nous ressusciterons d'entre les morts, nous nous reverrons, nous nous raconterons joyeusement tout ce qui s'est passé . . .[14]

[is it true what religion says, that we will be reborn from the dead, that we will all see each other again? Certainly we shall be reborn, we shall see each other again, we shall tell each other joyously everything that has happened.]

Using the ending of *Les Frères Karamazov* and the theist affirmations of 'Moralité un peu tardive', Camus is able to accuse Dostoevsky of betraying the absurd by using it as a 'tremplin d'éternité', a springboard to faith. He classes Dostoevsky as a Christian existentialist novelist who makes the illogical 'saut'. 'Ce n'est donc pas un romancier absurde qui nous parle, mais un romancier existentiel'['It is thus not an absurd novelist who speaks to us here but an existential novelist'].[15] Camus can thus claim that Dostoevsky is not an absurd novelist because he announces the possibility of faith as a solution to the absurd.[16]

By describing, as betrayals of the absurd, Dostoevsky's statements about immortality in the *Journal* and *Les Frères Karamazov*, Camus presumably hoped to illustrate by contrast his conception of the absurd novel. However, it is precisely as an attempt to illustrate such an idea that Camus's study of Dostoevsky is unsatisfactory. Since he discusses Dostoevsky solely in terms of ideas, his whole argument seems to be that if Dostoevsky had not introduced the idea of a religious solution to the problem of absurdity into his work, he would have been an absurd novelist. By limiting his focus to ideas, Camus merely succeeds in illustrating the philosophical content of the absurd novel as one in which we see man's passionate attempt to find a meaning for existence and his failure to do so.[17] The absence of faith or any other transcendent notion is the *sine qua non* of the absurd work of art. In this respect, Camus could argue that *Les Frères Karamazov* is not an absurd novel simply because the religious solution is advanced. However, the absurd novel is not simply defined by its contents. It has other characteristics which play no part in Camus's discussion of Dostoevsky as an absurd novelist for the unsurprising reason that Camus is completely absorbed by Dostoevsky's depiction of a world without grace. For example, Camus does not consider whether the act of writing a novel was gratuitous for Dostoevsky, as it should be for the authentic absurd novelist.[18] Neither does he examine whether Dostoevsky's descriptive and narrative art limits itself to the task, essential again, according to Camus, for the truly absurd writer, which is not to 'raisonner le concret' ['explain the concrete'] but to describe and report only the appearance of the physical world in all its variety and colour without any attempt to explain and make reference to essences. Nor is there any reference to the quantitative ethic to judge whether Dostoevsky is concerned, as a writer, to exhaust life's potentialities through vicarious hedonism and to augment the sense of existence by its fictional transpositions (for the absurd writer, in Camus's eyes, pursues quantity in the immediate, just like Don Juan and Sisyphus).[19]

The limits of Camus's discussion of Dostoevsky as an absurd novelist are most evident in his analysis of *Les Possédés*. Camus has no need to enter into any detailed examination of the claims of *Les*

Frères Karamazov to be an absurd novel since the religious thesis, offered by Aliocha, automatically excludes it from consideration. However, the case of *Les Possédés* is more problematic since the religious solution is not offered explicitly in the text. Camus, however, does not try to claim *Les Possédés* as an absurd novel. He restricts himself to stating that Stavroguine and Kirilov incarnate absurd attributes. Camus's study of Kafka is superior in this respect, for he feels able to claim that *The Trial* is a perfectly successful absurd novel.[20] Camus's reluctance to claim that *Les Possédés* is an absurd novel may well be explained by the fact that he knew something of the history of the composition of this work. He would thus have known that the absence of any pro-religious optic was the result of censorship and not part of Dostoevsky's original design. This involved a struggle between Divine and Demonic principles, with the former victorious. Stavroguine, the voice of atheism, representing the Anti-Christ, was to meet Tikhone, the bishop who embodies the Christian ethic in all its Dostoevskian paradoxical love and humour. The confrontation between the two was to take place in the chapter, 'Chez Tikhone', where Stavroguine was to read a confession of his sins to the bishop and the bishop was to triumph. However, owing to certain references concerning the violation of a child, the chapter was rejected by the *Russian Messenger,* the review publishing the work, and Dostoevsky had to prune the episode.[21] Be that as it may, it is the absence of any real discussion of the absurd novel *qua* novel, in the Dostoevsky study, which leads one to the view that, despite its positioning in the artistic section, Camus was far more interested in Dostoevsky as a writer/novelist who makes the existential leap into faith and betrays the absurd by intellectual suicide.

When he describes Dostoevsky as 'un romancier existentiel',[22] Camus is deliberately linking the Russian writer to the thinkers analysed in the earlier part of *Le Mythe de Sisyphe* who have already been charged by him with a betrayal of logic and reason, either by way of 'la raison humiliée' ['reason humiliated'] (Jaspers, Kierkegaard) or 'la raison triomphante' ['reason triumphant'] (Husserl).[23] Camus finds Dostoevsky's affirmation of faith as illogical as theirs and he does not miss the opportunity of reiterating his condemnation of them through Dostoevsky. In fact, Camus's condemnation of Dostoevsky is very strongly worded, almost as if Camus is actually disappointed and angered, as it were, by Dostoevsky's faith. He remarks: 'La réponse de Dostoïevski est l'humiliation, "la honte" selon Stavroguine' ['Dostoevsky's reply is humiliation, "shame" according to Stavroguine'].[24] Moreover, one feels that Camus is thinking of Dostoevsky specifically when he writes, in *Le Mythe de*

Sisyphe, just before the Dostoevsky study: 'Il y a tant d'espoir tenace dans le cœur humain. Les hommes les plus dépouillés finissent quelquefois par consentir à l'illusion.' ['There is so much tenacious hope in the heart of man. Even those who are stripped of it to the maximum sometimes end by giving in to illusion'].[25] His enthusiasm for Dostoevsky certainly ebbs at this point and he doesn't show the same level of interest in Dostoevsky's Christian heroes—Aliocha and Zosime—for example: he prefers those who try to live without faith and without denying their lucidity and their logic. Admittedly, Dostoevsky's anti-Christians are powerful creations in their own right: despite, and sometimes because of, their amoral proclivities and evil tendencies, they attract and fascinate. As M. T. Sajkovic rightly observes:

> Not a few critics have been drawn to the negative philosophy carried by the 'great rebels'. Their power and strength has fascinated, like Milton's Satan in *Paradise Lost,* and has occupied the critics rather than the sublime figures, Sonia, Prince Muishkin and Alyosha. The latter are 'pale' and 'ineffectual' beside the colossal atheists.[26]

However, Camus's interest goes deeper than this romantic fascination with the demonic; he sees the rebels as his allies in their determination to live without God. In Camus's eyes, Dostoevsky has betrayed his great atheists and his own lucidity of mind by yielding to divine temptation. This is the sense of Camus's remarks: 'Le créateur [Dostoïevski] choisit contre ses personnages' ['The creator [Dostoevsky] makes a choice in oppostion to his own characters'], and, later: 'La réponse de Dostoïevski est l'humiliation, "la honte" selon Stavroguine . . . Ainsi Kirilov, Stavroguine et Ivan sont vaincus. *Les Karamazov* répondent aux *Possédés.* Et il s'agit bien d'une conclusion' ['Dosteovsky's reply is humiliation, "shame" according to Stavroguine. *Les Frères Karamazov* is a reply to *Les Possédés.* And it is indeed a conclusion'].[27] These judgements concerning Dostoevsky's 'saut', his choice of 'humiliation' and his 'betrayal' of Ivan, Stavroguine and Kirilov, all spring from Camus's aversion to Christian existentialist apologetics. Whether it is Pascal, Dostoevsky, Jaspers or Kierkegaard that Camus has in focus, he loves their visions of life without God for their integrity, authenticity and power, but he strongly repudiates the religious hypothesis that they infer, of necessity, from the disgraced state. Dostoevsky then, in Camus's eyes, falls from grace paradoxically when he declares his faith in God. Camus prefers the rebels who would die rather than abandon their lucidity. They refuse to make the 'saut' and prefer the reality of this world to the illogical propositions concerning the next one. Dostoevsky's rebels display more intellectual authenticity than their creator, for they, like Camus's *l'homme absurde*, despite their nostalgia for faith, reject the 'dérobade', or the evasion through hope for and belief in the next world.

As with the Christian existentialists in general, Camus is not criticizing Dostoevsky's Christian faith as such but rather that faith which is born of acute awareness of the absurdity of life, that form of religious apologetics rooted in Pascal and Tertullian. Camus finds the logic which goes from absurdity to faith quite suspect. It is not surprising, therefore, to find that, having linked Dostoevsky to the Christian existentialists in the first part of his study, he goes on to question the reality of Dostoevsky's belief in God. He does this in two ways. First, he appears to believe that Dostoevsky's leap into faith is somehow related to the fact that he was a novelist. He says, for example, of Dostoevsky's declaration of faith: 'Ici encore le saut est émouvant, donne sa grandeur à l'art qui l'inspire' ['Here again the leap is moving, giving greatness to the art which inspires it'].[28] Translated literally, this implies that the leap is inspired by the novelist's art and Camus does, indeed, argue, in *Le Mythe de Sisyphe*, that the novel form is the one where 'la tentation d'expliquer demeure la plus grande, où l'illusion se propose d'elle-même, où la conclusion est presque immanquable' ['the temptation to explain remains greatest, where illusion proposes itself spontaneously, where to conclude is almost unavoidable'].[29] This is to explain Dostoevsky's faith in terms of the internal dynamics of the novel which relentlessly, for Camus, seek explanation, although the absurd artist must resist this temptation to explain. A second interrogative is placed before Dostoevsky's faith when Camus begins to probe the history of the composition of *Les Frères Karamazov*. He quotes Dostoevsky's famous letter of 1870:

> Parlant des *Karamazov*, Dostoïevski écrivait: 'La question principale qui sera poursuivie dans toutes les parties de ce livre est celle dont j'ai souffert consciemment ou inconsciemment toute ma vie: l'existence de Dieu.'[30] Il est difficile de croire qu'un roman ait suffi à transformer en certitude joyeuse la souffrance de toute une vie.[31]

> [Speaking of *The Karamazovs*, Dostoevsky wrote: 'The main question to be explored in all parts of this book is the one which has caused me suffering, consciously and unconsciously, throughout my life: the existence of God.' It is difficult to believe that a novel was enough to transform a life-long suffering into joyous certainty.]

Camus thus doubts that Dostoevsky shared Aliocha's certainty about immortality and he gleefully notes Boris de Schlœzer's comment that Dostoevsky composed the anti-theist parts of *Les Frères Karamazov* in just three weeks, in a state of exaltation, whilst the theist part took three months labour.[32] This is a more cogent and interesting thesis than the previous one about the inherent explanatory pressures of novelistic art and is central to Dostoevskyian critical debate especially since Bakhtin emphasized that polyphony was germane to Dostoevsky's world and that the author's voice is always in dialogue with many others in the text. Certainly, Dostoevsky's faith is far from comfortably secure. He admitted once that, to his dying day, he would remain 'l'enfant de l'incroyance et du doute' ['the child of disbelief and doubt'].[33] However, if Dostoevsky sometimes found it hard to believe securely in God, he was most certainly convinced of the impossibility of life without God and this schism in his faith generated the great tormented atheists of his best novels. Camus's suspicion of Dostoevsky's faith indicates that he was almost unable to believe that anybody who could describe absurdity with such power and depth could possibly transcend that reality. George Strem has aptly remarked:

> Camus does not seem to believe that anyone who has the ability to dissect the reasoning of the rebels—the social and especially the metaphysical rebels—with such consummate skill as Dostoevsky, could be sincere when he turned against that rebellion, discarding his reason to accept the solution dictated by faith.[34]

This is another way of saying that Camus simply cannot accept Christian existentialist apologetics, especially in the case of Dostoevsky. Dunwoodie opens up further perspectives on Camus's probing of the foundations of Dostoevsky's faith by bringing Bakhtin into the forefront of debate. Arguing that Camus is right to go beyond his apparent identification of Dostoevsky's voice with Aliocha's, Dunwoodie situates the question of Dostoevsky's faith in the interplay of voices operating between character and author in his novels. From this viewpoint the question of faith is, Dunwoodie claims, irreducible. He also cites, in support of his claim, Dostoevsky's statements, made on separate occasions, to the effect that *both* the theist and atheist parts of *Les Frères Karamazov* would be irrefutable culminating points of the novel. As Dunwoodie says:

> Réfuter l'irréfutable en deux points culminants d'un même roman, voilà bien l'image d'un débat irréductible.[35]

[To refute the irrefutable in two culminating points in the same novel, here indeed is the picture of an irreducible debate.]

It is most interesting to note that, in this discussion of the authenticity of Dostoevsky's Christianity, Camus does not concern himself directly with any of the mystical sources of Dostoevsky's faith. He is content to focus on what E. H. Carr defined as the 'pragmatic' aspect of his Christianity,[36] that aspect which is manifest in the Russian writer's declaration that immortality is not a consolation but a necessity and that in moments of anguish, such as when a member of the family dies, 'on a soif de la foi comme de "l'herbe déssechée" ' ['one thirsts after faith like "parched grass" '][37] and that one finds faith eventually 'parce que la vérité devient évidente dans le malheur' ['because truth becomes self-evident in misfortune'].[38] However, Dostoevsky also experienced moments of great peace and harmony when he felt at one with the world and, in these privileged moments, his faith was serene. In another famous letter of 1854, he remarked:

Dieu m'envoie parfois des instants où je suis tout à fait paisible; à ces instants-là, j'aime et je me sens aimé par les autres, et c'est à ces instants-là que j'ai formé en moi un *credo* où tout est clair et sacré pour moi. Ce credo est très simple, le voici: croire qu'il n'est rien de plus beau, de plus profond, de plus sympathique, de plus raisonnable, de plus viril et de plus parfait que le Christ; et je me dis avec un amour jaloux non seulement qu'il n'y a rien mais qu'il ne peut rien y avoir. Plus encore, si quelqu'un me prouvait que le Christ est en dehors de la vérité, et qu'il serait réel que la vérité fût dehors du Christ, j'aimerais mieux alors rester avec le Christ qu'avec la vérité.[39]

[God sometimes sends me moments when I am completely at peace; at such moments, I love and feel myself loved by others, and during such moments I have formulated within myself a credo where everything is clear and sacred for me. This credo is very simple, and this is it: to believe that nothing is more beautiful, more profound, more wise and more perfect than Christ; and I say to myself with a jealous love, not only that there is nothing but that there can be nothing. Furthermore, if somebody were to prove to me that Christ is outside of truth and that it would be convincing to believe that truth was outside of Christ, I would then prefer to stay with Christ than to be with the truth.]

These sacred moments of unshakeable faith were experienced by Dostoevsky during attacks of epilepsy. They are not regarded by

Dostoevskian criticism as the cause of his faith, or even at the root of it[40] but these seizures are certainly of importance in the artistic and philosophical *formulation* of Dostoevsky's notion of grace and transcendence. The Russian writer also injects traces of the ecstasy and harmony experienced during such epileptic moments of 'holy madness' into the characters of Kirilov and Muichkine.[41] Camus is not only well aware of these moments and most sensitive to their manifestations in these two characters who attract him, in large measure, precisely because of these characteristics. However, he never relates these experiences of harmony and serenity to Dostoevsky's religious beliefs. As we shall see in our later chapter on Kirilov, Camus actually assimilates these moments to his own notions of 'grace' without God, developed in the pagan/ Mediterranean lyricism of *Noces* and expressed in one of Camus's favourite statements in his early writings: 'Tout est bien' ['All is well']. These words constituted, for Camus, both the essence of Greek wisdom and *mesura* before fate (seen in Œdipus's acceptance of his punishment), the key to his own lucid hedonism before death, incarnated in Sisyphus, and were also central to the experience of Kirilov and Muichkine. However, by severing the link between Kirilov's notion of harmony and Dostoevsky's epilectic seizures as well as by ignoring the Russian writer's view of them as revelations of a transcendent reality, Camus is able to ally Kirilov's moments of serenity and equanimity to his own paganism and thus produce an unusual interpretation of the engineer as a positive and optimistic character. In doing so, he is trying to prove a point about Dostoevsky's faith, that it is pragmatic and unconvincing and that Dostoevsky's atheists do not share their creator's vision of a godless world as impossible for consciousness to bear.[42] In this way, it can be claimed that Dostoevsky's christian mysticism is hijacked by Camus and rerouted through his own hedonism and positivism. Camus would thus appear to be trying consciously to create a non-theist world which has all the ecstatic visionary power of Dostoevsky's Christian transcendence but is grounded in rational lucidity before fate. This will constitute his initial strategy for a way of responding to the challenge of Dostoevsky and producing an answer to him.

Having spread sufficient doubt to undermine the foundations of Dostoevsky's faith in his own mind, Camus is able to declare, at the end of his Dostoevsky study:

> Ce qui contredit l'absurde dans cette œuvre, ce n'est pas son caractère chrétien, c'est l'annonce qu'elle fait de la vie future. On

peut être chrétien et absurde. Il y a des exemples de chrétiens qui ne croient pas à la vie future.[43]

[What contradicts the absurd in this work, is not its Christian character but its declaration of an after-life. One can be Christian and absurd. There are examples of Christians who do not believe in the after-life.]

Claiming, in addition, that it is possible to ally New Testament writing with absurd sensibility, Camus states that Dostoevsky begins by arguing that existence is either 'mensongère *ou* éternelle' and ends with a surprising reply to the challenge of his atheists, especially to Kirilov, that 'l'existence est mensongère *et* elle est éternelle' ['Existence is either illusory *or* eternal . . . existence is illusory *and* eternal'][44]

Despite the doubts and whatever the ambiguity which Camus sensed at the root of Dostoevsky's faith, he has to concede that the Russian writer 'choisit contre ses personnages' ['chooses against his characters'] and that, in consequence:

Ce n'est pas d'une œuvre absurde qu'il s'agit ici, mais d'une œuvre qui pose le problème absurde . . . une œuvre absurde au contraire ne formait pas de réponse, voilà toute la difference.[45]

[It is not an absurd work that is in question here but a work which poses the problem of the absurd . . . an absurd work, on the contrary, formulates no reply, that is where the whole difference lies.

For all its general interest as an expression of Camus's enthusiasm for Dostoevsky, the Dostoevsky study, in the *Mythe de Sisyphe*, does not articulate adequately Camus's notion of the absurd novel or succeed in giving a clear picture of the road the absurd artist should follow in order to avoid repeating the 'saut' of Dostoevsky. What it does do, however, is to draw very clearly the lines of convergence and divergence between the two writers and to reveal the powerful attraction which Camus felt towards Dostoevsky's world and his disinclination to accept the authenticity of its transcendent dimension. However, the presence of Dostoevsky in *Le Mythe de Sisyphe* is not confined to the Dostoevsky study nor are the subjects of debate restricted to those explicitly tackled by Camus in this specific part of *Le Mythe de Sisyphe*. The whole of *Le Mythe de Sisyphe* can be said to function in diverse ways as a Camusian response to his reading of Dostoevsky.

3

Suicide and Logic
Camus's use of Dostoevsky's 'Jugement' and 'Moralité un peu tardive' in *Le Mythe De Sisyphe*

The very strong impression that *Le Mythe de Sisyphe* was conceived in a spirit of debate and opposition to Dostoevsky is not only conveyed by that section of the essay devoted to him. In addition to the explicit responses formulated by Camus to Dostoevsky's views on immortality and the absurd, the general lines of argument of *Le Mythe de Sisyphe* appear to contain an implicit challenge to Dostoevsky's concept of logical suicide. Camus discusses the idea of logical suicide in the early part of his essay but without reference to Dostoevsky, save for the single mention of Kirilov as one of the few people ever to carry their logic to its absolute conclusion. Despite the lack of explicit reference, however, a number of analogies and marked contrasts between the concept of logical suicide outlined in the essay and Dostoevsky's own treatment of the same subject suggest that Camus was, once again, defining himself in opposition to Dostoevsky in the earlier part of his essay. In the Dostoevsky study, Camus does, of course, mention the Russian writer's views on logical suicide but without actually challenging them or defining himself in opposition to them in that context. He certainly does not acknowledge that the question of logical suicide, raised in the opening section of *Le Mythe de Sisyphe*, has any link with Dostoevsky's world. Despite this, there are grounds for believing that Camus's treatment of the theme of suicide is an implicit reversal of Dostoevsky's and that the diametrically opposed conclusions which Camus and Dostoevsky draw from the absurd (Camus rejects both logical suicide and the inference of immortality, whereas Dostoevsky accepts both) indicate that *Le Mythe de Sisyphe* generally is written, in one sense, as a reply to Dostoevsky and, more precisely, as a reply to his ideas as they are expressed in 'Jugement' and 'Moralité un peu tardive'. This claim would suggest that Dostoevsky was a key figure in stimulating and crystallizing Camus's concept of the absurd, that his inclusion in *Le Mythe de Sisyphe* goes far beyond any consideration of Camus's predilection for the technique of illustration by contrast or of the historical circumstances relating to Kafka.

There are a number of reasons for isolating in this way these two extracts from Dostoevsky's *Journal d'un écrivain*, 'Jugement' and 'Moralité un peu tardive', both of which were known to Camus since they are both cited in the Dostoevsky study.[1] First, it is in these texts that the oppositions, despite a multitude of affinities, are grasped most clearly and that the idea of a debate most forcefully suggests itself. Secondly, by their concentration of argument and crucial lack of ambiguity, they can be said to be texts of considerable impact when it comes to grasping Dostoevsky's general lines of thought and are thus capable of crystallizing debate and opposition in a very focused way. As Sajkovic rightly states, 'Dostoevsky did not "systematize his dialectic" '[2] but these two articles do constitute a considerable move in that direction and they are often used by critics because of their pithiness, clarity and unique value as an expression of the Russian writer's world-view. Although Camus found, in Dostoevsky, not an abstract thinker but an artist capable of creating living characters who fascinated him (and nobody could deny the impact of these characters upon Camus), from the viewpoint of the general argument of *Le Mythe de Sisyphe* about logical suicide, 'Jugement' and 'Moralité un peu tardive', because of their propositional and discursive nature, should be accorded a special role as shaping and crystallizing agencies.[3]

A first general point to make in defence of the idea that *Le Mythe de Sisyphe* was written as a reply to 'Jugement' and 'Moralité un peu tardive' is that the two works in question postulate, as logical deductions from a belief in the absurdity of life, the very two standpoints which Camus endeavours, in *Le Mythe de Sisyphe*, to refute as illogical. In his *Journal* entries, Dostoevsky argues that it is impossible to love life if one considers it to have no meaning: suicide or faith, he claims, are logical deductions from the absurd:

Sans la conviction de son immortalité sur terre, les liens de l'homme avec la terre se relâchent, deviennent plus fragiles, pourrissent, et la perte du sens supérieur de la vie, lequel peut fort bien n'être ressenti que sous forme de nostalgie, conduit sans aucun doute au suicide. C'est pourquoi voici la moralité de mon article d'octobre ['Jugement']. Si la foi en l'immortalité est aussi nécessaire à l'être humain, c'est donc qu'elle est l'état normal de l'humanité. Puisqu'il en est ainsi, l'immortalité de l'âme humaine existe sans aucun doute. En un mot, l'idée de l'immortalité, c'est la vie même, la vie vivante, sa formule définitive, la source principale de la vérité pour le genre humain et de la conscience de ce qui est juste.[4]

[Without the conviction of one's immortality on Earth, the links between man and Earth slacken, become more fragile, decay, and the loss of the sense of life's higher meaning, which may well only be felt in the form of nostalgia, inevitably leads to suicide. That is the moral of my October article ('Jugement'/'The Verdict'). If faith in immortality is so necessary to human beings, this is because it is the normal state of humanity. Because this is so, the immortality of the soul exists without any doubt whatsoever. In short, the idea of immortality is life itself, the life living, its definitive formulation, the principal source of truth for the human race and of awareness of what is finite.]

In the same section, Dostoevsky attacks those intellectuals, alienated from Russian culture and religious traditions, who, with their 'concepts de fer' ['cast-iron concepts'] and 'doutes positifs' ['positivist doubts'], believe in the imperative 'vivre à tout prix' ['live whatever the price may be'].

Camus develops diametrically opposed viewpoints in *Le Mythe de Sisyphe*. As well as objecting to the logic which goes from absurdity to faith and describing it as an illogical leap, he denies that suicide is a logical reponse to the absurd and argues that life is all the more precious because it is finite. Suicide betrays the logic of the absurd by destroying the lucid awareness that gives rise to it. Suicide is thus akin to the Christian existentialist leap into faith: it runs away from the truth. Moreover, recognition that the absurd is inescapable logically, either through suicide or faith, provides mankind with a powerful incentive to enjoy life as much as possible before death, as this world is our only world. Absurd awareness and love of life are not only compatible, contrary to Dostoevsky's most powerful conviction, but are logically linked or, as Camus puts it:

[La vie] sera d'autant mieux vécue qu'elle n'aura pas de sens.[5]

[(Life) is all the better lived for having no meaning at all.]

and

On ne découvre pas l'absurde sans être tenté d'écrire quelque
manuel de bonheur . . . Le bonheur et l'absurde sont deux fils de
la même terre. Ils sont inséparables.[6]

[One does not discover the absurd without being tempted to write
a manual of happiness . . . Happiness and the absurd are two sons
of the same soil. They are inseparable.]

Not only this, but if the absurdity of life renders it more precious
and pleasurable, religious faith and a belief in immortality would, in
consequence, according to Camus, devalue life and rob it of its
passionate intensity. In Dostoevsky, then, awareness of the absurd
is a corrosive anguish, alienating humanity from pleasures and love
and condemning us to a sense of futility and even to suicide unless
we yield to the logical necessity of faith. Camus, however, rejects
both suicide and faith and argues that the absurd, far from being an
inescapable source of anguish for the non-believer, can unleash the
greatest of passions for life. This diametrical opposition between
the two writers and the precise antithetical relationship between the
arguments of the *Journal* and those of *Le Mythe de Sisyphe* lend
support to the idea of a reply and a debate. This does not mean, of
course, that Camus is exclusively replying to Dostoevsky or that his
views concerning love of life are only directed at the Russian writer.
Camus defines himself in opposition to Christian existentialists
generally and there is a general anti-Christian offensive in his early
work, linked to the idea that belief in the next world weakens our
attachment to this one.[7] Nevertheless, Dostoevsky's part in stimulating Camus's thought in the essay should be considered significant
for a number of reasons. First, 'Jugement' and 'Moralité un peu
tardive' were well known to Camus and he quotes substantially from
them in his Dostoevsky study. Both Dostoevsky's texts are a powerful
and concentrated statement of the principal issues raised in *Le Mythe
de Sisyphe* about suicide, logic and love of life. Additionally, one must
take into account and try to give some meaning to the remarks
which Camus makes about his encounter with the works of
Dostoevsky at the age of twenty. The 'ébranlement', of which he
spoke, indicates that he was both stimulated and disturbed by his
reading of Dostoevsky and thus emphasizes the Russian writer's role
as a crystallizer. In *Le Mythe de Sisyphe* itself, Camus says of
Dostoevsky:

personne sans doute comme Dostoïevski n'a su donner au monde absurde des prestiges si proches et si torturants.[8]

[without a doubt nobody like Dostoevsky has managed to give the world of absurdity such close and tormented brilliance.]

and

Voici une œuvre où dans un clair-obscur plus saisissant que la lumière du jour, nous pouvons saisir la lutte de l'homme contre ses espérances.[9]

[Here is a work where, in a twilight more dazzling than the light of the day, we can seize the struggle of man against his hopes.]

These remarks testify to his deep involvement in Dostoevsky and it is noteworthy that Camus makes no comparable remarks about other writers analysed in *Le Mythe de Sisyphe*. It is not unreasonable, therefore, to accord a privileged status to Dostoevsky's work as a crystallizing voice in Camus's early formation.

Several other points can be made to defend the idea that *Le Mythe de Sisyphe* was written partly as a reply to 'Jugement' and 'Moralité un peu tardive'. The first is related to the theme of logical suicide itself. It may well be, as Strem and others have suggested,[10] that the entire thematic of logical suicide, in the early Camus, originates in Dostoevsky's 'Jugement', 'Moralité un peu tardive' and *Les Possédés* (through the character of Kirilov). Suicide is certainly a dominant theme in the early work, although it is replaced by murder, in large measure, during the revolt period, possibly indicating that neither is a 'personal' theme.[11] Apart from being the major theme of *Le Mythe de Sisyphe*, suicide appears in *Le Malentendu*,[12] *Caligula*,[13] and haunts Camus momentarily in *L'Envers et l'endroit*[14] The question has to be asked: why are there so many references to suicide in Camus's early work which, he tells us from the beginning, will only express his 'amour de vivre'[15] and when he also declared, in countless interviews, such as the one with É. Simone in *Actuelles* I:

Je suis né pauvre, sous un ciel heureux, dans une nature avec laquelle on sent un accord, non une hostilité. Je n'ai donc pas commencé par le déchirement, mais par la plénitude.[16]

[I was born poor, under a felicitous sky, in a natural order with which one feels accord not conflict. I did not begin my life with a sense of being torn apart but with one of plenitude.]

If Camus's love of life and feelings of plenitude are real enough, the thematic of suicide would best be described as a dramatic device, allowing him to give full expression to his love by rejecting suicide. If this is so, then it could be further argued that Camus's pre-occupation with suicide, in his early work, does not result from or reflect any deeply felt interest or temptation but is rather more an intellectual preoccupation, with Dostoevsky as one of its major crystallizing agents.

It is worth noting that Quilliot and Faucon take different positions on the question of Camus and suicide. Quilliot is inclined to the view that the theme is functional and used to underline love of life:

> Pourquoi vivre? De *l'Envers et l'endroit* au *Mythe de Sisyphe*, la même question retentit dans son œuvre . . . Mais la réponse est dans la question même. En fait, Camus ne s'est jamais demandé: dois-je continuer à vivre? faut-il se suicider dans le monde tel qu'il est? mais plutôt: pourquoi ai-je continué de vivre?[17]

> [Why live? From *L'Envers et l'endroit* to *Le Mythe de Sisyphe*, the same question resounds in his work . . . But the reply is in the question itself. In fact, Camus never asked himself: must I continue to live? is it necessary to kill oneself in this world as it is? but rather: why have I continued to live?]

Suicide for Quilliot, as for Thody, who says Camus uses the suicide theme 'principally to begin the essay in as startling and dramatic a way as possible',[18] is, basically, affirmation of life by contrast.[19] Faucon, however, argues that Camus probably thought seriously about committing suicide between 1936 and 1937 (an unhappy period of Camus's life, despite the Algerian setting) and that *Le Mythe de Sisyphe* was conceived at that time, in some measure, as a result of this personal temptation:

> En 1936 et 1937, écarté par la maladie des objectifs qu'il avait choisis, voué à la routine des besognes alimentaires, déçu dans ses adhésions politiques, meurtri par son échec conjugal, Camus a pu être frôlé par la tentation du suicide.[20]

> [In 1936 and 1937, prevented by illness from pursuing his chosen objectives, completely sucked into the routine of earning his daily bread, disappointed in his political allegiances, bruised by conjugal failure, Camus may well have been touched by the temptation to commit suicide.]

Camus, of course, states in *Le Mythe de Sisyphe*, that any normal person contemplates suicide, and this would strengthen Faucon's view that the suicide theme is of personal origin. Then, there is the very important entry in *Carnets*, in March 1936, the period referred to by Faucon, which concerns a man tempted by suicide:

> Il posait tous les soirs cette arme sur la table. Le travail fini, il rangeait ses papiers, approchait le revolver et y plaquait son front, y roulait ses temps, apaisait sur le froid du fer la fièvre de ses joues. Et puis il restait ainsi un long moment, laissant errer ses doigts le long de la gachette, maniant le cran d'arrêt, jusqu'à ce que le monde se tût autour de lui et que, somnolent déjà, tout son être se blottit dans la seule sensation du fer froid et salé d'où pouvait sortir la mort. Dès l'instant où l'on ne se tue pas, il faut se taire sur la vie. Et lui se réveillant, la bouche pleine d'une salive déjà amère, léchait le canon de l'arme, y introduisit sa langue et, râlant d'un bonheur sans fond, répétait avec émerveillement: 'ma joie n'a pas de prix.'[21]

> [Every evening, he would place this weapon on the table. His work finished, he would tidy his papers, draw the revolver near, stick his forehead against it, roll his temples around it, calm the fever of his cheeks against the cold of its metal. And then he would stay there for a long time, letting his fingers wander along the trigger, operating the safety-catch until the world went silent about him and, already drowsy, his whole being would cradle itself into the simple sensation of the cold salty metal which could let loose death. From the moment one does not kill onself, one should keep silent about life. And, waking up again, his mouth already full of bitter saliva, he would lick the weapon's barrel, stick his tongue into it and repeat with amazement in a gasping death-rattle of infinite bliss: 'my joy is priceless'.]

This passage, which poses certain difficulties of interpretation,[22] could conceivably be the result of personal temptation. However, it was written as part of Camus's unfinished *La Mort heureuse*[23] and could, thus, equally well be seen as part of an intellectual thematic.

Clearly, it is difficult to establish just how strongly Camus was tempted by suicide and whether this accounts for the widespread presence of the subject in his early work. However, so much of Camus's early work is devoted to expressing his love of life that one is more inclined towards Quilliot's position than Faucon's. This would suggest that the suicide theme has an insistent presence in the early work because it provided Camus with a means to negate it by proclaiming his love of life. If this is the case, the claim could certainly be advanced that the whole suicide question, as it appears in Camus's early work and in *Le Mythe de Sisyphe*, is very much related to his reading of Dostoevsky and his dialogue with him. The Russian writer helps to shape Camus's understanding of the possible links between suicide and the absurd and generates, in Camus, a determination to produce a counter-offensive to Dostoevsky's treatment. The central thesis of *Le Mythe de Sisyphe*, that suicide is not a logical response to the absurd, would be a direct answer to 'Jugement' and 'Moralité un peu tardive' (the case of Kirilov, as we shall see in Chapter 5, is made more complex by Camus who is determined to see the engineer's suicide in a positive light as a proclamation of freedom and joy for mankind without God).

A number of points can be made in support of the above. First, it should be remembered that, of all the writers mentioned in *Le Mythe de Sisyphe*, it is only Dostoevsky who solicits Camus's attention because of the theme of logical suicide—the others are studied exclusively in the context of 'philosophical' suicide. Secondly, the main concern in the Dostoevsky study is, precisely, his treatment of suicide and its links with the absurd and this is exactly the subject matter of *Le Mythe de Sisyphe* generally, and of 'Jugement' in particular. Furthermore, Dostoevsky himself refers to the suicide in 'Jugement' as 'le suicide logique' and, although Camus does not himself actually use this expression in *Le Mythe de Sisyphe*, the question formulated by the essay is: 'Y a-t-il une logique jusqu' à la mort?'—does awareness of the absurd logically and crucially lead to suicide?[24] Apart from such fairly obvious considerations, parallels between Camus's treatment of suicide and Dostoevsky's, both in 'Jugement' and elsewhere, are frequently visible. Curiously, it is worth noting that the passage about suicide quoted from the *Carnets*[25] appears to rework part of one of Dostoevsky's most bizarre and amusing short stories, 'Le Songe d'un homme ridicule', where the protagonist sits at a table with a revolver, contemplating suicide (admittedly, it is a classic situation).

> Cette fois, je m'assis à la table en silence, pris le revolver et le posai à côté de moi . . . je savais que cette nuit-là, je me tuerais en toute certitude, mais combien de temps devais-je rester assis à une table en attendant le dernier moment?[26]

> [This time, I sat down at the table in silence, took the revolver and placed it beside me . . . I knew that I would kill myself for certain that night, but how long was I to remain sitting at the table waiting for the last moment?]

It is possible that Camus's *Carnets* entry contains an intertextual echo of this passage from Dostoevsky. 'Le Songe d'un homme ridicule' is incorporated in the *Journal d'un écrivain* as part of the entry for avril 1877.[27] Camus had read the *Journal* (he mentions it in *Le Mythe de Sisyphe*), but it is not possible to date the year of reading precisely. He uses the 1927 Chuzeville translation and so he could have read it in the early thirties and certainly by 1936, the date of the *Carnets* entry. Of course, the *Journal* is long and Camus may not have read the whole of it, although 'Le Songe d'un homme ridicule' is placed quite near in the text to 'Moralité un peu tardive'.[28]

Be that as it may, there are a number of reasons for believing that, in addition to the suicide theme, 'Jugement' may well have been instrumental in giving shape to Camus's general description of the absurd as it appeared in *Le Mythe de Sisyphe*. The writer of 'Jugement' is described by Dostoevsky as 'un matérialiste' ['a materialist'] who kills himself 'par ennui' ['out of boredom'] but also according to a Cartesian logical argument, referred to as 'le raisonnement', which is the text itself. He is, thus, a nineteenth-century rationalist and atheist. Camus's 'raisonnement absurde' ['absurd reasoning'] also aspires to describe 'l'état métaphysique de l'homme conscient' ['the metaphysical state of conscious man'] or, in other words, to claim that the absurd is the inevitable by-product of the relationship between reasoning consciousness and the material world.

The writer of 'Jugement' locates the source of all his troubles in consciousness which puts him out of harmony with the natural world, makes him dissatisfied with the normal pattern of existence (described as eating, drinking, sleeping, procreating and building up a home), which is animalistic and mechanical and generally causes him pain and metaphysical *angst*:

> Mieux vaudrait [he writes] que je fusse créé à l'image des autres animaux, c'est-à-dire vivant, mais n'ayant de moi-même aucune conscience raisonnable. Ma conscience n'est précisément pas une harmonie, mais une désharmonie, puisque c'est grâce à elle que je suis malheureux. Considérez où sont les heureux de ce monde et quels sont les hommes qui consentent à vivre? Justement ceux qui sont parcils aux animaux et leur ressemblent le plus grâce au peu de développement de leur conscience. Ils consentent volontiers à vivre, à condition de vivre comme des animaux, c'est-à-dire de manger, boire, dormir, faire son nid et proliférer.[29]

> [It would have been better if I had been created to be like other animals, that is to say alive but without any rational consciousness of myself. My consciousness is precisely not harmony but a

disharmony because it is as a result of it that I am unhappy. Consider who are the happy people in the world and who are the people who consent to live? Precisely those who are similar to animals and are most like them because they have little conscious development. They willingly consent to live, on the condition that they live like animals, that is to say eating, drinking, sleeping, building a nest and proliferating.]

At the beginning of *Le Mythe de Sisyphe*, Camus stresses the primary role of the questioning consciousness in producing the sense of absurdity in the midst of the mechanical, repetitive patterns of existence:

Il arrive que les décors s'écroulent. Lever, tramway, quatre heures de bureau ou d'usine, repas, tramway, quatre heures de travail, repas, sommeil, et lundi mardi mercredi jeudi vendredi et samedi sur le même rythme, cette route se suit aisément la plupart du temps. Un jour seulement le 'pourquoi' s'élève et tout commence dans cette lassitude teintée d'étonnement. 'Commence,' ceci est important. La lassitude est à la fin des actes d'une vie machinale, mais elle inaugure en même temps le mouvement de la conscience . . . Car tout commence par la conscience et rien ne vaut que par elle.[30]

[The scenery suddenly collapses. Getting up, tramway, four hours in the office or factory, tramway, four hours work, meal, bed and Monday Tuesday Wednesday Thursday Friday Saturday at the same regular pace, this is a road readily followed most of the time. One day, though, the 'why' confronts us and everything begins with this weariness tinged with bewilderment. 'Begins', this is important. Weariness is at the end of a life of mechanical actions but it initiates, at the same time, the moment of awareness . . . For everything starts with awareness and nothing counts without it.]

In both texts, consciousness is the prime agent, alienating man from his surroundings, disrupting familiar patterns of existence and forcing to the forefront of life the question of its ultimate purpose; in both works 'le "pourquoi" s'élève', as Camus put it (the writer of 'Jugement' asks 'A quoi bon organiser sa vie et consacrer tant d'efforts à s'établir dans la société?' ['What's the point of organizing one's life and making so much effort to get established in society?'])[31] For the writer of 'Jugement', consciousness is necessarily suffering but he does not wish to suffer for no evident purpose. Since nature will not tell him this purpose, existence is an humiliating 'comédie' which man must reject in suicide:

Je condamne cette nature qui avec un si impudent sans-gêne m'a fait naître pour souffrir—je la condamne à être anéantie avec moi. Mais comme je ne peux supprimer la nature, je me supprimerai donc moi-même uniquement par dégoût d'avoir à supporter une tyrannie qui n'est de la faute de personne.[32]

[I condemn this nature which with such impudent lack of concern brought me into the world in order to suffer—I condemn it to be destroyed with me. But since I cannot destroy nature, I shall therefore destroy myself expressly to show my disgust at having to endure a tyranny which cannot be ascribed to anyone.]

In *Le Mythe de Sisyphe*, Camus writes:

On continue à faire les gestes que l'expérience commande pour beaucoup de raisons dont la première est l'habitude. Mourir volontairement suppose qu'on a reconnu, même instinctivement, le caractère dérisoire de cette habitude, l'absence de toute raison profonde de vivre, le caractère insensé de cette agitation quotidienne, et l'inutilité de la souffrance.[33]

[We continue to carry out the actions which experience dictates for many reasons, the primary one being habit. To die by act of will implies that one has recognized, even instinctively, the derisory character of the habit, the absence of any deep reason for living, the senseless nature of our daily agitations and the futility of suffering.]

In both texts, the derisory nature of existence is stressed as is the futility of suffering through awareness.

Arguments about the inevitable frustrations of our consciousness's natural aspirations for unity with the world are also dominant features of both texts. In 'Jugement' we find:

La nature, par le moyen de la conscience, m'annonce une certaine harmonie avec le grand tout. La conscience humaine a fait de ce message des religions. Elle me dit que moi, tout en sachant fort bien que je ne puis participer à l'harmonie du tout, n'y participerai jamais et même ne comprendrai jamais ce que cela veut dire—je n'en dois pas moins obéir à ce message, me réconcilier, accepter la souffrance en vue de l'harmonie avec le tout et consentir à vivre.[34]

[Nature, through the agency of consciousness, brings me a certain idea of harmony with the whole of being. Human consciousness has used this idea to build religious faiths. It also tells me that I, whilst knowing full well that I cannot share in this harmony in any way, will never be able to share in it nor ever understand what it means, must nonetheless accept this idea, reconcile myself to it, accept suffering as part of the harmony with everything and agree to live.]

He finds no answer to his questions in nature: 'La nature, non seulement ne me reconnaît pas le droit de lui demander des comptes, mais ne me répond même pas' ['Nature not only does not grant me any right to demand accountability for its actions but does not even reply to me'].[35]

Camus's concept of the absurd also stresses man's frustrated desire for unity born of the encounter between 'l'appel humain et le silence déraisonnable du monde' ['humanity's appeals and the unreasonable silence of the world'].[36] For Camus, our basic desire is to realize a conscious unity with the natural world which would embrace and explain, in a unique formula, our total experience:

Si la pensée découvrait dans les miroirs changeants des phénomènes, des relations éternelles qui les puissent résumer et se résumer elles-mêmes en un principe unique, on pourrait parler d'un bonheur de l'esprit dont le mythe des bienheureux ne serait qu'une ridicule contrefaçon. Cette nostalgie d'unité, cet appétit d'absolu illustre le mouvement essentiel du drame humain.[37]

[If thought could discover in the changing mirrors of phenomena, timeless relationships which can both explain these phenomena and the relationships themselves by reference to a unique principle, one could then speak of a happiness of the mind which would make the one promised by the myth of the faithful look like some silly joke. This craving for unity, this desire for an absolute, illustrate the essential movement of the drama of humanity.]

The futility of human endeavour, of love and of happiness before the absolute fact of death is stressed in both texts. Dostoevsky's character cannot accept that human society or, indeed, any activity, is worthwhile if man and all his works are to be converted into primitive nothingness at death:

A quoi bon organiser sa vie et consacrer tant d'efforts à s'établir dans la société des hommes d'une façon régulière, raisonnable et parfaitement juste? . . . je sais que demain tout cela doit être anéanti. Moi-même, et tout ce bonheur et tout l'amour et toute l'humanité —nous retournerons au néant, au chaos primitif.[38]

[What's the point of organizing one's life and making so much effort to get established in society in an ordered, rational and perfectly just way? . . . I know that tomorrow all this is to be destroyed. Myself, and all the happiness and all the love and humanity in its entirety, we shall all return to nothingness and the primal chaos.]

He feels himself to be a victim of 'les lois inanimées de la nature' ['the inanimate laws of nature'] and, because of this, happiness, pleasure or sustained love of others are simply impossible. He does not blame God for his wretched state, since he is a rationalist, but he is further vexed by the idea that there is no-one to blame.

Le Mythe de Sisyphe contains echoes of the same preoccupations:

Sous l'éclairage mortel de cette destinée, l'inutilité apparaît. Aucune morale ni aucun effort ne sont *a priori* justifiables devant les sanglantes mathématiques qui ordonnent notre condition.[39]

[In the deadly light of this destiny, futility arises. No moral theory nor any endeavour are *a priori* justifiable before the gory mathematics which govern our condition.]

Further support for the claim that 'Jugement' occupies an important place in Camus's description of the absurd in *Le Mythe de Sisyphe* is indirectly provided by the play, *Le Malentendu*. The causes of Martha's suicide, in *Le Malentendu*, recall the world of Dostoevsky's 'Jugement'. Martha cries out to Maria:

Nous sommes volés, je vous le dis. A quoi bon ce grand appel de l'être, cette alerte des âmes? Pourquoi crier vers la mer ou vers l'amour? Cela est dérisoire . . . Priez votre Dieu qu'il vous fasse semblable à la pierre. C'est le bonheur qu'il prend pour lui, c'est le seul vrai bonheur. Faites comme lui, rendez-vous sourde à tous les cris, rejoignez la pierre pendant qu'il en est temps.[40]

[We've been robbed, I tell you. What's the use of this great appeal of being, this agitation of souls? Why cry out to the sea or to love? It is derisory . . . Ask your God to make you like stone. That's the happiness he reserves for himself, that's the only true happiness. Be like him, deafen yourself to all cries, become like stone again while you still have time.]

Despite the evident Camusian leitmotifs, there are palpable traces of Dostoevsky here: consciousness as anguish, making us ask questions we cannot answer; the sense of humiliation, revolt and outrage; the desire to escape from the suffering of mind and to find peace in death. (Martha kills herself in a gesture of rebellion: 'Je quitterai ce monde sans être réconciliée' ['I shall leave this world without being reconciled'].)[41] The writer of 'Jugement' similarly asks:

> Au fait, de quel droit la nature m'a-t-elle mis en ce monde, à la suite de quelles *lois éternelles* que l'on dit siennes? J'ai été créé avec une conscience et *j'ai conscience* de cette nature: de quel droit m'a-t-elle mis au monde, sans ma volonté, moi qui suis conscient? Le conscient est par conséquent le souffrant; je ne veux pas souffrir, car en vertu de quoi acccepterais-je de vivre?[42]

> [In fact, by what right has nature placed me in this world, by virtue of what *eternal laws* that are said to be hers? I have been created with consciousness and I am conscious of this nature: by what right has she placed me in this world, without my will, I who am conscious? The conscious individual is in consequence the suffering person; I don't want to suffer, for in the name of what should I accept to live?]

He further argues that only animals can be happy: 'Si j'étais fleur ou vache, moi aussi je jouirais' [If I were a flower or a cow, I too would enjoy myself'],[43] and he decides to kill himself 'par dégoût' ['out of disgust'] and explains 'je trouve cette comédie de la part de la nature tout à fait stupide . . . et . . . même j'estime humiliant de ma part d'accepter de la jouer' ['I find this farce on the part of nature utterly stupid . . . and . . . even consider it humiliating on my part to agree to participate in it'];[44] both characters kill themselves in bitterness and despair at the frustration caused by the relationship between consciousness and the world order. They feel locked up and oppressed by the limits of their awareness. Of course, Martha's whole perception of the absurd as oppressive and life-destroying runs counter to Camus's ultimate rejection of suicide in *Le Mythe de Sisyphe* and to his final assessment of the absurd as a pathway to a lucid and passionate happiness. But Martha's standpoint is fully in conformity with the tortured world of Dostoevsky's materialist in 'Jugement' and of his desperate non-believers in general. Camus actually appears to have created, in Martha, a very Dostoevskian expression of the suicide theme as it appears in 'Jugement'[45] and this can be claimed to strengthen the argument about the importance of 'Jugement' in the elaboration of Camus's early work.

The various similarities mentioned make it possible to argue that 'Jugement' and 'Moralité un peu tardive' engage Camus in a dialogue which helps to cystallize his understanding of the absurd. Admittedly, such ideas are not uncommon and Camus himself says in *Le Mythe de Sisyphe*, when speaking of absurd notions: 'Ils courent à travers toutes les littératures et toutes les philosophies. La conversation de tous les jours s'en nourrit. Il n'est pas question de les réinventer' ['They run through all literature and all philosophy. They are the bread and butter of everyday conversation. I do not claim them as my own'].[46] On the other hand, the Dostoevsky texts in question group together and express propositionally, in a condensed and particularly striking and challenging way, the very essence of absurd sensibility. Not only this, they advance, as necessary consequences of absurd awareness, the very thesis that Camus is out to refute in his equally logic-obsessed conceptualization of *l'homme absurde* and Sisyphus. For this reason it seems conceivable that, when Camus read 'Jugement' and 'Moralité un peu tardive', it brought him into a sharply defined position of engaged opposition to Dostoevsky's thought, despite the strong sense of convergence and affinity which he felt with the Russian writer generally. Camus's will to live, his general pursuit of happiness and pleasure existed and persisted in powerful form despite and, indeed, because of his belief in the absurd. He could not accept that logic of the absurd which condemns man to suicide and despair. Nor could he accept the inference of immortality as part of absurd logic. *Le Mythe de Sisyphe* can be seen, in one sense, as a result of this challenge from Dostoevsky: Camus's reply emphasizes that love of life is not only sustainable in an absurd world but is logically deducible from it. Life is all the more passionately enjoyed because death is final and there is no afterlife. It is not suicide that is logical in an absurd world (indeed, suicide is illogical, a contradiction), but an affirmation of life. Consciousness is not only pain and anguish but a source of energy and lucidity, offering us the pleasure of plenitudinous existence. A passion for living and absurd awareness can co-exist for Camus by force of a logical necessity and inner dynamic which simultaneously excludes and condemns both suicide and immortality as illogical. This is to turn Dostoevsky's world upside-down and to reformulate its paradigms in a new antithetical synthesis

The idea that Camus wrote *Le Mythe de Sisyphe* in a spirit of debate with Dostoevsky and, particularly, to challenge and refute the arguments of 'Jugement' and 'Moralité un peu tardive', is necessarily a speculative one. Certainly, Camus himself cannot be said to be consistently and entirely conscious that this may have been so. It is hoped that the claim can now be seen as a defensible one. Advancing it, however, does not in any sense mean that one can neglect the other writers analysed in *Le Mythe de Sisyphe*: to state the importance of Dostoevsky is not to overstate it, nor to understate the relevance of others. In any case, it is too early in our study to draw final conclusions, for there is a great deal more to Camus's general preoccupation with Dostoevsky during the early period than has been revealed so far by the isolation of 'Jugement' and 'Moralité un peu tardive'. The whole question of Camus's response to Dostoevsky's rebels must be addressed.

4

Camus and Dostoevsky's Rebels

So far, Camus's interest in Dostoevsky has been examined mainly in terms of the differences and oppositions between the two writers and it has been suggested that Dostoevsky provides Camus with both a means of illustrating his own thought by contrast and a powerful stimulant in the crystallization of his thought in the early 1940s. It is now time to discuss Camus's interest in terms of affinity and convergence with the Russian writer and to focus on similarities which exist between them, despite the formal difference concerning the conclusions to be drawn from a belief in the absurdity of life.

Our analysis in this chapter will be related also to an examination of Camus's preoccupation with Dostoevsky's rebels, Kirilov, Ivan and Stavroguine, the characters who are very much to the foreground in the expression of Camus's early enthusiasm for Dostoevsky. It has been noted that Camus was almost disappointed by Dostoevsky's espousal of Christianity and sceptical about its authenticity: it constituted a betrayal of his lucidity and, consequently, of the ideas expressed by the anti-theists, Kirilov, Ivan, and Stavroguine. Camus can, therefore, be said to have more in common with Dostoevsky's great rebels than with Dostoevsky himself: he also, like they do, prefers lucidity to faith. Just as *l'homme absurde* turns away in disappointment from those who have recourse to the irrational and use the 'tremplin d'éternité' ['springboard to faith'], so Camus turns away from Dostoevsky himself and moves towards the faithless rebels, displaying little interest in the Christian heroes.

The very strong attraction which Camus felt towards the rebels was highlighted in an earlier chapter but is conveniently recalled here. In *Le Mythe de Sisyphe*, referring to Ivan, Kirilov and Stavroguine, Camus wrote:

Mais quelle prodigieuse création que celle où ces êtres de feu et de glace nous semblent.si familiers! Le monde passionné de l'indifférence qui gronde en leur cœur ne nous semblent en rien monstrueux. Nous y retrouvons nos angoisses quotidiennes. Et personne sans doute comme Dostoïevski n'a su donner au monde absurde des prestiges si proches et si torturants.[1]

[But what an extraordinary creation is this one, where beings of fire and ice seem so familiar to us. The passionate world of indifference which rumbles in their hearts does not seem in any way monstrous to us. We rediscover there our daily anxieties and to be sure nobody like Dostoevsky has managed to give the world of absurdity such close and tormented brilliance.]

This impression of familiarity and of consciously felt affinity which Camus experienced when reading Dostoevsky and which he referred to again in 'Prière d'insérer des *Possédés*' in 1959 ('Les créatures de Dostoïevski, nous le savons bien maintenant, ne sont ni étranges ni absurdes. Elles nous ressemblent, nous avons le même cœur' ['The creatures of Dostoevsky, we now well know, are neither strange nor absurd. They are like us, we have the same heart']),[2] is one of the most interesting aspects of Camus's preoccupation with the Russian writer. No doubt, Dostoevsky's great genius enabled him to create powerful and convincing characters, but Camus appears to be deeply receptive to the lives and ideas of the great rebels. He tends to treat them as real people. They haunt his subjective life and his work and are key figures in the expression of his thought. It is certainly not simply as embodiments of particular ideas that the rebels fascinate him but as flesh and blood individuals involved in the general dramas of existence. What are the underlying causes of this fascination?

In 1945, in the course of an interview in which Camus repudiated the idea that he was an existentialist, he said he was interested in 'tous ceux qui ne vivent pas dans la grâce' [all those who live without grace'].[3] What draws Camus to Dostoevsky's world initially is its dramatic and intense expression of the idea that life is absurd without God and its general exploration of the problems of life without faith. It is, perhaps, sometimes necessary to recall that there is no self-evident relationship between the idea that life is absurd and the inability to believe in God. Bertrand Russell and Julian Huxley are famous examples of non-believers but they in no way considered life absurd, meaningless or futile. A. J. Ayer was quick to point out, in the famous *Horizon* article of 1946,[4] that the whole of Camus's argument in the *Le Mythe de Sisyphe* is based on the *preconceptions* of a sensibility given to looking at life in terms of expectations of meanings and explanations. Camus's world, in a very basic way, is structured emotionally and conceptually like the world of Dostoevsky's rebels: they are determined to live in a world without faith, although they believe that world to be without ultimate meaning and absurd. Dostoevsky's rebels are fed by Dostoevsky's own religious, emotional and intellectual dilemmas and conflicts. For Dostoevsky, life is not only meaningless without faith but 'quelque chose de contre-nature, un intolérable non-sens' ['something unnatural, an unbearable nonsense'].[5] His inner struggle for faith is referred to in the famous letters of 1854 and 1870 which provide the terms of the passionate debate between the author and his protagonists about life with and without God:

> Je vous dirai de moi-même que je suis un enfant du siècle, l'enfant de l'incroyance et du doute, je le suis à ce jour et (je sais cela) jusqu'à la pierre tombale. Que d'atroces tortures m'a coûtées et me coûte encore maintenant cette soif de croire qui est d'autant plus forte en mon âme qu'il y a en moi plus d'arguments contraires.[6]

> [I will tell you of myself that I am a child of the age, the child of disbelief and doubt, I remain so to this day and (I know this) will remain so until I die. What countless atrocious torments has this thirst to believe cost me and continues to cost me, a thirst which is all the greater in my soul because there are in me so many counter-arguments.]

Later, alluding to the unwritten novel, *La Vie d'un grand pécheur*, Dostoevsky writes:

> Le problème principal qui traversera toutes les parties est celui qui m'a tourmenté, sciemment ou inconsciemment, toute ma vie— l'existence de Dieu.[7]

> [The main problem which will stretch across all parts is the one which has tormented me, consciously or unconsciously, all my life —the existence of God.]

Just like Stavroguine, Dostoevsky, when he believes, doesn't believe that he believes and when he doesn't believe, he doesn't believe that he doesn't believe. If Dostoevsky does eventually opt for God, finding inspiration in Christian existentialist apologetics and the intuitions of epilepsy, it is not without the greatest of difficulties, because the logic and power of atheist sensibility will not stop gnawing at the foundations of his faith.[8]

Dostoevsky may be said then to have provided Camus with a vivid and intensely drawn canvas of life without God, through which the young Algerian was able to explore his own problems, emotions and reactions. On a far less important scale, Camus's interest in the heroes of Roger Martin du Gard can be accounted for in the same way. Jean Barois, Antoine and Jacques Thibault, like Dostoevsky's rebels, seek a foundation for existence outside a framework of religious belief and attract Camus as prototypes of the absurd man. It is not without significance that Camus also directly compares Martin du Gard's heroes to those of Dostoevsky in the preface that he wrote for the writer's collected works: he refers to Antoine as a middle-class Kirilov and states that the Thibault family, in their passion for life, reminded him of the Karamazovs.[9]

If a romantically formulated metaphysic of disbelief is thus the dominant episteme of Camus's encounter with the rebels, it should still be noted that this is not how Camus himself explained his early responses to Dostoevsky: in 1955, he claimed that it was the psychological aspect of Dostoevsky's fiction that interested him (as it did Gide):

> J'ai d'abord admiré Dostoïevski à cause de ce qu'il me révélait de la nature humaine. . . . De plus, il satisfaisait chez moi un goût assez complaisant de la lucidité pour elle-même.[10]

> [I first admired Dostoevsky because of what he revealed to me about human nature . . . In addition, he satisfied in me a fairly self-indulgent craving for lucidity for its own sake.]

By the time Camus staged *Les Frères Karamazov*, in 1938, psychological interest has been transcended, if not replaced, by wide-ranging metaphysical preoccupations. No doubt the purely dramatic potential of the Russian novel interested Camus but the *Théâtre de L'Équipe* which produced it, aimed to give expression to:

> les grands sentiments simples et ardents autour desquels tourne le destin de l'homme . . . amour, désir, ambition, religion . . . Les sentiments de tous et de tout temps dans des formes toujours jeunes, c'est à la fois le visage de la vie et l'idéal du bon théâtre.[11]

> [the great feelings, simple and passionate, around which human destiny revolves . . . love, desire, ambition, religion . . . The feelings

45

of all and of all time in forms ever fresh, this is the face of life and the ideal of good theatre.]

Thus, psychological factors were quickly supplanted by metaphysical ones as Camus grew to maturity and after his recurrent attacks of tuberculosis which must have been a significant factor in the determinants of the shape of his early thought.

The early references to Dostoevsky in the *Carnets* also testify to Camus's pronounced interest in the rebels in terms of metaphysics. In August 1938, shortly after the staging of *Les Frères Karamazov*, Camus refers to Ivan and his view that morality is essentially a religious concept and perishes in a godless world:

> L'homme vraiment libre est celui qui acceptant la mort comme telle, en accepte du même coup les conséquences—c'est-à-dire le renversement de toutes les valeurs traditionnelles de la vie. Le 'Tout est permis' d'Ivan Karamazov est la seule expression d'une liberté cohérente. Mais il faut aller au fond de la formule.[12]

> [The truly free person is the one who accepting death as it is, accepts simultaneously the consequences—namely the overturning of all traditional notions of values in life. Ivan Karamazov's 'Everything is permitted' is the only expression of coherent freedom. But it is imperative to get to the bottom of the statement.]

In December of the same year, a further reference occurs, this time to Kirilov and suicide: 'Kirilov a raison. Se suicider c'est faire preuve de sa liberté' ['Kirilov is right. To commit suicide is to prove your freedom'].[13] Evidently, by 1938 at least, Camus's interest in Dostoevsky was principally metaphysical and not psychological. It is equally clear that Camus's general interest in literature, at this time, is dominated by metaphysical considerations. Both in his review of *La Nausée*[14] and his general discussion of the novel form in *Le Mythe de Sisyphe*,[15] he expresses his admiration for novelists who are also philosophers and use the novel to pose existential problems—and he particularly refers to Dostoevsky in this respect in *Le Mythe de Sisyphe*. R. M. Albérès believes that all Camus's literary tastes were determined by metaphysical considerations and not by aesthetics or the desire to possess a comprehensive knowledge: he says that, from Democritus to Kafka, Camus simply read those writers who deal primarily with what Albérès calls 'l'essentiel du drame humain pris à sa racine' ['the essential elements of humanity's drama captured at its root']. Dunwoodie, likewise, refers to 'cette logique philosophique

[qui] colore aussi ses préférences esthétiques' ['this philosophical reasoning which also colours his aesthetic preferences'].[16]

By 1942 and the period of composition of the Dostoevsky study in *Le Mythe de Sisyphe*, Camus feels able to give Dostoevsky the status of a modern writer because of his metaphysical preoccupations. Distinguishing between classical and modern sensibility, Camus argues that the former is more concerned with moral problems, whereas the latter's dominant preoccupation is metaphysical. Dostoevsky, with his predilection for what Camus calls elsewhere 'l'abîme' ['the abyss'] clearly belonged to the modern world:

> Tous les héros de Dostoïevski s'interrogent sur le sens de la vie. C'est en cela qu'ils sont modernes: ils ne craignent pas le ridicule.[17]

> [All Dostoevsky's heroes ask themselves questions about the meaning of life. This is what makes them modern: they do not fear ridicule.]

This Camusian affirmation of the philosophical relevance of Dostoevsky to the modern world has itself a curiously Dostoevskian ring to it: it is Stavroguine who states, in his letter to Dacha, just before his suicide, 'ce n'était pas la peur du ridicule,—je suis au dessus de cela' ['it was not through fear of ridicule—I am above that'],[18] whilst the protagonist of the story, 'Le Songe d'un homme ridicule', reveals that he ceased to fear being 'ridicule' once he realized that death made life futile and that he was 'indifférent' to everything.[19] The affirmation also underscores the fact that a primary source of his early interest in Dostoevsky was the Russian writer's evocation of a world without grace, a point well made by one of Camus's Christian critics, A. Blanchet, when he writes:

> Camus a souffert dans sa chair et dans son esprit de ne trouver aucun sens à la vie. C'est par cette souffrance que, en dépit de moyens infiniment plus modestes, il peut être rapproché de Dostoïevski dont il a d'ailleurs subi la fascination.[20]

> [Camus suffered physically and mentally from not finding any meaning in life. It is through this suffering that, despite his infinitely more modest abilities, he can be likened to Dostoevsky whose work, moreover, fascinated him.]

Another general feature of the Dostoevskian rebels' sensibilities which appeals to Camus and makes him feel close to their world is their strong determination to act authentically and live according to their beliefs and logic, an attitude which Camus clearly shared. Kirilov is mentioned early in *Le Mythe de Sisyphe* as one of those rarest of thinkers who act according to their philosophy and the context of the remark expresses Camus's contempt for those who cheat or practise hypocrisy:

> C'est un lieu commun de comparer les théories philosophiques et la conduite de ceux qui les professent. Mais il faut bien dire que, parmi les penseurs qui refusèrent un sens à la vie, aucun sauf Kirilov qui appartient à la littérature, Pérégrinos[21] qui naît de la légende et Jules Lequier[22] qui relève de l'hypothèse, n'accorda sa logique jusqu'à refuser cette vie.[23]

> [It is a well-worn track to compare philosophical theories with the behaviour of those who profess them. But it is very necessary to point out that among the thinkers who claimed that life was meaningless, none apart from Kirilov, who is a literary character, Peregrinos, who is from legend, and Jules Lequier whose example is partly hypothetical, follows their logic to the point of killing themselves.]

Camus makes 'l'honnêteté' his ruling consideration in *Le Mythe de Sisyphe*, explaining why it draws him to Nietzsche ('s'il est vrai, comme le veut Nietzsche', writes Camus approvingly 'qu'un philosophe, pour être estimable, doive prêcher d'exemple' ['if it is true, as Nietzsche claims, that a philosopher, to be admired, must serve as an example']) and alienates him from Schopenhauer who praised suicide 'devant une table bien garnie' ['sitting at a table full of fine fare'].[24] For Camus, the absurd is not simply an idea but an experience of great emotional impact, 'une passion, la plus déchirante de toutes' ['the most tearing passion of all'],[25] which should govern one's life; any evasion from the truth makes one 'un tricheur' ['a cheat']:

> Si je tiens pour vrai cette absurdité qui règle mes rapports avec la vie, si je me pénètre de ce sentiment qui me saisit devant les spectacles du monde, de cette clairvoyance qui m'impose la recherche d'une science, je dois tout sacrificier à ces certitudes et je dois les regarder en face pour pouvoir les maintenir. Surtout je dois leur régler ma conduite et les poursuivre dans toutes leurs conséquences. Je parle ici d'honnêteté.[26]

> [If I accept as true this absurdity which governs my relationships with existence, if I am permeated with this feeling which seizes

me when I observe the world and with this lucidity which dictates my quest for knowledge, I must sacrifice everything to these certainties and I must look at them directly in order to be able to keep them in focus. Above all I must base my conduct on them and pursue them in all their consequences. I am talking here of integrity.]

Camus is drawn to Kirilov precisely because of this 'honnêteté' ['integrity'] and because he will be 'logique jusqu'au bout' ['logical to the end']. Kirilov explains to Piotr Stépanovitch:

> Toute ma vie j'ai voulu que ce ne fussent pas seulement des mots. C'est pour cela que j'ai vécu. Et maintenant encore, je désire chaque jour que ce ne soient pas des mots.[27]

[All my life, I have wanted it to be not just a question of words. That is what I have lived for. And even now, each day I do not want it to be merely a question of words.]

Kirilov wants to wed thought to action and Camus admires his fundamentalism because:

> Il existe un fait d'évidence qui semble tout à fait moral, c'est qu'un homme est toujours la proie de ses vérités . . . Un homme devenu conscient de l'absurde lui est lié pour jamais.[28]

[There is a self-evident fact which appears entirely moral, which is that a man is always the prey of his own truths . . . A man who has become aware of the absurd is tied to it for evermore.]

Dostoevsky's rebels generally, in the same way as Kirilov, want to make their thought 'real' and constitute it as the basis of action, not posture. As Mochulsky says of Dostoevsky's rebels, 'they tempestuously and dramatically *experience* their ideas'[29] and their philosophies govern their lives. Dmitri Karamazov tells Aliocha that he cannot sleep at all at night because he is tormented by the socialist Rakitine's theory that morality is only a relative notion and that absolute virtue does not exist:

> En effet, qu'est-ce que la vertu? Réponds-moi, Alexeï. Je ne me représente pas la vertu comme un chinois, c'est donc une chose relative? Ou bien, n'est-elle pas relative? Question insidieuse! Tu ne riras pas si je te dis que ça m'a empêché de dormir durant deux nuits. Je m'étonne qu'on puisse vivre sans y penser.[30]

[In effect, what is virtue? Answer me, Aliocha I don't think of virtue like a Chinaman, is it therefore a relative thing? Or isn't it relative? Impossible question. You won't laugh if I tell you that all this has prevented me from sleeping for two nights. I am amazed that one can live without thinking about it.]

Such restless and obsessive preoccupation is the lot of many of Dostoevsky's characters. They are racked by metaphysical problems which they cannot put to one side and their lives are ruled by the conclusions which spring from their perceptions and analyses. Kirilov commits suicide to demonstrate the truth of 'son idée' ['his idea'] and Camus, in one sense, admires him for the authenticity of the action. Ivan Karamazov struggles to live according to the idea that if God does not exist or one rejects Him or does not believe in Him, all is permitted. Camus responds to Ivan's desire to live according to his own logic: 'Ivan . . . vit réellement ses problèmes' ['Ivan . . . lives his problems for real'],[31] he says, in *L'Homme révolté*. Stavroguine shows his real contempt for conventional standards of behaviour and respectability because, unable to believe in God, he cannot convince himself of the reality of Good or Evil. He pulls Gaganoff by the nose because of the man's unfortunate habit of adding, as a sort of appendix to any discussion, the words: 'Non, on ne me mène pas par le bout du nez, moi' ['No, nobody leads me by the nose, not me'].[32] Also, he seizes and passionately embraces another man's wife at a social function[33] and his marriage to a cripple is partly the result of a friend's wager that he would not dare to do it.[34] He breaks codes in a spirit of ironic revolt because there are no absolute rules in a godless world. No evasions work for Stavroguine whose lack of belief and fundamental pessimism about life's absurdity slowly but surely lead to terminal 'accédie' ['accidie']. Kirilov, like Dmitri, never sleeps at night but spends the time pacing up and down, turning over the main points of his philosophy. He cannot stop thinking about his ideas:

Chacun pense successivement à diverses choses; moi j'ai toujours la même idée dans l'esprit, et il m'est impossible de penser à une autre. Dieu m'a tourmenté toute ma vie . . .[35]

[Everybody thinks about different things one after the other: me, I always have the same idea in my head and I cannot think of anything else. God has tormented me throughout my life . . .]

Dostoevsky's rebels are thus intensely and hyperactively *engaged* by their metaphysical preoccupations. They live almost exclusively for their ideas and are not in the least concerned with social success or material comfort, as Nina Gourfinkel rightly points out:

> Une seule chose importe vraiment aux héros de Dostoïevski: s'expliquer avec l'au-delà, qu'il s'agisse de l'enfer ou du ciel. Leur angoisse métaphysique est inextinguible.[36]

> [Only one thing truly matters to Dostoevsky's heroes: to come to terms with the next world, whether it be hell or heaven. Their metaphysical anguish is never-ending.]

George Steiner has also commented on these aspects of Dostoevsky's characters:

> Dostoevsky's characters—even the neediest among them—always have leisure for chaos or unpremeditated total involvement. They are available day and night; no one need go and ferret them out of a factory or an established business.[37]

The world of Dostoevsky's rebels is well tuned, in terms of intensity and authenticity, to the aspirations and experiences of the young Camus. They, like himself, want to live according to the dictates of logic and lucidity. They wish to deny nothing and to face the truth of existence. This fictional universe was indeed 'prodigieuse' ['prodigious'] in the eyes of Camus, for, with its 'clair-obscur plus saisissant que la lumière du jour' ['twilight more dazzling than the light of the day'], it provided him with a highly productive medium, tailor-made for him, through which he could nourish and explore his own favourite ideas, a world of intensity and extremes, posing problems with all or nothing absolutism.

A further important similarity between Camus and Dostoevsky's rebels relates to their appetites for life in general. In this case, however, it is really a matter of a deep and significant affinity between the two writers, for if Dostoevsky separated himself from his rebels by denying the absurd and accepting faith, his rejection of their experience and atheistic rationalism did not prevent him from imparting to them a passionate love of life which, in turn, is a striking feature of Camus's response to existence, especially in his early work. It has already been noted, in Chapter 3, that Camus and Dostoevsky are diametrically opposed in the way they relate their love of life to their general philosophies. Absurdity and the passionate desire to live and exhaust life's potentialities are logically connected, for Camus, in a dialectic which energizes and lyricizes his early thought. For Dostoevsky, however, love of life, without a belief in immortality, will quickly destroy itself and become hollowed out with negativity and sterile self-absorption. Furthermore, Dostoevsky, in both his letters and his fiction, stated that love of life was a source of revelation. Zosime expresses the idea, in *Les Frères Karamazov*, when he advises:

> Aimez toute la création dans son ensemble et dans ses éléments, chaque feuille, chaque rayon, les animaux, les plantes. En aimant chaque chose, vous comprendrez le mystère divin dans les choses.[38]

> [Love all creation in its entirety and in all its elements, each leaf, each ray of the sun, the animals, the plants. In loving individual things, you will understand the divine mystery to be found in things.]

Although Camus rejected the divine implications of Dostoevsky's notion of love of life, he was very acutely sensitive to the expression of this love in Dostoevsky and it appears to play a major role in stimulating his interest in the Russian writer and his rebels. In addition, in *Le Mythe de Sisyphe* and *L'Étranger*, Camus chooses, to illustrate his own intense love of life and that of his character, Meursault, an image absolutely fundamental to Dostoevsky's picture of the world, that of the *condamné à mort*. It is necessary, therefore, to look at the expression of the theme of love of life in Dostoevsky and Camus and to explore the links between them.

Dostoevsky constantly voices his love of life in his correspondence[39] but nowhere with greater force, and quite understandably so, than when he wrote to his brother, Mikhaïl, in December 1849, having experienced the fear and will to live of the man condemned to death. Dostoevsky came within seconds of being shot by the Imperial Guards, as a punishment for being involved in subversive political activity in the Petrashevski circle, but suddenly found himself spared when the Tzar's envoys explained that his sentence had been commuted to eight years exile in Siberia. Undaunted by this grim prospect, Dostoevsky could write:

> Je ne suis ni abbatu ni découragé. La vie est partout la vie, la vie est en nous-mêmes, et non à l'extérieur. . . . La vie, c'est un cadeau, la vie, c'est le bonheur, chaque minute pouvait être une éternité de bonheur.[40]

> [I am neither depressed nor demoralized. Life is life wherever it is, life is in ourselves and not in external things . . . Life is a gift, life is happiness, every minute could be an eternity of happiness.]

The source of Dostoevsky's triumphant affirmation was his close encounter with death. He went on to relate the most significant parts of his experience at the time in *L'Idiot*, where Muichkine speaks of an acquaintance who suffered Dostoevsky's fate and declares:

> L'incertitude, l'horreur de l'inconnu qi'il sentait si proche étaient quelque chose d'épouvantable, mais rien, disait-il, ne lui avait été alors plus pénible que cette incessante pensée: 'Si je ne mourais pas? Si la vie m'était rendue? Quelle éternité. Et tout cela serait à moi! Oh! alors, chaque minute serait pour moi une existence entière, je n'en perdrais pas une seule, je tiendrais compte de tous mes instants pour n'en dépenser aucun inutilement.'[41]

> [The uncertainty, the horror of the unknown which he felt to be so imminent, were dreadful things, but nothing, he said, was then more painful to him than this constant thought. 'What if I were not to die? What if life were given back to me? What an eternity. And it would all be mine. Oh! Every minute then would be a whole existence for me, I would take account of every instant I had so as not to waste any one of them.']

Hippolyte Térentieff, of the same novel, agrees with Muichkine that only the man condemned to death knows the real value of life; others squander it flippantly, enjoy it nonchalantly, but only the *condamné* (and, by implication, himself, for he is condemned to tuberculosis) could live life with the intensity which befits its value.[42] Dostoevsky loved life with that intensity. Not only did he respond powerfully to all the registers of existence but he loved nature, a fact often overlooked by those who see Dostoevsky as a great town novelist. In the *Journal d'un écrivain*, Dostoevsky could write:

> De ma vie je n'ai rien tant aimé que la forêt avec ses champignons et ses haies sauvages, ses insectes et ses oiseaux, ses hérissons et ses écureuils, avec l'humide et tendre odeur de ses feuillages pourrissants.[43]

> [In all my life I have loved nothing so much as the forest with its mushrooms and wild hedges, its insects and its birds, its hedgehogs and its squirrels, with the soft, damp smell of its rotting leaves.]

There is no need to emphasize that an equally passionate love of life underpins Camusian experience. From the outset, he tells us, what he had to express was his love of life itself 'à [sa] façon' ['in (his) own fashion']. Like Dostoevsky, he considered each moment of life precious and capable of delivering a pagan sense of the eternal:

53

L'Éternité est là et moi je l'espérais . . . Chaque minute de
vie porte en elle sa valeur de miracle et son visage d'éternelle
jeunesse.[44]

[Eternity was there and I was awaiting it . . . Each minute of life
carries within it its value as a miracle and its face of eternal youth.]

As in the case of Dostoevsky, it appears that Camus's intense love
of life was a natural and spontaneous one which was enhanced by
the sudden possibility of death. Camus's attacks of tuberculosis
intensified his vision and love of existence as it did for Gide's Michel
and as the experience of capital punishment did for Dostoevsky.
Indeed, the whole of Camus's early work amounts to an imperative
to enjoy life's every moment before death, in its finality, ends all our
pleasures[45]

Both these writers, therefore, really did feel a very great passion
for life and Camus was well aware of his similarity to Dostoevsky in
this respect. In September 1949, he wrote in the *Carnets* II:

Il faut aimer la vie avant d'en aimer le sens, dit Dostoïevski. Oui
et quand l'amour de vivre disparaît, aucun sens ne nous en
console.[46]

[One must love life before loving its sense, says Dostoevsky. Yes
and when love of life disappears, no sense consoles us for it.]

Camus is evidently referring here to *Les Frères Karamazov* and to
Aliocha's agreement with Ivan that love of life precedes logic and
reason. However, it is really through Dostoevsky's characters and
not through Dostoevsky himself, who links love of life to faith, that
Camus articulates and explores his great affinity with the Russian
writer on this subject. All the Karamazov family love life, a point
which did not escape Camus's attention for he refers to it explicitly
in his Martin du Gard preface when he brings in Dostoevsky.[47] Ivan
tells Aliocha:

Souvent je me suis demandé s'il y avait au monde un désespoir
capable de vaincre en moi ce furieux appétit de vivre.[48]

[Often I have asked myself if there was in this world a despair
capable of vanquishing in me this furious appetite for life.]

In a way which is in itself Camusian, Ivan expresses thus his response
to the natural world: 'j'aime les tendres pousses au printemps, le ciel

bleu' ['I love the delicate buds of spring, the blue sky'].[49] Kirilov tells Stavroguine that he loves life and explains his ecstasy at the sight of an autumn leaf.[50] Camus, it should be stressed, considered this aspect of both characters to be sufficiently important to note it when analysing them,[51] and this area of Camus's interest in these two rebels will need to be explored further when Camus's response to them is considered in the detailed study later. It is true that Stavroguine is an exception to the claim that Dostoevsky's rebels display enormous love of life, but he is, by Dostoevsky's standards, in an advanced state of disaffection from existence when we first meet him, a fact suggested by the mask-like appearance of his face.[52] Stavroguine really illustrates, from the outset, Dostoevsky's profound conviction that, without faith, man's love of life, his ties with creation and his spontaneous pleasures will all atrophy and die. Kirilov's suicide and Ivan's madness also illustrate, but in differing ways, this central thesis, although we shall see that Camus endeavours to propose an alternative interpretation.

Both the shared intensity of their responses to existence and their preoccupation with death and capital punishment make one suspect, as various critics have pointed out,[53] that Camus uses Dostoevsky's image of the *condamné* as a suitable vehicle for the expression of his own love of life. In *Le Mythe de Sisyphe*, Camus argues that the absurd man should love life like a condemned prisoner whose revolt against the certainty of death gives life its true and authentic value. He writes:

[L'Absurde] échappe au suicide, dans la mesure où il est en même temps conscience et refus de la mort. Il est, à l'extrême pointe de la dernière pensée du condamné à mort, ce cordon de soulier qu'en dépit de tout il aperçoit à quelques mètres, au bord même de sa chute vertigineuse. Le contraire du suicidé, précisé- ment, c'est le condamné à mort. Cette révolte donne son prix à la vie.[54]

[(The Absurd), escapes suicide, to the extent that it is simul- taneously consciousness and refusal of death. It is, at the very limit of the last thought of the man condemned to death, this shoelace which in spite of everything he sees a few metres before him, on the very edge of his dizzy fall. The opposite of the man who commits suicide is precisely the man condemned to death. This revolt against death gives life its value.]

Although the decisive contrast made by Camus between the man who commits suicide and the *condamné* is graphically and pointedly of his own invention, it seems difficult to resist the view that Camus's general use of the *condamné* image engages in dialogue with and, indeed, embodies a reply to Dostoevsky. Camus had read *L'Idiot*[55] and responded to Muichkine's evocation of the man condemned to death. Admittedly, the image of the *condamné* in Dostoevsky, as well as coming from his personal experience, has links with Victor Hugo's *Le Dernier Jour d'un condamné à mort* and Pascal's famous *Pensée*, both of which were obviously also known to Camus. However, despite the common intertextual sources, Dostoevsky appears to have played a significant role in shaping Camus's image of the *condamné* and providing a powerful metaphor to convey his passionate love of life. Confirmation of the above suggestion can clearly be seen in *L'Étranger*. A number of critics[56] have commented on the striking parallels between Muichkine's observations on the man condemned to death and those of Meursault in prison. Muichkine, as we have seen, speaks of the condemned man's hopes for escape and his intense will to live, adding, in an evocation of torture designed to highlight the full torment of the last moments before execution:

> Figurez-vous . . . un homme mis à la torture: son corps est couvert de plaies; par suite la douleur physique le distrait de la souffrance morale, si bien que, jusqu'à la mort, ses blessures seules constituent son supplice. Or la principale, la plus cuisante souffrance n'est peut-être pas causée par les blessures, mais par la conviction que dans une heure, puis dans dix minutes, puis dans une demi-minute, puis dans un instant votre âme s'envolera de votre corps, que vous ne serez plus un homme, et que cela est certain; le pire, c'est cette *certitude*. Le plus horrible, ce sont ces trois ou quatre secondes durant lesquelles, la tête dans la lunette, vous entendez au-dessus de vous glisser le couperet.[57]

> [Imagine . . . a man who is tortured: his body is covered in wounds; as a result, the physical suffering distracts him from the moral suffering so that, until he dies, his wounds alone constitute his torment. However, the worst, the most agonizing pain is not perhaps caused by the wounds but by the knowledge that in an hour, then in ten minutes, then in thirty seconds, then in an instant your soul will leave your body, that you will no longer be a person, and that this is certain; the worst thing is that *certainty*. The most horrible thing is those three or four seconds during which, your head in the aperture, you can hear the blade sliding down above you.]

Dostoevsky uses Muichkine to voice his opposition to capital punishment, which was not part of the Russian penal code, to condemn it as a far worse crime against humanity than murder itself and to single out the guillotine as a particularly atrocious form of torture, since it so mechanically robs the *condamné* of all hope of its failure. Dostoevsky also uses this moment in *L'Idiot* to bring up the question of a man condemned in this way who is suddenly let off and how this torment and grace is linked to Christ's suffering and the general Christian notion of hope.

Meursault, who is also Camus's mouthpiece when it comes to opposition to capital punishment,[58] regrets that he has not paid more attention to executions:

> Je ne sais combien de fois je me suis demandé s'il y avait des exemples de condamnés à mort qui eussent échappé au mécanisme implacable, disparu avant l'exécution, rompu les cordons d'agents. Je me reprochais alors de n'avoir pas prêté assez d'attention aux récits d'exécution. On devrait toujours s'intéresser à ses questions. On ne sait jamais ce qui peut arriver . . . Là, peut-être, j'aurais trouvé des récits d'évasion. J'aurais appris que dans un cas au moins la roue s'était arrêtée, que dans cette préméditation irrésistible, le hasard et la chance, une fois seulement, avaient changé quelque chose.[59]

> [I don't know how many times I asked myself if there were examples of condemned men who had escaped from the implacable machine, who had disappeared before the execution, broken free of the police ranks. I then blamed myself for not having paid enough attention to accounts of executions. One should always take an interest in these matters. You never know what can happen . . . Perhaps I would have found there some descriptions of escape. I might have learnt that, in one case at least, the wheel had jammed, that in that irresistible premeditation, hazard and chance, once at least, had changed something.]

It is likely that Camus was recalling Dostoevsky's fate at this moment. Meursault also speaks of 'ce bond terrible que je sentais en moi à la pensée de vingt ans de vie à venir'['this terrific surge that I felt within me at the thought of twenty more years of life to come'][60] which appears to echo Muichkine's observations about the *condamné's* desire to live—'Si je pouvais ne pas mourir! Si la vie m'était rendue! quelle éternité s'ouvrirait devant moi . . .' ['Were I not to die! If life was given back to me! What an eternity would open up before me . . .'].[61] Muichkine also states that a man whose throat is cut by brigands preserves, to the last moment, the hope of escape, but this does not exist for the condemned man whose death is inescapably certain and, therefore, unbearable and inhuman.[62] Meursault speaks of a similar hope of escape from certainty:

> Ce qui comptait, c'était une possibilité d'évasion, un saut hors du rite implacable, une course à la folie qui offrit toutes les chances de l'espoir . . . l'espoir, c'était d'être abattu au coin d'une rue, en pleine course, et d'une balle à la volée.[63]

> [What mattered was a possibility of escape, a way of leaping out of this implacable ritual, a mad dash offering all the chances of hope . . . hope, this meant being killed by a stray bullet whilst rushing madly round a street corner.]

Meursault also concludes that if he had the power to change the law, he would arrange executions which would allow the prisoner a chance of escape:

> l'essentiel était de donner une chance au condamné. Une seule sur mille, cela suffisait pour arranger bien des choses.[64]

> [the essential thing was to give the condemned man a chance. Only one in a thousand, that was enough to sort out a lot of things.]

Further manifestations of this parallelism appear in the *Carnets*. It is interesting to note that the 1936 entries (when Camus is fully engaged in reading Dostoevsky) include reference to a projected 'histoire d'un condamné à mort' to be narrated by Patrice of *La Mort heureuse*.[65] Later, in December 1938, the following extract appears, containing reflections on capital punishment which Camus finally used both in *Le Mythe de Sisyphe* and *L'Étranger* (although originally intended for *La Mort heureuse*) and which bears an evident relationship to the quoted speeches of Muichkine:

> Il n'y a qu'un cas où le désespoir soit pur. C'est celui du condamné à mort (qu'on nous permette une petite évocation). On pourrait demander à un désespéré d'amour s'il veut être guillotiné le lendemain, et il refuserait. A cause de l'horreur du supplice? Oui. Mais l'horreur naît ici de la certitude—plutôt de l'élément mathématique qui compose cette certitude. L'absurde est ici parfaitement clair. C'est le contraire d'un irrationel. Il a tous les signes de l'évidence. Ce qui est irrationnel, ce qui le serait, c'est l'espoir passager et moribond que cela va cesser et que cette mort pourra être évitée. Mais non l'absurde. L'évident c'est qu'on va lui couper le cou et pendant qu'il est lucide - pendant même que toute sa lucidité se concentre sur ce fait qu'on va lui couper le cou.

Kirilov a raison. Se suicider c'est faire preuve de sa liberté. Et le problème de la liberté a une solution simple. Les hommes ont l'illusion d'être libres. Les condamnés à mort n'ont pas cette illusion. Tout le problème est dans la réalité de cette illusion. Avant: 'le cœur, ce petit bruit qui depuis si longtemps m'accompagne, comment imaginer qu'il cessera, comment l'imaginer surtout à la seconde même . . .' 'Ah! le bagne, le paradis du bagne.'[66]

[There is only one case where despair is pure. It is that of a man condemned to death (please allow us a short evocation). One could ask somebody dying of love if he wants to be guillotined the next day, and he would refuse. Because of the horror of the torment? Yes. But the horror is born here of the certainty, rather the mathematical element which constitutes this certainty. The absurd is here perfectly clear. It is the opposite of anything irrational. It has all the signs of the obvious. What is irrational, or what would be so, is the fleeting and lifeless hope that this is going to stop and that this death will be able to be avoided. But not the absurd. What is obvious is that someone is going to cut his head off whilst he is perfectly lucid—during the very moment when all his lucidity is concentrated on the fact that he is going to have his head cut off. Kirilov is right. To commit suicide is to demonstrate proof of your freedom. And the problem of freedom has a simple solution. Men have the illusion of being free. Condemned men do not have this illusion. The whole problem is in the reality of this illusion. Before: 'the heart, this little noise which has been my companion for so long, how to imagine that it will cease, how to imagine it at the very moment . . .' 'Ah! the prison, the paradise of prison.']

The intertextual links with Muichkine's speech are, again, quite striking. Both passages use the words 'certitude' and 'supplice' and both make the point that the real suffering comes from the certainty that death is unavoidable rather than the actual pain. Both passages deal with a man who is to be guillotined and both are concerned with the question of the last moments of subjective life. Finally, the mention of 'le paradis du bagne', at the end of the Camus extract, also recalls Dostoevsky's great sensation of relief when he escaped capital punishment and went instead to prison in Siberia, whilst the reference to Kirilov demonstrates that the whole suicide/*condamné* argument and opposition in Camus's work is developing with Dostoevsky's world very much in his mind.

Intense love of life, then, is coupled, in Dostoevsky, with his experience of the death sentence and execution provides both an image of our conditon and evokes the notions of Christ's crucifixion and our rebirth through hope to an eternity of life. Dostoevsky's description of the *condamné* and of the whole world of execution (trial, cell, waiting for death and imagining the final moment etc.) appear to have affected Camus profoundly, not only because he shared all the Russian writer's opposition and revulsion to capital punishment but because it provided him with a rich source of metaphorical and literal thoughts about the link between love of life, death and the inhuman, mechanical processes of execution. The whole of Camus's early work and the key arguments of *Le Mythe de Sisyphe* and *L'Étranger* are really designed to give emphatic and vivid expression to the idea that the bloody mathematical certainty of death must dynamize our determination to live fully and that we should have the pure passion for life of the *condamné* and put away all thoughts of suicide, either actual or intellectual. Dostoevsky is a central presence and a major voice in Camus's world when he elaborates these arguments, helping to shape his picture of *l'homme absurde* and Meursault in prison. This love of life, which Dostoevsky bequeathed to the sensibilities of his great rebels, and its symbolic expression through the image of the *condamné*, provide a significant bridge between the world of the two writers, despite their oppositions in other respects, and constitutes a major line of convergence and dialogue between them.

Both Dostoevsky's and Camus's fictional and philosophical worlds are thus haunted by death and execution, giving their works that stark, fundamentalist, dramatic expression which is part of their appeal. Camus ponders capital punishment and the image of the *condamné*, both as a judicial issue and as a metaphor of existence, in a debate with Dostoevsky. The originality of Camus, in this particular moment of dialogue with Dostoevsky, emanates from the fact that, whilst retaining all the power and moral logic of Dostoevsky's opposition to capital punishment, he is able to rework and refashion the description of the *condamné* into a new image, capable of articulating his positive philosophy of happiness in the kingdom of this world. This new image of the man condemned to death will both serve as a major point of contrast to the *suicidé* and incarnate, through Sisyphus, *l'homme absurde* and especially Meursault in prison, a reply to Dostoevsy's world of Christian hope and rebirth in the next world. In one sense, it could be argued that a major focus of Camus's intentions in *L'Étranger* is to borrow Dostoevksy's image of the *condamné* in order to promote an alternative Christ figure in Western literature: Meursault will kick God's representative, if not God himself (or herself) out of his cell or the prison of his existence, reject hope as evasion and declare his solidarity with this world in a triumphant moment of self-affirmation before death/execution/ crucifixion. He will not bow down to guilt or repent, yield to divine authority or surrender to madness, suicide or despair.

It is perhaps important to stress that if Camus is reworking Dostoevsy's image of the *condamné* in his early work, this is not to be seen in terms of Camus simply borrowing a Dostoevskian icon because of its emotive and moral power and using it to promote his new Christ in a dramatic way. Camus is genuinely haunted by the idea of the *condamné* and execution in his own right.[67] However, the haunting is given enormously enhanced impact and range of application through the agency of his dialogue with Dostoevsky. Camus assimilates the paradigms of Dostoevsky's world of execution to refomulate them in a new synthesis which will carry the full charge of his ethic of individualist and ecstatic self-affirmation before the crushing walls of the absurd.[68]

The attention paid by Camus to the theme of love of life in Dostoevsky should make it clear that it is not simply the picture of despair and anxiety which draws Camus to Dostoevsky's world and characters. R. M. Albérès's view,[69] supported by R. M. Batchelor,[70] that Dostoevsky represents, for Camus, 'la méditation de la mort' or 'l'homme mis au pied du mur, devant l'humiliation, la souffrance, la condamnation' ['the meditation of death' or 'man against the wall, confronted with humiliation, suffering, condemnation'], whereas Nietzsche represented 'la méditation de la vie' ['the meditation of life'], is clearly an oversimplification and fails to recognize the positive and life-enhancing dimension of Camus's experience of reading Dostoevsky. Dostoevsky appealed to Camus both as an analyst of the absurd and as a man who loved existence with an intensity equal to his own. The euphoric and, indeed, beatific dimension of Dostoevsky's world brought it to life for Camus and helped to provide the great rebels with their haunting fascination for him.

Three general areas of affinity have been explored in order to account for Camus's attraction to Dostoevsky's rebels: the experience of the absurd or life without God, the desire to confront the experience with honesty and lucidity and a passionate attachment to life itself mediated through images of death and execution. Dostoevsky finally abandons lucidity, for faith but the rebels live in the same philosophical world as the young Camus. Their major aim, like Camus's own, is to come to terms with the experience of the absurd, without denying its reality. They share with him a commitment to the truth and reason and will not yield to inauthentic hope. However, although the rebels have certain features in common, both with themselves and Camus, they are, nonetheless, individuals and their assimilation of the absurd is not identical. Dostoevsky creates each character to voice their own particular conclusions from the common experience and to incarnate the absurd in a specific way. They are thus made to offer a range of options and perspectives on a world without God. Because of this, Camus himself is attracted to each rebel in a different way and it is the particular response of Camus to each of them which will form the basis for the next two chapters.

One final point needs to be made about Camus's interest in the rebels in general. Whatever the links between Camus and these Dostoevskian characters, he does not arrive at the same conclusions as they do. The relatively contented *homme absurde* who emerges from the pages of *Le Mythe de Sisyphe*, Sisyphus himself, Don Juan etc., these are exemplars of Camus's view of the absurd and they are quite unlike the rebels in the final analysis. For Camus, or so the unlikely argument goes, the absurd should be, can be, and is, a source of happiness for mankind. The absence of God is both compatible with and even necessary to eternal enjoyment of the present (a belief in God distracts from intense involvement with the world). Dostoevsky's rebels, for all their power and glory, live in a hapless state: Kirilov and Stavroguine kill themselves, Ivan goes insane. Despite Camus's attempts to interpret the rebels 'positively' in *Le Mythe de Sisyphe*, the absurd does eventually lead them to despair and they come to illustrate Dostoevsky's conviction that life is impossible without faith, an attitude radically at variance with Camus's own. Meursault and *l'homme absurde* are non-believers but they do not live unhappily: they articulate Camus's answer to Dostoevsky and represent his attempt to create an exit from the impasses of his world, but they could not have been produced by his mind. Dostoevsky's non-believers want to believe, but cannot, because their reason and their questioning consciousness form a barrier to faith. Unable to find God, but with a deep need to believe, they despair and fall into the torments of the Underground Man, Ivan, Dmitri, Stavroguine, Hippolyte and Kirilov; either this, or they are converted like Raskolnikov. Consciousness of the absurd leads them to suicide, paralysis of the will, moral nihilism, bitterness and madness. Although Camus claimed that *l'homme absurde* is not without nostalgia for faith, it is not a nostalgia comparable to that of Dostoevsky's great rebels: Camus's anti-theist heroes, in the early period, find happiness despite and because of the odds. They are new Tzars or Nietzschian supermen who can say 'yes' to everything.

Their kingdom is entirely of this world and, to be sure, they are the only Christs we deserve.

This does not mean (or at least, it did not mean for Camus) that Camus's positive heroes are less tragic than Dostoevsky's rebels, since the two writers have different views of tragedy. For Dostoevsky, characters of great qualities fall into despair, commit suicide or go mad because they cannot find God. Camus, on the other hand, considered one type of man more tragic than a desperate one: paradoxically, he believed, at the time of his early work, that tragedy was centred in happiness He wrote, for example, in *Noces*:

> Tout ce qui exalte la vie accroît en même temps son absurdité. Dans l'été d'Algérie, j'apprends qu'une seule chose est plus tragique que la souffrance et c'est la vie d'un homme heureux.[71]

> [Everything which exalts life, augments simultaneously its absurdity. In the Algerian summer, I understood that only one thing is more tragic than suffering and that is the life of a happy man.]

Tragedy, in both writers, is born of the absurd, as is comedy in large measure, but, for Camus, the picture of a man snatching happiness from the absurd and treasuring it before death is more tragic than that of the individual overwhelmed by a graceless state and a sense of futility, the hall-mark of Dostoevskian tragedy.

Yet Camus did, of course, create certain desperate atheists at this time and did so precisely in the tragedies that he wrote for the theatre. The tragedy of the happy man is reserved for the novels and the early philosophical essays. Caligula and Martha, of *Le Malentendu*, are desperate non-believers: the absurd, for them, is no great pathway to happiness but a destructive passion which turns them into murderers and eventually brings them to suicide. Both are humiliated and injured by the absurd and live in a bleak world which recalls that of Dostoevsky's atheists and is a long way from the happiness of Sisyphe or Meursault. The particular links between these two characters and Dostoevsky's rebels will be explained in the chapters on Kirilov and Ivan but it should be noted, at this stage, that Camus's dramatizations of the absurd, in *Caligula* and *Le Malentendu*, force the question: how confident and secure are the foundations of Camus's Mediterranean world of happiness in the immediate, in this world when they are challenged and haunted so powerfully by Caligula and Martha? In other words, how confident and secure an answer to Dostoevsky are *Le Mythe de Sisyphe* and *L'Étranger*?

63

5

Freedom and the Man-God
Camus and Kirilov in *Le Mythe De Sisyphe*

It is usually Ivan Karamazov who is singled out as the Dostoevskian character with whom Camus has the greatest sense of identity and who made the greatest impact upon him. Camus himself tended to take this view when he spoke of the staging of Copeau's adaptation of *Les Frères Karamazov*.[1] However, although Ivan is a very significant presence in the life of the young Camus and an even greater one in the post-war period, at the time of the composition of *L'Homme révolté*, it is the bizarre suicide project of the engineer, Kirilov, of *Les Possédés*, which dominates Camus's interest in Dostoevsky at the time of *Le Mythe de Sisyphe*. Jean Onimus has pointed out the significance of Kirilov in the thought of Camus during the early period ('c'est peut-être à Kirilov que Camus doit le plus . . . on se demande si toute la métaphysique de Camus n'est pas sortie d'un tel texte' ['it is perhaps to Kirilov that Camus is most indebted . . . one asks oneself if all Camus's metaphysic does not come out of this text'])[2] and several articles have appeared on the subject, attempting to give substance to Onimus's claim. George Strem, Ervin Brody, Kriztina Horvath, Nadine Natov, Julie Vincent and myself,[3] have been among the most interesting appraisals of Camus's fascination with Kirilov, although these articles contain widespread variations of approach. Brody is the most enthusiastic in his response to Camus's analysis of Kirilov, claiming it to be a 'unique interpretation',[4] whilst Julie Vincent argues that the inadequacies of the French translations used by Camus blinded him to certain negative aspects of the character and made him idealize Kirilov, although she does admit that this, in itself, created 'a new tradition for the character'.[5] Dunwoodie aims to take a different line of approach from these comparative studies when he centres his own analysis on retracing 'l'activité de Camus- lecteur [de Dostoïevski]' ['the activity of Camus as reader (of Dostoevsky)'] and on 'le dialogue auteur-personnage que Camus ausculte' ['the author-character dialogue that Camus is listening to'].[6] In this interpretation, Camus's attempts to depict Kirilov as a positive hero of the absurd are considered as part of a strategy to disengage Kirilov's voice from Dostoevsky's and to read *Les Possédés* in a polyphonic, Bakhtinian way. However, there is a lot more to Camus's response to Kirilov than an attempt to depict his suicide in a more favourable light than Dostoevsky, the author, subjectively intended. The present appraisal of Camus's response to Kirilov, building on existing critical analysis, endeavours to define this interest both in terms of affinities and to place it in the context of the notion of a debate between the two writers and to explain Camus's rather eclectic and unusual interpretation as a function of that debate.

Camus's interest in Dostoevsky's rebels may be said to vary according to the particular problems analysed by Camus at a given moment. Camus's interest in Kirilov is most pronounced in the early 1940s and the greater part of the Dostoevsky study in *Le Mythe de Sisyphe* is devoted to an analysis of the engineer's suicide. Ivan and Stavroguine are also mentioned in the essay but they do not have the same amount of space devoted to them as Kirilov. By 1951, however, the case is altogether different, for it is then Ivan, *Le Grand Inquisiteur* and Chigalev who most preoccupy Camus, and Kirilov is placed in the background. His greater interest in Kirilov during the earlier period evidently reflects Camus's probing of the themes of suicide and the absurd in *Le Mythe de Sisyphe*, as he elaborates the foundations of his lucidity-based hedonism, whilst the more detailed attention paid to Ivan and Chigalev in the later period complements his search, from 1943 onwards, for a moral imperative within the framework of the absurd and for a grounding value system for his political philosophy situated somewhere between complacency ('la conformité' or accepting things as they are) and revolution (saying no to everything in the existing social order).

Camus's general response to Kirilov is, perhaps, best illustrated by contrasting it with that of another critic, Ronald Hingley. Camus is moved by the engineer and calls his philosophy 'une indicible aventure spirituelle' ['an indescribable spiritual adventure'].[7] Hingley, however, comments:

> With regard to Kirillov who bears the main burden of 'philo-sophising' in the novel, the suggestion must be made that, like

Ippolit Terentyev in the *The Idiot*, he is one of Dostoevsky's most overrated characters. Dostoevsky was barely capable of creating a nonentity, and Kirillov, with his black lustreless eyes, his curious unidiomatic Russian (a symbol of his estrangement from the soil) and the preoccupation with tea-drinking, which serves as his leitmotiv, is not easily forgotten. But his argument that because God does not exist he must prove that he himself is God by killing himself, and such pseudo-profound statements as God is the fear of the pain of death, contribute some of the least interesting pages of *The Devils*.[8]

For Hingley, only with the passages describing his suicide does Kirilov cease to be 'the most tedious figure in the book'.[9] Even R. Curle, who finds Kirilov one of the most appealing characters in *Les Possédés*, believes that the engineer's obsessive personality is 'quite foreign' to Western European man or 'l'homme moyen sensuel' ['the average sensual man'].[10] Why, then, should Camus have such a high regard for the engineeer's philosophy, treating him with admiration and almost affection, as though he were a real person, and pinning upon his chest what E. Brody has called 'a "croix d'honneur" ['cross of honour'] for his visionary dream about the regeneration of mankind'?[11]

The first major reason for Camus's attraction to Kirilov and for his decision to integrate the example of the engineer into the framework of *Le Mythe de Sisyphe* is linked to the fact that Camus did not consider Kirilov's act of suicide to represent a pessimistic end to a non-religious philosophy committed by a desperate character. On the contrary, Camus links Kirilov's thought to the main thesis of *Le Mythe de Sisyphe*, that the absurd can bring passionate happiness to mankind, to the idea that:

> On ne découvre pas l'absurde sans être tenté d'écrire quelque manuel de bonheur . . . Le bonheur et l'absurde sont deux fils de la même terre. Ils sont inséparables.[12]

> [One doesn't discover the absurd without being tempted to write a manual of happiness . . . Happiness and the absurd are two sons of the same soil. They are inseparable.]

Kirilov attracted Camus because, for him, his philosophy contained a similarly powerful expression of optimism within the absurd.

In *Le Mythe de Sisyphe*, the substance of Camus's view of Kirilov's suicide is that it should be called 'un suicide pédagogique' ['a pedagogical suicide'].[13] Kirilov dies to teach us a truth which contains 'le secret absurde dans toute sa pureté' ['the absurd secret in all its purity'].[14] It is not madness or metaphysical despair which, in Camus's eyes, drives Kirilov to suicide. This was, he states, the reason for the suicide of the writer of 'Jugement'[15] but, with Kirilov, it is the desire to show people that the non-existence of God and, indeed, life without God hold great advantages for us: 'Ce n'est pas le désespoir qui le pousse à la mort', writes Camus, 'mais l'amour du prochain pour lui-même' ['It is not despair which drives him towards death but love of his fellow man for its own sake'].[16] Camus defends this interpretation with two of Kirilov's statements: 'Si tu sens cela [that is to say the advantages born of the non-existence of God], tu es un tsar et loin de te tuer, tu vivras au comble de la gloire', and 'Moi, je suis malheureux, parce que je suis *obligé* d'affirmer ma liberté' [in order to teach man the truth] ['If you feel this, you are a tzar and, far from killing yourself, you will be at the height of glory' and 'I, I am unhappy because I am *obliged* to affirm my freedom'].[17] Kirilov must take his own life, according to Camus, not through despair but because he is the sole possessor of a truth which is capable of leading mankind to a new glory, but this truth can only be communicated by his suicide. To understand the source of this truth and why Camus considered it to reveal 'le secret absurde dans toute sa pureté',[18] it is necessary to recall the main lines of Kirilov's suicide plans. The outline of the engineer's philosophy which follows will concentrate initially on those parts from which Camus himself draws his analysis. This is because Kirilov does explain his suicide in terms of communicating a truth to mankind but, as will be indicated at the end of the chapter, there are other forces at work on the engineer which Camus does not discuss and which cast a totally different light on his action. For the moment, it is sufficient to flesh out Camus's view of the character.

Kirilov believed that man, in his present state of development, is unhappy because he is haunted by the fear of suffering and of death. He tells the narrator: 'La vie est une souffrance, la vie est une crainte, et l'homme est un malheureux' ['Life is suffering, life is fear, and man is unhappy'].[19] Kirilov, however, believes that fear can be overcome and his suicide, at one level, will demonstrate the triumph of man over the fear of death.[20] Moreover, fear of death, in Kirilov's eyes, is the source of God: man created God to relieve the terror of the fear of the finality of death: 'Dieu est la souffrance que cause la crainte de la mort' ['God is the suffering caused by the fear of death'].[21] Consequently, the person who conquers fear of death by suicide also eliminates the need for God by destroying the source of His existence. Furthermore, if man invented God through fear, he is comforted by a lie and Kirilov's suicide will thus also demonstrate that we can live without the lie of God and in full knowledge of the facts of existence: 'Qui ose se tuer a découvert où gît l'erreur' ['He who dares to kill himself has discovered where the error lies'].[22] Finally, in destroying God, man also affirms that his will is subject to none greater than his own: 'Si Dieu existe,' claims Kirilov, 'tout dépend de lui, et je ne puis rien en dehors de sa volonté. S'il n'existe pas, tout dépend de moi, et je suis tenu d'affirmer mon indépendance' ['If God exists,' claims Kirilov, 'everything depends on him and I can do nothing outside of his will. If he doesn't exist, everything depends on me and I am obliged to affirm my independence'].[23] By destroying the source of God, man can become a God on Earth because he is subject to no master or any superior will: 'Celui qui se tuera pour tuer la crainte, celui-là deviendra dieu aussitôt' ['He who kills himself to kill fear, he will straightaway become God'].[24]

With God dead and man's reign established on Earth, Kirilov believed that the long period of human suffering and fear would end and a new era would commence. We would be physically transformed from weak, wretched beings into strong and proud ones and the source of our strength would be the conquest of fear:

> L'Homme à présent n'est pas encore ce qu'il doit être. Il viendra un homme nouveau, heureux et fier. Celui à qui il sera égal de vivre ou de ne pas vivre, celui-là sera l'homme nouveau.[25]

> [Man is not yet what he is to be. A new man will come, happy and proud. He for whom to live or die is a matter of indifference, he will be the new man.]

Present man, however, is unaware of these great possibilities, so Kirilov will commit suicide to inaugurate the new era and show man a new awareness of his condition. He will sacrifice himself and only he needs to do this:

> Mais celui-là seul, qui est le premier, doit absolument se tuer; sans cela, qui donc commencera et prouvera? C'est moi qui me tuerai absolument, pour commencer et prouver.[26]

> [But only he who is first must kill himself without fail; if this is not so, who will begin and demonstrate? It is I who will kill myself without fail, to begin and to demonstrate.]

Kirilov himself has, of course, already achieved the new state of awareness and appears to be reaping its benefits. If man, by eliminating God, becomes a God on Earth, he will experience immediately the joys promised to those who enter the Kingdom of God. Kirilov thus tells Stavroguine, who questions whether his ecstasy is linked to a belief in the next world, that he believes in eternity on Earth. Stavroguine asks: 'Vous croyez maintenant à la vie éternelle dans l'autre monde?' ['You now believe in eternal life in the next world?'] and Kirilov replies:

> Non, mais à la vie éternelle dans celui-ci. Il y a des moments, vous arrivez à des moments où le temps s'arrête tout d'un coup pour faire place à l'éternité.[27]

> [No, but in eternal life in this one. There are moments you attain, moments when time suddenly stops to make way for eternity.]

Kirilov can, therefore, conclude optimistically with a phrase that Camus found particularly interesting and which he felt to be expressive of the essence of absurd philosophy: 'Tout est bien' ['All is well'].[28] Kirilov expands on this state of mind later to Chatov:

> Il y a des moments,—et cela ne dure que cinq ou six secondes de suite, où vous sentez soudain la présence de l'harmonie éternelle . . . C'est un sentiment clair et indiscutable. Il vous semble tout à coup être en contact avec toute la nature et vous dites: Oui, c'est bien comme ça, cela est vrai.[29]

> There are moments—and this only lasts for five or six seconds on end—when you suddenly feel the presence of eternal harmony. It is a clear and certain feeling. It suddenly seems to you that you are in contact with the whole of nature and you say: Yes, it is fine like this, this is true.]

Kirilov's message to mankind then is that if he can conquer the fear of death which produces the lie of God, he will achieve freedom, joy and glory in this world immediately.

In *Le Mythe de Sisyphe*, Camus links Kirilov's ideas to those incarnated in his own creation, *l'homme absurde*. He says:

> Kirilov est donc un personnage absurde—avec cette réserve essentielle cependant qu'il se tue. Mais lui-même explique cette contradiction, et de telle sorte qu'il révèle en même temps le secret absurde dans toute sa pureté. Il ajoute en effet à sa logique mortelle une ambition extraordinaire qui donne au personnage toute sa perspective: il veut se tuer pour devenir dieu.[30]

[Kirilov is thus an absurd character—with the basic reservation, however, that he kills himself. But he himself explains this contradiction and in such a way that he reveals at the same time the absurd secret in all its purity. He adds, in effect, to his mortal logic an extraordinary ambition which gives the character his full perspective: he wants to kill himself to become God.]

Camus then goes on to analyse Kirilov's theory of the Man-God and the undoubted implication is that Camus considered this idea to contain 'le secret absurde dans toute sa pureté'. One could justifiably assume from this that Camus's and Kirilov's thought converged on this matter but the contrary seems true and it is worth considering why before continuing with the analysis.

Kirilov's philosophy embraces a conception of freedom quite unlike Camus's own and there can be no real justification for a *rapprochement* between the theory of the Man-God and *l'homme absurde*. Kirilov's freedom has metaphysical origins since it is based on the idea that if God does not exist, there is no will greater than man's. Man is a God on Earth because there is no God in Heaven. Camus, however, states quite explicitly in *Le Mythe de Sisyphe* that metaphysical liberty is a meaningless idea within his own philosophical framework:

Savoir si l'homme est libre commande qu'on sache s'il peut avoir un maître. L'absurdité particulière à ce problème vient de ce que la notion même qui rend possible le problème de la liberté lui retire en même temps tout son sens.[31]

[To know if man is free demands that one knows if he might have a master. The particular absurdity of this problem comes from the fact that the very notion which makes possible the problem of freedom simultaneously robs it of any sense.]

Kirilov's suicide was meant to represent the denial of God and the consequent affirmation of man's freedom. Camus and *l'homme absurde* do not deny God: they do not believe in Him, but the possibility of His existence is not excluded. Because Camus is an agnostic rather than an atheist, awareness of the absurd cannot lead to the supremacy of man's will on Earth. The kind of freedom which springs from Camus's position is quite different: the absurd man knows that he is going to die and considers death final. Consequently, he decides to live entirely for the present and, in so doing, he achieves freedom of action— the sort of freedom which comes from not having to sacrifice the present to future considerations.[32]

Despite these differences, Camus says of Kirilov's theory: 'Devenir Dieu c'est seulement être libre sur cette terre, ne pas servir un être immortel' ['To become God means only to be free on this earth, not to serve an immortal being'].[33] In claiming that Kirilov's freedom comes simply from not serving God, Camus is once again linking him to *l'homme absurde*, whom he defined as 'celui qui sans le nier ne fait rien pour l'éternel' ['he who, without denying God, does nothing for the eternal'].[34] But Kirilov's freedom does not merely consist in not serving a God: it is based on a complete denial of God and could not exist with even the possibility of a God. The root of this confusion seems to lie in the fact that Dostoevsky is a Christian writer and poses the problem of free-will and God's omnipotence in his works, whereas Camus felt such problems to be meaningless from his own particular standpoint. This has been commented upon by Joseph Marek:

> C'est de la liberté que part Dostoïevski, c'est elle qu'il tente d'élucider et de justifier. Au contraire, chez Camus, la notion de la liberté n'intervient que parmi les conséquences qui découlent du postulat de l'absurde: le problème de la liberté n'est plus central. L'homme que nous propose Camus décide de vivre en homme libre une fois qu'il a reconnu l'absurdité de sa position; mais il n'est pas voué originellement à la liberté, il ne se définit pas essentiellement comme liberté. Sur ce point Camus s'oppose radicalement à Sartre et aux autres existentialistes, alors que ceux-ci se rapprochent de Dostoïevski.[35]

> [It is from freedom that Dostoevsky starts, it is freedom which he tries to clarify and justify. On the contrary, with Camus, freedom only arises as one of the consequences which flow from the postulation of absurdity: the problem of freedom is no longer central. The man who Camus proposes to us decides to live as a free person once he has recognized the absurdity of his position; but he is not originally destined for freedom, he isn't essentially defined as freedom. On this point Camus distinguishes himself radically from Sartre and the other existentialists, who stand closer to Dostoevsky.]

The same confusion is also notably evident in a reference to Kirilov and freedom in the *Carnets* in 1938. Here Camus wrote:

> Kirilov a raison. Se suicider, c'est faire preuve de sa liberté.

> [Kirilov is right. To commit suicide is to prove your freedom.]

But then he adds:

> Et le problème de la liberté a une solution simple. Les hommes ont l'illusion d'être libres. Les condamnés à mort n'ont pas cette illusion. Tout le problème est dans la réalité de cette illusion.[36]

> [And the problem of freedom has a simple solution. Men have the illusion of being free. Men condemned to death do not have this illusion. The whole problem is in the reality of this illusion.]

At first, in this quotation, Camus appears to accept that suicide provides a proof of freedom but then he claims freedom is an illusion, presumably because of death. If it is an illusion, how can suicide be a proof of it?

Notwithstanding these important differences in their notions of freedom, Camus is determined to abstract Kirilov from Dostoevsky's Christian metaphysic of the will, to project him as a positive hero of absurd freedom as defined by his own framework and to see incarnated in this character the possibility of ecstatic happiness combined with a lucid appraisal of the fact of death. Kirilov's suicide provides, in this way, a key to human happiness.

> Mais si ce crime métaphysique suffit à l'accomplissement de l'homme [to kill God within oneself by overcoming fear of death leads to glory for man on Earth] pourquoi y ajouter le suicide? Pourquoi se tuer, quitter le monde après avoir conquis sa liberté? Cela est contradictoire. Kirilov le sait bien, qui ajoute 'Si tu sens cela, tu es un tzar et loin de te tuer tu seras au comble de la gloire.' Mais les hommes ne le savent pas. Ils ont besoin qu'on leur montre le chemin et ne peuvent pas se passer de la prédication. Kirilov doit donc se tuer pour l'amour de l'humanité mais lui mort, les hommes enfin éclairés, cette terre se peuplera de tzars et s'illuminera de la gloire humaine . . . Ainsi ce n'est pas le désespoir qui le pousse à la mort mais l'amour du prochain pour lui-même.[37]

> [But if this metaphysical crime is sufficient for the fulfilment of humanity, why add suicide to it? Why kill oneself, leave the world after having acquired one's freedom? This is a contradiction. Kirilov knows it well, and adds: 'If you feel this, you are a tzar and far from killing yourself you will be at the height of glory.' But men do not know this. They need somebody to show them the way and they cannot do without a prophet. Kirilov must then kill himself for the love of humanity but once he is dead and people are fully enlightened, the earth will be peopled with tzars and bathed in

human glory . . . Thus it is not despair which drives him towards
death but love of humanity for its own sake.]

Kirilov's suicide is thus endorsed by Camus in the name of a
pedagogy which will yield greater human happiness. It delivers us
the Kingdom of this world, a world which Kirilov enjoyed and would
have continued to enjoy, had it not been for the necessity of his
illuminating sacrifice. Leaving aside, for the moment, the question
of the validity and coherence of Camus's analysis of Kirilov, it is
clear that Camus's attraction to the character is related to the
question of the engineer's lucidity before death and his enigmatic
state of contentment expressed in the familiar 'tout est bien'. An
analysis of these two areas of interest will enable a clearer picture to
be formed of the general impact of Kirilov in the crystallization of
Camus's early thought on both themes.

Both Kirilov and the young Camus, whatever the origins of their
respective notions of freedom, are moved by a strong desire to face
the facts of existence and, in particular, to face the fact of death.
Kirilov's claims that God is the fear of the pain of death, that we
must overcome lies to escape our wretched state, and that courage
is rooted in lucidity, are echoed everywhere in Camus's early work.
Although it is true that, in *Le Mythe de Sisyphe*, Camus rejects faith
largely because God's existence cannot be proved empirically, in
L'Envers et l'endroit and *Noces*, the anti-religious arguments take a
different form and seem permeated with Kirilovian elements.

Religion, in the early *essais* is seen mainly as a degrading escape
from impotence, illness, loneliness and death. It is compensation for
the diminishing forces of life, man's only true kingdom. As Roger
Quilliot says:

C'est une pauvre religion que Camus a connue dans son entourage,
tout entière liée à la peur de la mort.[38]

[It was an impoverished religion which Camus knew from his
background, linked in its entirety to the fear of death.]

In 'L'Ironie', for example, Camus refers to an old woman who is
'libérée de tout sauf de Dieu, livrée toute entière à ce mal dernier'
['liberated from everything but God, totally given over to this final
ill'] and this is reminiscent of Kirilov's attitude to God and freedom.[39] Like Kirilov, Camus believed that one of man's basic longings
is to escape the conviction that death is final[40] and he too considers
such fear undignified. Death, although unpleasant, like the absurd,

should be faced honestly and with dignified courage.[41] Camus also dreams of the coming of a new race of men who will not tolerate the indignity of fearing death ('le seul progrès de la civilisation, celui auquel de temps en temps un homme s'attache, c'est de créer des morts conscientes' ['the only progress that civilization can make, that progress occasionally yearned for by men, is to create conscious deaths']).[42] and this echoes Kirilov's vision of a new man, proud and free. In fact, it is tempting to believe that Camus thought he found in his Algerian countrymen a race of people similar to the one Kirilov hoped to see emerge. 'L'Été à Alger' represents a eulogy of the values of courage, lucidity and honesty before fate; Camus talks of the Algerians as people 'nés pour l'orgueil et la vie' ['born for pride and life'],[43] and goes on:

> Ces hommes n'ont pas triché. Dieux de l'été, ils le furent à vingt ans par leur ardeur à vivre et le sont encore, privés de tout espoir. J'en ai vu mourir deux. Ils étaient pleins d'horreur, mais silencieux. Cela vaut mieux ainsi.[44]

> [These men have not cheated. They were gods of the summer at twenty by their passion for life and they are still gods now, devoid of all hope. I saw two of them die. They were filled with horror, but kept silent. It is better this way.]

He also praises their refusal to dress in pleasant myths their horror of death[45] and this again seems to parallel Kirilov's wish to kill the lie of God. Kirilov would surely have reacted favourably to the Algerians, at least as Camus depicts them, for they have that very pride and strength, coupled with lucidity, which forms the essence of his new man.[46] Camus's Mediterranean mythology of a perishable race of young Algerian Gods of the summer is shot through with Kirilov's vision of the Man-God and of a new dawn of human self-affirmation before death.

Another work by Camus which brings out particularly well the way in which his attitude to death, courage and lucidity coincides with the engineer's is *Caligula*, a play originally entitled *Caligula ou la Mort*. *Caligula*, like *Le Malentendu*, is rooted in Camus's absurd cycle of works and crystallizes, as a play, essentially at the same time as *Le Mythe de Sisyphe*. Both plays bear strong traces of Camus's reading of Dostoevsky. Camus's conception of the Roman Emperor contains several elements which recall Kirilov's ideas. Caligula attempts to reveal the reality of the human condition to the patricians. He dislikes lies and wants man to recognize the truth that 'Les hommes meurent et ils ne sont pas heureux' ['Men die and they are not happy'].[47] When his servant, Hélicon, explains that the truth does not prevent people from eating their lunch, he replies:

> Alors, c'est que tout, autour de moi, est mensonge, et moi, je veux qu'on vive dans la vérité. Car je sais ce qui leur manque, Hélicon. Ils sont privés de la connaissance et il leur manque un professeur qui sache ce dont il parle.[48]

> [Then, this is because I am surrounded by lies and I want people to live in the truth. For I know what they need, Helicon. They are deprived of knowledge and they need a teacher who knows what he is talking about.]

Caligula, like Kirilov, wants to bring man to a new awareness and he considers himself a teacher (speaking to Caesonia, he describes his actions as 'de la pédagogie'[49] recalling Camus's reference to Kirilov's suicide as 'un suicide pédagogique'). Caligula also wants to transform man and make him happy:

> Je serai transformé et le monde avec moi, alors enfin les hommes ne mourront pas et ils seront heureux.[50]

> [I shall be transformed and the world with me, then at last men will not die and they will be happy.]

Furthermore, Caligula feels he is guiding man along the road to freedom; like Kirilov, he considers himself the only free man and he wants to teach this freedom to others, although he does this by tyranny and not suicide. Caligula's freedom is also born of a certain indifference to death, and, like the engineer, he admires lucidity, courage and strength of mind before destiny.[51] In this respect, it should be noted that Camus described Caligula's death as 'un suicide supérieur' ['a higher form of suicide'], and he uses the same expression to refer to Kirilov's suicide in *Le Mythe de Sisyphe*, as though unconsciously linking the two characters.[52] Finally, the Emperor shares the restlessness of the engineer; he is obsessed with the absurd and, like Kirilov, spends the night in agitated meditation.[53]

Clearly, Kirilov and the young Camus appear to possess some striking affinities when it comes to the subject of death. Camus appears to have assimilated the visionary pronouncements of Dostoevsky's engineer and to have fed them into his early *essais* and *Caligula* in order both to formulate his own philosophy of the new man and eventually to dramatize the possible dangers of such individualism.

A further very interesting affinity between Camus and Kirilov is related to the engineer's statement, 'tout est bien', and the ecstatic mood which governs it. Kirilov's frame of mind, when uttering these words, seems to have held a particular fascination for Camus; he refers to it on several occasions in Le Mythe de Sisyphe and calls it 'absurde'.[54] Indeed, it seems possible that Camus himself sometimes experienced moods which he identified with Kirilov's and this appears to be a major factor in his preoccupation with the engineer and with Dostoevsky generally in the early period. There can be little doubt that Kirilov's 'tout est bien' emanates, in a general sense, from that love of life which was enjoyed by Dostoevsky and which we have already examined as a specific affinity between Camus and the Russian writer. However, the statement 'tout est bien' is also indicative of a more profound apprehension of existence.

Kirilov's 'tout est bien' is uttered in moments of ecstatic communion with nature and all aspects of creation; at these times he feels at one with the world and imagines that he is experiencing on Earth the joys of the Kingdom of Heaven, the joys available to all men who become Gods in this world. In the exchanges made with Stavroguine (quoted on p. 69), Kirilov states his belief in eternal life in this world, revealed to him in these moments, an atemporal sensation of harmony with everything, a point particularly noted by Camus.[55] This sensation of timeless, joyful communion with the world order produces, in Kirilov, a serenity tantamount to indifference to all human suffering and evil. He accepts all aspects of life, whatever they may be: 'Et si l'on meurt de faim, et si l'on viole une petite fille, . . . c'est bien aussi?' ['And if one dies of starvation, and if a young girl is raped, . . . is that alright as well?'] asks Stavroguine, and Kirilov replies: 'Oui. Tout est bien pour quiconque sait qu'il est tel' ['Yes. All is well for anyone who knows that this is so'].[56]

In 1937, when speaking of Tibetan mystics, Camus made the following remark about lucidity and ecstasy:

> Coutumes respiratoires des yogis du Thibet. Ce qu'il faudrait, c'est apporter notre méthodologie positive à des expériences de cette envergure: avoir des 'révélations' auxquelles on ne croit pas. Ce qui me plaît: porter sa lucidité dans l'extase.[57]

> [Respiratory habits of Tibetan yogis. What is wanted is to apply our positivist method to experiences of this scale: to have

'revelations' which we do not believe in. *What I like:* maintaining one's lucidity in ecstasy.]

Camus does, in fact, seem to have experienced this state of lucid and ecstatic communion with the world order. He describes the different aspects of it in the early *essais*, whilst the memory of it informs part of his thinking in *Le Mythe de Sisyphe*. It also underpins the characterization of Scipion in *Caligula* and helps to define the notion of 'le royaume' ['the kingdom'] in other parts of his work such as 'La Femme adultère'. It is Camus's response to the world at these particular moments which recalls Kirilov's mood when he says, 'tout est bien'. A number of parallels can be made here.

As Camus himself points out in *Le Mythe de Sisyphe*, Kirilov's 'tout est bien', which Camus describes as 'un mot aussi vieux que la souffrance des hommes' ['an expression as old as human suffering'] and significantly as 'la formule de la victoire absurde' ['the formula which expresses the victory of the absurd attitude'],[58] expresses, in one sense, a mood of reconciliation with destiny. It is based on the conviction that life brings man both pleasure and pain, and that the dark destructive forces of the world order are counterpoised and compensated by the other side of life's cloth. It also springs from the feeling that man is, at least, the moral master of his destiny if he shows courage, does not give in to despair or run away from the challenge thrown down by fate. For Camus, this mood of reconciliation, attained by Kirilov, represented the very essence of Greek wisdom before destiny.[59] Both Œdipus and Sisyphus, in his view, arrive at Kirilov's attitude in their final judgement of life, despite all their torments[60]. It is also the conclusion reached by Tarrou in *La Peste*[61] and, of course, it is at the root of Camus's attitude in the early *essais* and *Le Mythe de Sisyphe*, permeating his conception of *l'homme absurde*, Don Juan, the Conqueror and the Actor. As an expression of this mood of reconciliation, Kirilov's 'tout est bien' seems to sum up Camus's early views on man and destiny, and in *Le Mythe de Sisyphe*, as we have noted, he actually refers to it as 'la formule de la victoire absurde',[62] epitomizing our power to live and face our destiny fully alone without grace or hope.

The personal experiences which underlie Camus's observations on Kirilov and the Greeks in *Le Mythe de Sisyphe* are fully described in *Noces*, and many other similarities with the engineer's state of mind become apparent. For example, Camus experienced, like Kirilov, moments of accord and harmony with the order of creation. The whole of *Noces* celebrates the joyful communion and supreme accord which Camus achieves with nature and all aspects of life. This feeling of harmony also leads Camus, like Kirilov, to a kind of serenity, although Camus's serenity is admittedly not as sublime as the engineer's whose ecstasy finally leads to ethical insensibility and prevents the perception of evil and suffering. Yet although Camus was acutely sensitive to the suffering of others, there is definitely a trace of Kirilov's serenity in his early thought, a point Camus made himself in the preface to *L'Envers et l'endroit*, where he speaks of the 'indifférence naturelle' ['natural attitude of indifference'] which did not in any way predispose him to social engagement on behalf of others.[63] The indifference mentioned here would appear to be similar to Kirilov's in that it originates not from insensitivity but from this feeling of accord with creation. At least this seems to be the sense specifically of the essay 'L'Ironie', and also to be one of the major ideas of the early *essais* in general captured in the following quote:

> Tout ça ne se concilie pas? La belle vérité. Une femme qu'on abandonne pour aller au cinéma, un vieil homme qu'on n'écoute plus, une mort qui ne rachète rien et puis, de l'autre côté, toute la lumière du monde. Qu'est-ce que ça fait si on accepte tout?[64]

> [All this cannot be reconciled? What nonsense. A woman whom one abandons to go to the cinema, an old man whom nobody listens to any more, a death which redeems nothing and then, on the other side, all the light in the world. What does it matter if one accepts everything?]

In addition, Camus also experiences in *Noces* the sensation of timelessness, of living in the eternity of the present, a fundamental aspect of Kirilov's mood.[65] This feeling correspondingly produces, in both Camus and Kirilov, an indifference to the future: at Djémila, says Camus, the word 'future' has no meaning[66] and Kirilov's ecstasy is so strong that he believes he has achieved the timeless state mentioned in the New Testament when man will cease to procreate.[67] Camus noticed Kirilov's indifference to the future, and, in *Le Mythe de Sisyphe*, describes such indifference as an essential feature of *l'homme absurde*, so he was well aware of his similarity to Kirilov in this respect.[68] He also points out that it is this very mood which led Kirilov to allow his suicide to be used by the nihilist group in *Les Possédés* to provide them with a cover for the murder of Chatov—such is Kirilov's confidence before fate.[69] In both cases, the sense of eternity in the present moment is linked to the heightened awareness of death. Camus, at Djémila, evokes the image of the *condamné* to designate his sense of intensity: 'Oui, je suis présent. Et ce qui me frappe à ce moment, c'est que je ne peux aller plus loin. Comme un homme emprisonné à perpétuité—et tout lui est présent' ['Yes, I am present. And what strikes me at this moment is that I cannot go any further. Like a man serving a life-sentence for whom all time is present time'].[70] Camus injected the sense of an eternal present into Meursault during his *emprisonnement*, for Meursault claims that even if he had to spend the rest of his life in a dry tree-trunk, he would not mind as long as he had a sight of the sky above and could contemplate it. This certainly echoes Kirilov's sense of the mystical and possibly also Muichkine's, who claims that man can live a boundless life even in prison (Muichkine, as we shall see, embodies all the essential features of epilepsy interpreted as a mystical experience giving access to oneness).[71]

There would appear to be, then, a considerable number of striking parallels between Camus's pagan mysticism in *Noces* and the state of mind achieved by Kirilov in *Les Possédés*. Both experience a state of harmony and spiritual tranquillity before fate, charged with a lucid intensity when facing the fact of death; both have sensations of timelessness linked to ecstasy within the absurd and this produces an indifference to the future and a certain serenity and detachment before traditional notions of value and evil. These convergences of mood, added to their similar responses to death, religious lucidity, honesty and courage, and their wish to see a new race of men emerge confidently, proudly and triumphantly from the ruins of God's Kingdom, provide the basic keys to Camus's interest in Kirilov. Kirilov emerges from this analysis as a powerful crystallizing element in the formulation of Camus's early work, helping to sharpen his ideas on death, religion and hedonistic self-affirmation, and providing a model of lucid ecstasy within the framework of absurd awareness and of a deep sense of contentment before fate. Camus's reading of Kirilov may be said, generally, to remind Camus of the way his own particular feelings and ideas about the world could be framed to form a philosophical attitude and to promote a vision of a new man and an alternative Christ figure.

Whatever may be said of Camus's interest in Kirilov, no study of his response to the engineer would be complete without referring to his eclectic view of the character. It is certainly difficult to accept Carina Gadourek's assertion that Camus's analysis of Kirilov is 'penetrating' and 'explains the character well'[72] or Brody's claim that it has a 'unique' value.[73]

The first major point that needs to be made is that, even taking into account Bakhtine's polyphonic readings which make ambiguity central to Dostoevsky's world, Dostoevskian criticism does not interpret Kirilov positively or optimistically. Kirilov may promise us a new Kingdom through his mystical atheism and his theory of the Man-God but he remains a desperate character. Hingley, for example, considers that Kirilov's suicide, like Stavrougine's, ultimately illustrates Dostoevsky's viewpoint that, without belief in immortality, life is impossible for man: 'Kirillov', he writes, 'represents anti-Dostoyevskianism carried to what Dostoevsky liked to think of as its logical conclusion in suicide.'[74] Marek felt that Kirilov was a 'very desperate person'[75] and George Steiner makes the more precise point that 'Kirilov kills himself in abject despair, because he could not kill himself in an affirmation of freedom'.[76] Moreover, in depicting Kirilov as a teacher who will produce the Tzars, Stavroguine and Ivan, Camus inverts the psychology and pedagogy of the text because Kirilov is Stavroguine's pupil and creature as, ideed, are Chatov and Verkhovensky junior.[77] Stavroguine is the centre of *Les Possédés* and his all pervasive atheism and indifference 'poison' and fragment his associates who become possessed like the Gadarene swine. Stavroguine has fed Kirilov with the thesis of the Man-God and suicide and provoked an obsessional crisis in the character, as Chatov knows only too clearly.[78] The fact that Kirilov is also an engineer and has been to America, the country of Western technological decadence and spiritual bankruptcy for Dostoevsky, are additional contingent factors used to support a negative view of the character.

If Kirilov kills himself in despair, why then, Camus would presumably argue, does he say ecstatically, 'tout est bien' and assert that man can achieve greatness without God? K. Mochulsky's interpretation seems to me to provide a good answer. Kirilov, he claims, suffers from a fatal dichotomy of mind and heart. Far from achieving happiness within awareness of the absurd, Kirilov is unable to reconcile the conclusions of his reason with the joyful and optimistic feelings which spring from the heart, and he is torn apart by this dualism in his character. With the heart, Mochulsky argues, Kirilov experiences religious ecstasy, but with the mind he arrives at the negation of God and the necessity of suicide. He illustrates the drama of a man who feels that Christianity is true but his believing heart is powerless before the disbelief of reason.[79]

Kirilov certainly does appear to be divided between the claims of reason and religious belief, and he reveals this struggle between lucidity and faith, a struggle which was, of course, experienced by Dostoevsky himself, when he tells Piotr Stépanovitch:

Dieu est nécessaire et par conséquent doit exister . . . Mais je sais qu'il n'existe pas et qu'il ne peut exister. Comment ne comprends-tu pas qu'avec ces deux idées-là, il est impossible à l'homme de continuer à vivre?[80]

[God is necessary and thus must exist . . . But I know that he does not and cannot exist. Why do you not understand that with those two ideas, it is impossible for man to continue to live?]

Camus did notice this remark, but either failed or, what is more likely, chose not to develop its implications fully, and his portrait of Kirilov remains incomplete because it does not take account of all the particulars of the text.

Because it is structured upon this basic despair, the philosophy of the Man-God, for all its Romantic appeal, is fragile and vulnerable at the centre. This seems a more logical interpretation, for Dostoevsky was hardly likely to create a happy atheist, believing as he did that life is impossible for man without God. His faith may have been imperfect, but his conviction that without faith man could do nothing was absolute. In trying to fit Kirilov into his analysis of *l'homme absurde*, Camus thus not only extricated Kirilov from his creator's Christian vision but also glossed over the religious conflict within him. As was previously noted, an essential difference between Camus's *l'homme absurde* and Dostoevsky's rebels lies in their attitude towards a godless world. Dostoevsky's atheists are unhappy; whatever the intensity of their rebellions, they want to believe but cannot. This is not the case with Camus's characters, with the exception of Caligula, Martha and Clamence, who all resemble Dostoevsky's rebels and do not have Camus's total sympathy. The real heroes —Meursault, Rieux, Tarrou, Jan and Kaliayev—do not despair in their disbelief and maintain a stoical resolve in adversity.

As well as ignoring the fatal schism between heart and reason which undermines the foundations of Kirilov's 'optimistic atheism' (to coin a phrase), Camus also, both in his interpretation of Kirilov and in his dramatization of the character in his adaptation of *Les Possédés*, pays no attention to the actual circumstances of Kirilov's suicide in the novel, where Dostoevsky is at pains to underline the desperate, jumpy nervousness of Kirilov as he wildly edges towards his death. In fact, Kirilov's grand plan is undermined in its execution and more resembles the despair of the writer of 'Jugement'[81] than an affirmation of freedom. George Strem has commented upon this:

> It is interesting that Camus did not seem to understand or, what is more likely, chose to ignore the true significance of Kirilov's suicide, which turned out to be, under the masterly hand of Dostoevsky, an ardent demonstration of the futility of any rebellion against God, the very opposite of the message it had intended to convey.[82]

Dostoevsky certainly does emphasize Kirilov's religious yearnings: the keen eye of Stavroguine sees to the heart of the engineer's dilemma when he tells him that he will soon believe in God because he needs to do so badly,[83] whilst the convict Fedka is impressed by Kirilov's Christian feelings when he reads the *Book of Revelation* to him.[84] Camus takes Kirilov's religious dimension and elevates it to an expression of non-theist optimism about life on Earth in the immediate. He makes Kirilov into a Cartesian apologist of the absurd as a key to happiness, rather than the suffering and divided person that he is for most other critics. In other words, he rescues Kirilov from Dostoevsky's all-embracing Christian messianism and allows him to triumph over his creator and affirm the possibility of a coherent atheism and hedonism.

Strem raises the point of the fidelity of Camus's aproach to the novel by referring to the possibility that Camus 'did not understand' or 'more likely, chose to ignore' the true significance of Kirilov's suicide. Another critic refers to Camus's 'interprétation inclinée' ['slanted interpretation'][85] of Kirilov, whilst another blames the inadequacy of the French translations available to Camus, which did not fully convey the speech impediments of Dostoevsky's character and his alienation from the Russian soil.[86] This latter point seems overstated: it may be that Kirilov's Russian is not adequately captured by the translators but Kirilov's conflicts and basic despair are fully apparent and, in any case, French critical interpretation of Kirilov in general does not coincide with the Camusian response. It has already been stated that Camus was often interested in other people's thinking less for its intrinsic value than for those particular moments when it either coincided or entered into conflict with his own. This appears to have led Camus to concentrate on the positive potentialities of Kirilov and to disregard the unstable foundations of his philosophy and its religious ambiguities. He perhaps produces, in this way, a far more challenging and dangerous Kirilov than Dostoevsky intended to produce or could ever have produced, a real Man-God and an answer to the Christ who was crucified in the name of an illusory next world, governed by a God who does not exist.

In view of the similarities indicated between the state of mind of

Kirilov and that of Camus in *Noces*, it is very interesting to note Mochulsky's argument that Kirilov experiences the world in his heart as a Christian. What appeared, to Camus, to be the essence of Greek wisdom before fate and an expression of modern hedonistic individualism without God was, in fact, for Dostoevsky, part of the experience of epileptic seizure. Kirilov's 'tout est bien' is clearly very close to the mood and state of mind of Prince Muichkine which, as was already noted, is produced by epilepsy and formed part of the mystical element in Dostoevsky's otherwise pragmatic faith. When Kirilov explains his ecstatic feelings to Chatov, Chatov warns him that he may be suffering from epilepsy,[87] and, in this way, Dostoevsky is able to make quite explicit the links between Kirilov and the prince and the way in which their moods are related to epilepsy and Christianity.

It is surely significant that Muichkine, whom Gide described as having attained 'l'état chrétien par excellence' ['the Christian state *par excellence*'],[88] is the only one of Dostoevsky's positive Christian characters to interest Camus, and it was precisely because of this state of mind. Camus wrote of the prince in *Le Mythe de Sisyphe* (and the phraseology is worth noting):

> Malade, ce dernier vit dans un perpétuel présent, nuancé de sourires et d'indifférence et cet état bienheureux pourrait être la vie éternelle dont parle le prince.[89]

> [This latter person, being ill, lives in a perpetual present, laced with smiles and indifference and this blissful state could be the eternal life to which the prince refers.]

For Dostoevsky, the epileptic experience constituted a foretaste of the Kingdom of Heaven: a great synthesis occurred in which he felt at one with God. Since Camus's experience in *Noces* was also one of unity and feeling at one with the world, it is difficult not to think of his reference to the Tibetan mystics ('avoir des "révélations" auxquelles on ne croit pas . . . porter sa lucidité dans l'extase'['to have "revelations" which we do not believe in . . . maintaining one's lucidity in ecstasy']). Could the experience in *Noces* have been such a 'révélation'? It was certainly a vital experience for Camus and represents a kind of pagan mysticism. Although it had no transcendental significance for him, there is some proof of the fact that he associated it with religious experience: having called Kirilov's state of mind 'absurde', Camus concludes the Dostoevsky study in *Le Mythe de Sisyphe* with the paradoxical remark that one can be 'chrétien et absurde' ['Christian and absurd'], and speaks of the 'absurdité de l'Evangile' ['the absurdity of the New Testament'].[90]

It seems possible to deduce from all this that Camus experienced moments comparable to Dostoevsky's moments of grace, but without believing in God. André Blanchet, a Christian critic, has pointed out that Camus deliberately places a Christian complexion on his experience in *Noces* to show that moments of ecstasy similar to religious grace are possible for the non-believer, and he sees this as a further aspect of the anti-Christian tendency of the work.[91] This idea of attributing to such moments the appearance of grace may well have been suggested to Camus by Kirilov who could thus be said to be providing Camus with a key to a reply to Dostoevsky's world of Christian grace and this reply would be pagan ecstasy in the immediate.

One final point should be made on this issue: the Christian moods of Kirilov and Muichkine also seem related to Meursault's. Meursault appears to live in harmony and accord with the world order if not the social one. He is tender, serene and indifferent in the same way as Kirilov and the prince. He lives with only a vague sense of time, and Camus may well have been trying to communicate through Meursault that feeling of all being present described in *Noces*. P. Thody has pointed out the many similarities between Meursault's mood and that of Camus in the early lyrical works,[92] and Sartre did, of course, notice a parallel between Muichkine and Meursault and refers to their tranquillity and serenity,[93] an affinity also seized upon by Boisdeffre.[94] One might add that Meursault is a strong and proud individual, does not give in to fear or despair and achieves a state of contentment with the world order premissed on death and its lucid recognition. Camus also compared Meursault to a Christ figure, as he did Kirilov, and it may well be that the engineer's concept of the Man-God made its mark upon *L'Étranger* in this way. In this respect, it is worth noting that, once again, Camus fails to notice or simply ignores the fact that Kirilov's state of mind embraces an indifference to ethical distinctions which is dangerous, to say the least. Kirilov's epileptic state, it should be stressed, is different in ethical terms from Muichkine's who retains a clear perception of evil and suffering.[95] Camus does, of course, mention certain aspects of Kirilov's indifference (indifference to the future, stoical attitude towards death) but the ethical dimension is unexplored in favour of the idea of the positive atheist. Camus evidently perceives Kirilov and creates Meursault through the perspectives of his own experiences in *Noces* which are also characterized by moments of ethical insensibility and are at the root of the hedonistic individualism of the early period. Camus's overall aim throughout this period is to define the absurd in terms of happiness. His interpetation of Kirilov is a function of that objective and of his determination to provide an answer and an alternative world-view to Dostoevsky's theism. Camus appears to want a philosophy with all the mystical power and ecstasy of Dostoevsky's world of grace without any of its divine trappings. To achieve this, he very consciously engages Dostoevsky's work in dialogue, hijacks its mystical dimensions, expressed through Kirilov, Muichkine and Dostoevsky himself, reroutes them through his own pagan mysticism in *Noces* and creates a new Man-God and semi-Christ-like figure, Meursault, to answer the challenge of Dostoevsky's world.[96] As the ethical dimension of Camus's thought develops after 1942, Kirilov becomes far less important in his work at the same time as the attitude of Meursault looks increasingly inadequate to the challenges of history and society. Kirilov's lucid contentment as conceptualized by Camus, Sisyphus's happiness and the alternative Christ appear increasingly unreal and limited as the world goes to war.

Camus's selective and highly angled approach to Kirilov transformed Dostoevsky's character from a person in desperate need of faith and suffering from a fatal dichotomy of mind and heart into a hero of the absurd and an incarnation of authentic freedom. His fascination with Kirilov was great but it was with a Kirilov very much seen through the lenses of his own thought and sensibility. This does not alter the fact that Kirilov is a principal element in Camus's dialogue with Dostoevsky and a vey real presence in his early work.

6

Two Tzars of the Absurd
Stavroguine and Ivan in
Le Mythe De Sisyphe

Camus refers specifically to two more of Dostoevsky's rebels in *Le Mythe de Sisyphe*, Stavroguine of *Les Possédés* and Ivan Karamazov, but they are not analysed to the same extent as Kirilov. This is perhaps because their ideas and eventual fates in the novels cannot be made to blend with or reflect the optimistic line of thought developed in Camus's discussion of the absurd. Whereas Kirilov's suicide could be presented in a positive light and have some value as a paradigm of absurd happiness, Stavroguine's suicide and the note that accompanies it, together with Ivan's insanity, do not constitute an invitation to find happiness in the absurd. They are more difficult to rescue from the general pessimism which Dostoevsky felt at the thought of existence without God. Nonetheless, Camus does still present them as positive exemplars of the absurd, as Kirilovian 'tzars' of a godless world, whose fates offer further dimensions and facets of absurd thought and sensibility. Kirilov is seen by Camus as the intellectual father of Stavroguine and Ivan. After his opening remarks about the engineer, Camus observes:

> Notons seulement avant d'aller plus loin que Kirilov rebondit dans d'autres personnages qui engagent eux-mêmes de nouveaux thèmes absurdes. Stavroguine et Ivan font dans la vie pratique l'exercice des vérités absurdes.[1]

> [Let us at least note before continuing that Kirilov rebounds in other characters who in themselves express new absurd themes.

86

Stavroguine and Ivan, in their everyday lives, practise the truths of the absurd.]

Despite their tragic ends (which Camus is inclined to dismiss as proving nothing), Stavroguine and Ivan are capable of shedding light on other regions of the absurd and join Don Juan, the Conqueror, the Actor, Sisyphus and Kirilov himself in Camus's portrait gallery of absurd exemplars. At the same time, Camus's analysis of each character provides perspectives which help to explain the nature of his preoccupation with them and how they fit into the general pattern of Camus's interest in and dialogue with Dostoevsky.

In the Dostoevsky study, Camus argues that the 'vie ironique' ['ironic life'][2] which Stavroguine leads and his absolute indifference (he calls Stavroguine a 'tzar dans l'indifférence' ['tzar of indifference'][3] as though he were part of Kirilov's progeny),[4] are both absurd characteristics. Camus also argues that Stavroguine's assertion in his letter to Dacha, that he could not hate anything ('Je n'ai rien pu détester')[5] is the key to his personality and again reflects an absurd attitude:

> Stavroguine mène une vie 'ironique', on sait assez laquelle. Il fait lever la haine autour de lui. Et pourtant, le mot-clé de ce personnage se trouve dans sa lettre d'adieu: 'Je n'ai rien pu détester.' Il est tzar dans l'indifférence.[6]

> [Stavroguine leads an 'ironic' life of the kind we know only too well. He arouses hatred all around him. And yet the key to this character is to be found in his farewell letter: 'I have not been able to hate anything.' He is a tzar of indifference.]

In pinpointing indifference emanating from the absurd as the key to Stavroguine, Camus is interpreting Stavroguine in conformity with Dostoevsky's own conception of the character[7] but the two writers' estimation of this indifference is, in some respects, quite different.

First of all, it must be pointed out that when Camus refers to Stavroguine's 'indifférence' as an 'absurde' characteristic, the reader inevitably links this indifference to that of *l'homme absurde* and expects to find an affinity between Stavroguine and Camus's absurd hero. However, this is far from being the case. *L'homme absurde* is a man of passion, determined to use every moment of life in pursuit of action and pleasure. He discovers a basic contentment in existence and his indifference is really to the future and to the possibility of the next world: death is the only reality for *l'homme absurde* and produces the imperative to exhaust life's possibilities now, since to mortgage the future is an uncertain wager. Dostoevsky's Stavroguine is quite a different expression of indifference. Stavroguine's will to live, to enjoy life or to do anything at all is actually enfeebled, not dynamized, by awareness of the absurd. Stavroguine's sense of the futility of life is like Romantic abulia, but abulia in its most powerful form, when it becomes a spiritual sickness leading to inertia and paralysis of the will, a comprehensive alienation from the forces of life and love. He says to Dacha, in his letter:

> Mes désirs n'ont pas assez de force pour me diriger. On peut traverser une rivière sur une poutre et non sur un copeau . . . Tout est toujours faible et mou . . . Jamais je ne pourrais croire aussi passionnément [que Kirilov] à une idée. Bien plus, il m'est impossible de m'occuper d'idées à un tel point.[8]

> [My desires are not strong enough to give me direction. One can cross a river on a wooden beam but not a shaving . . . Everything is always feeble and soft . . . I could never believe in an idea with the passion (of Kirilov). Moreover, I find it impossible to be preoccupied with ideas to such an extent.]

Stavroguine's indifference also displays a lofty contempt for the man of action and others in general.[9] He cannot act with conviction because life, for him, is completely futile, even including its pleasures: he has reached a terminal state of *veulerie* [chronic loss of the will to act]. Thus, the common experience of the absurd produces two very different expressions of indifference in Stavroguine and *l'homme absurde*: one is paralysed and torpid, finding pleasure in nothing, happiness impossible and the fact of life itself unimportant; the other is all passionate determination to exhaust the present moment and to find happiness within the limits of death. If Stavroguine is a 'tzar', and there can be no doubt that he is a powerful and dominant figure in *Les Possédés*, it is certainly not in the land of Sisyphus and *l'homme absurde*, despite their occasional points of convergence when it comes to their indifference and contempt for convention.

As to Stavroguine's inability to hate, this can be more readily linked to the attitude of *l'homme absurde*. 'Tout est bien' ['All is well'], the formula of absurd victory, has been seen to be the expression of absurd spiritual tranquillity before the 'déchirement' ['tearing conflicts'] of existence. All is accepted in the dialectic of pain and pleasure which is life. *L'homme absurde* is without bitterness or hatred: like Meursault, he achieves a state of reconciliation, 'une trêve mélancolique' ['a melancholy truce'][10] with the order of destiny. The young Camus himself was imbued with this sense of reconciliation in his early work and wrote, in the preface to *L'Envers et l'endroit*:

> quand une grave maladie m'ôta provisoirement la force de vie qui, en moi, transfigurait tout—je pus connaître la peur et le découragement, jamais l'amertume.[11]

> [when a grave illness robbed me for a moment of my life force which, for me, could transform anything—I possibly experienced fear and demoralization but never bitterness.]

Camus appears to have been attracted to Stavroguine because of this serene lack of hatred and sovereign detachment and indifference which he believed to be the key to the character. However, Stavroguine is both unable to hate or to love anything: he is neither hot nor cold but suffers from acedia and will have to be spat out.[12] Stavroguine, then, cannot be placed in the front-line in support of Camus's positive arguments about the absurd but he can be made to illuminate aspects of absurd sensibility not directly expressive of Camus's own ideas.

A good example of the way in which Camus refers to those aspects of Dostoevsky's works which reflect his own immediate interests is also provided by Stavroguine. Camus uses the character to make an oblique criticism of Dostoevsky's religious apologetics and his acceptance of Christian faith. He argues that Stavroguine would find his creator's rejection of reason and espousal of Christian truth shameful: 'La réponse de Dostoïevski', writes Camus, 'est l'humiliation, la "honte" selon Stavroguine' ['Dostoevsky's reply is humiliation, "shame" according to Stavroguine'].[13] This interpretation of the character is valid: Stavroguine does tell Chatov, as Dostoevsky told Vizine's wife, that even if Christ's existence were mathematically proved untrue, he would still believe in it.[14] However, he is eventually unable to sustain this position and later confesses to Dacha that he could never abandon reason and thus never shamefully betray himself.[15] Once again, reason is the obstacle to faith and Stavroguine provides a model for Camus of a person who could not make the leap into faith, and is thus an authentic absurd hero. Camus evidently sympathizes with Stavroguine's refusal to deny this logic and joins forces with him in repudiating those who do, including Dostoevsky himself. Stavroguine will be 'malheureux mais avec la vérité', not 'heureux avec le mensonge' ['unhappy with 'the truth', not 'happy with falsehood'].[16] Stavroguine does not find Camus's pathway out of absurd despair but he will not surrender to

Christian existentialist temptations. In this, he is superior to his creator who has shamefully sold out to God!

It is interesting to see that Camus places the following additional reference to Stavroguine as an epigraph to that section of *Le Mythe de Sisyphe* dealing with his conception of *l'homme absurde*: 'Si Stavroguine croit, il ne croit pas qu'il croie. S'il ne croit pas, il ne croit pas qu'il ne croie pas' ['If Stavroguine believes, he doesn't believe that he believes. If he doesn't believe, he doesn't believe that he doesn't believe'].[17] It is Kirilov who uses these words in order to explain to Piotr Verkhovensky the nature of the problems tormenting Stavroguine.[18] Stavroguine's dilemma is, of course, the one known so well to Dostoevsky himself, the inability to believe perfectly or to come to terms with atheism. It is difficult to explain what Camus's purpose was in linking Stavroguine to *l'homme absurde* in this way but it is established that the quotation only appears late on in the composition of the text of *Le Mythe de Sisyphe*.[19] G. Strem argues that Camus considered Stavroguine's 'scepticism towards life typical of the absurd attitude'[20] but the statement is vague and no examples are given of *l'homme absurde*'s scepticism nor is it clear what is meant by Stavroguine's 'scepticism towards life'. Stavroguine is a sceptic in the philosophical, Pyrrhonian sense: he doubts the existence and the non-existence of God. This is not quite true of *l'homme absurde* who does not deny the existence of God but who is strongly convinced of his disbelief. Camus may well say that *l'homme absurde* is not without nostalgia for faith but it is very unlikely that this nostalgia is comparable to Stavroguine's, who seeks but cannot find his father in Heaven. He, like Kirilov, needs to believe but cannot, a fact which he reveals to Chatov.[21] Only faith can save Stavroguine but *l'homme absurde* can find happiness in his own terms.

If Strem's argument, on the face of it, seems implausible, how is one to account for Camus's desire to accentuate the link between Stavroguine and *l'homme absurde* by the use of the epigraph? It is possible that Camus is formulating the whole concept of '*l'homme absurde*' as a life-line to Stavroguine, as a pathway out of his inertia, paralysis and unresolved scepticism. This would mean that the epigraph is used more to draw attention to the oppositions in the final formulation of the attitudes of Stavroguine and *l'homme absurde* than to point to similarities, as Strem suggests. Stavroguine really constitutes a powerful and haunting challenge to Camus's world since he embodies Dostoevsky's view of consciousness as leading to paralysis of the will and loss of attachment to love and to life when the anchor of faith is missing. *L'homme absurde*, on the other hand, incorporates Camus's idea that passion and action spring from consciousness of the absurd. In fact, the whole *l'homme absurde* section is introduced with the closing remarks of the previous part: 'Ce qui précède définit seulement une façon de penser. Maintenant il s'agit de vivre' ['What precedes only defines a way of thinking. Now it is a question of living'].[22] It is paradoxical to find a reference to Stavroguine immediately after this since he is so negative about action. This would further strengthen the idea that the epigraph is designed to promote and express a debate, rather than identify a similarity.

Dunwoodie adds to this discussion by arguing first, and uncontroversially, that Camus's use of the epigraph 'permet à Camus de signaler d'autres liens entre l'Œuvre dostoïevskienne et sa propre pensée' ['allows Camus to identify other links between Dostoevsky's work and his own thought']. He sees Stavroguine as '[une] grande figure subversive et déchirée . . . l'âpre alter ego de l'esprit enthousiaste et exigeant de Kirilov' ['(a) looming figure of subversion and division . . . the rasping alter ego of Kirilov's enthusiastic and demanding attitude']. He haunts, he says, the pages of *Le Mythe de Sispyhe*, not as a positive example of an absurd hero but 'comme être maléfique, objet de fascination, attrait de la stérilité et du vide' ['as a maleficent being, an object of fascination, embodying the magnetism of sterility and the void'].[23] Describing Stavroguine as a 'Sispyhe de la négation', Dunwoodie identifies the character as '[un] signe de l'abîme où s'enfonce l'homme absurde européen, la terrible réalité contre laquelle Camus pose d'œuvre en œuvre des garde-fous' ['Sisyphus of negation, (a) sign of the abyss into which European absurd man is falling, the terrifying reality which Camus is trying to keep in check from work to work'].[24] This appears to tie in well with the argument that Camus's *Le Mythe de Sispyhe* is consciously written to lead the Stavroguines of this world out of their despair and their internal conflict, where Dostoevsky places them, towards a new promised land of absurd fulfilment. If Stavroguine haunts Camus in the way that Dunwoodie suggests, it once again underlines the fragility of the Camusian response to Dostoevsky's world: it is doubtful that Stavroguine would display anything but contempt for *l'homme absurde* or even Meursault; his spiritual disaffection and sense of abandonment have proportions to rival those of Pascal and Eliot put togther, although not every critic sees him in these terms.[25]

A further point of interest concerning Stavroguine is that Dostoevsky had Don Juan in mind when creating the character (as well as Prince Hal and Hamlet)[26] and Camus was himself very preoccupied with Don Juan. It is Piotr who first describes

Stavroguine as a kind of Don Juan[27] and Stavroguine himself later declares: 'J'ai expérimenté avec la débauche sur une grande échelle et j'y ai épuisé mes forces, mais je ne l'aime pas et elle n'était pas mon but' ['I have tried debauchery on a grand scale and spent my strength on it but I didn't like it and it wasn't my goal'].[28] Part of Stavroguine's 'vie ironique' is to try to displace metaphysical anxiety by sexual debauchery—his sexual hyperactivity is not related to any physical or psychological malfunction! Camus certainly spotted the tendency of some Dostoevskian characters to seek relief from 'l'écharde dans la chair', or the thorn of existential anguish in their flesh, through intensity of emotion and sexual immorality (he refers, for example, to the 'Remarque curieuse et pénétrante de Gide: presque tous les héros de Dostoïevski sont polygames' ['A curious and penetrating observation by Gide to the effect that almost all Dostoevsky's heroes are polygamous']).[29] Camus's own conception of Don Juan is also rooted in metaphysical anguish: the character is not overcompensating through impotence or seeking psychological reassurance by seduction. However, Camus's Don Juan is at the same time very different from Dostoevsky's as incarnated in Stavroguine: Camus's figure doesn't seek escape from the absurd through debauchery—he loves life, enjoys the life of the seducer because it offers repetitive quantity and, indeed, he has all his pleasures enhanced and intensified by awareness of absurdity and death. Camus's Don Juan is also an affirmation of human freedom and innocence and this is far from the guilt-obsessed world of Stavroguine and his preoccupation with the failure to respond to the appeal of the child, Matriocha. In fact, Stavroguine as a Don Juan figure more resembles Clamence of *La Chute* than the vibrant seducer of *Le Mythe de Sisyphe*. Clamence tries to escape from awareness of his problems by debauchery, describing it as a 'long sommeil' ['a long sleep'][30] and he is also full of guilt because of his failure to respond to human suffering. As we shall see, in a later chapter, it is possible to cite Stavroguine, whom Camus refers to, in 1959, as 'un héros contemporain' ['a contemporary hero'][31] as one of the many Dostoyevskian voices speaking through Clamence in *La Chute*, a work which was possibly going to be called *Un héros de notre temps* (like the work of Lermontov whose protagonist was said, by Camus, to possess, like Dostoevsky's heroes, 'le cœur moderne' ['a modern heart']).[32] There certainly does appear to be a link between Camus and Dostoevsky via Don Juan, and the Don Juan of *Le Mythe de Sisyphe* can legitimately be seen as an answer to Stavroguine's escapist Don Juanism and another, perhaps more recondite, feature of the Camus/Dostoevsky dialogue at work in the text.

Whatever Camus's interest in Stavroguine, and clearly he reacts to the gravitational pull of Dostoevsky's ailing superman, it is not possible to claim that he responds to him in the same detailed and profound way as to Kirilov and Ivan. Whereas these two latter characters play important parts in *Le Mythe de Sisyphe* and *L'Homme révolté* respectively, Stavroguine receives limited attention in the first and is not referred to at all in the later essay. However, it should be noted that as Camus's understanding of *Les Possédés* evolved and he started to regard it as a prophetic novel about nihilism and totalitarianism, so his assessment of the relative importance of Stavroguine and Kirilov changed, possibly as a result of reading Berdiaiev on Dostoevsky when he was doing his background research for the adaptation. He came to realize that in the same way that Nicholas Spechniov, an influential political radical in the Petrashevski circle, was a model for Stavroguine, so Stavroguine, in *Les Possédés*, creates a vast philosophical and political progeny in Kirilov, Chatov and Verkhovensky and that he is the real centre of the novel. Consequently, he structures his adaptation of *Les Possédés* on the central significance of the 'Confession de Stavroguine' and the role of the character in generating metaphysical and political nihilism.[33]

This particular 'tzar of indifference' came eventually to be seen by Camus, much as he was seen by Dostoevsky, despite all the qualities he might possess as a superman, as a potential monster, threatening society with chaos and oppression and engendering the political evils of Verkhovensky junior and Chigalevism. In the early period, it is better to see Stavroguine as somebody who haunts Camus as a possible negative and pessimistic response to the absurd, something to be avoided at all costs. It is really Stavroguine's disregard of conventional values, his 'ironie', and his detachment from the routine of social order which lie at the heart of Camus's interest in him during the early period. However, whilst Stavroguine did interest Camus, it is not possible to claim that the character possesses the same crystallizing and inspirational presence in his early thought as Kirilov, except in terms of defining *l'homme absurde* in opposition to him. Trace elements of Stavroguine's contemptuous indifference are visible both in the composition of Meursault[34] and in the death speeches of Caligula[35] but no great emphasis should be placed on this as, in the final analysis, Stavroguine's indifference is a life-denying vicious circle and this is ultimately very much at variance with Meursault's 'ça m'est égal' ['it's all the same to me'] philosophy of pleasure or Caligula's energetic and self-destructive pedagogy which has the aim of trying to wake people up. George Steiner has observed that Stavroguine is a difficult character to identify with or understand: 'Few figures in literature draw us closer to the limits of understanding'.[36] It may be for this reason that Camus himself does not appear to become as involved with Stavroguine, despite his interest, as he does with Kirilov or Ivan. This is the view of J. Madaule in his study of Camus and Dostoevsky, where he states:

> Nous nous reconnaissons mal en Stavroguine, parce qu'il est démesuré, parce qu'il fait le mal avec une plénitude dont nous sommes tout à fait incapables.[37]

> [We find it difficult to identify with Stavroguine, because he is beyond our measure, because he commits evil with a fullness of which we are incapable.]

Camus, no doubt, was well able to understand the familiar monster of Stavroguine which lurked in modern sensibility but his love of life and pleasure set him on a different track from the Dostoevskian character.

If Stavroguine is a 'tzar dans l'indifférence' for Camus and a possible fulfilment of Kirilov's vision of the Man-God, so is Ivan Karamazov: he is a tzar of intelligence by his refusal 'd'abdiquer les pouvoirs royaux de l'esprit' ['to abandon the sovereign powers of the mind'].[38] Although receiving less attention than Kirilov in *Le Mythe de Sisyphe*, Ivan is, beyond doubt, the character in Dostoevsky's work who most fascinates and attracts him. By way of explanation, Strem maintains that Camus powerfully identified with Ivan and adds:

> In fact, [Camus] had the extraordinary chance of finding in this literary figure the expression of his own inner reality. The impulses, thoughts, actions and reactions of Dostoevsky's hero correspond intimately to what we know about Camus's own.[39]

Strem's view is echoed by Joseph Marek who considers Camus's sensibility to be of a similar nature to Ivan's[40] and also by Jacques Madaule who refers to Camus's and to Ivan's common experience of 'pitié' ['pity'] which he describes as:

> un ébranlement profond de notre être par où nous communions à la souffrance de l'autre, par où nous nous sentons solidaires de la condition humaine dans ce qu'elle a de plus inadmissible.[41]

[a profound stirring of our being through which we participate in the suffering of the other and feel solidarity with man's condition in its most inadmissible aspects.]

Camus's interest in Ivan, as we have already seen, manifested itself early on in his life, in 1938, when he staged the Copeau adaptation of *Les Frères Karamazov* for the *Théâtre de l'Equipe* and chose to play the part of Ivan. His previously noted comments on the whole period of *L'Équipe* and on the roles which he played confirm Strem's idea of identification:

> J'ai aimé par dessus tout Ivan Karamazov. Je le jouais peut-être mal, mais il me semblait le comprendre parfaitement. Je m'exprimais directement en le jouant.[42]
>
> [Above all else, I loved Ivan Karamazov. I didn't perhaps play him well but it seemed to me that I understood him perfectly. I was expressing myself directly when playing him.]

However, despite the early interest, the true range and depth of Camus's involvement with Ivan does not find full expression in his work until after the Second World War with the publication of *La Peste* and, especially, *L'Homme révolté*. Camus's understanding of the significance of Ivan and of his story of the legend of the Grand Inquisitor widened and deepened as he confronted the complexities of the political and historical circumstances of his time, especially during the Cold War and the era of Stalinism. The spheres of application of Ivan's 'tout est permis' ['everything is permitted'] are also not fully appreciated until the experience of war, Nazism and post-war politics have been adequately digested by him. Ivan looms large enough in Camus's early views on moral freedom and the absurd but he looms even more largely in the context of Camus's discussion of metaphysical revolt and political nihilism. Indeed, Camus's whole moral and political development occurs, in one way or another, in relation to his preoccupation with Ivan and to the ideas of Dostoevsky as embodied in the character. Nowhere is the notion of a debate and a dialogue between Camus and Dostoevsky more clearly grasped than in analysing Camus's response to Ivan Karamazov. The remaining part of this chapter will, therefore, explore Camus's preoccupation with Ivan in the early period and set the parameters for the next chapter on Camus's integration of Ivan and of the Grand Inquisitor story into the body of arguments advanced in *L'Homme révolté*.

In *Le Mythe de Sisyphe*, Ivan is presented by Camus positively and very lyrically as an absurd hero who refuses to make the existential leap into faith and to deny the powers of reason. Ivan is a tzar because he will not, unlike his creator or his brother Aliocha, humiliate himself before God or surrender to the irrational:

> A ceux qui, comme son frère, prouvent par leur vie qu'il faut s'humilier pour croire, il pourrait répondre que la condition est indigne.[43]

> [To those who, like his brother, prove by their lives that you must humiliate yourself in order to believe, he could reply that the condition is unworthy.]

Although Ivan does not actually say this, his attitude certainly implies it and Camus is clearly ardently in support of Ivan against Aliocha and Ivan against Dostoevsky. He also appears to believe that Dostoevsky is more impressed by Ivan than either Aliocha or, indeed, Dostoevsky himself! Ivan is Dostoevsky's most powerful expression of reasoned disbelief and this, in a general sense, attracts Camus to the character and provides the eulogizing framework of his response.

Camus's major arguments against religious belief in *Le Mythe de Sisyphe* are principally empirical and Ivan too is first and foremost an empiricist. For example, Ivan tells Aliocha that the rational mind will not concern itself with whether God's existence is a fact or not and puts the following statement to his younger brother:

> J'ai décidé . . . de ne pas chercher à comprendre Dieu. J'avoue humblement mon incapacité à résoudre de telles questions; j'ai essentiellement l'esprit d'Euclide, terrestre, à quoi bon vouloir résoudre ce qui n'est pas de ce monde? Et je te conseille de ne jamais te creuser la tête là-dessus, mon ami Aliocha, surtout au sujet de Dieu: existe-t-il ou non? Ces questions sont hors de la portée d'un esprit qui n'a que la notion des trois dimensions.[44]

> [I have decided . . . not to try to understand God. I humbly confess my inability to resolve such questions; basically, I have a Euclidian mind, one of this world, what is the point of trying to reason what is not of this world? And my advice to you is not to wrack your brain on that subject, Aliocha, especially on the question of God. Does he exist or not? These are questions beyond the range of a mind which only possesses three dimensions.]

Camus echoes Ivan's logic in *Le Mythe de Sispyhe*:

Je ne sais pas si ce monde a un sens qui le dépasse. Mais je sais que je ne connais pas ce sens et qu'il m'est impossible pour le moment de le connaître. Que signifie pour moi une signification hors de ma condition? Je ne peux comprendre qu'en termes humaines. Ce que je touche, ce qui me résiste, voilà ce que je comprends.[45]

[I do not know if this world has a transcendent meaning. But I do know that I do not have access to this meaning and that it is impossible for me at this moment to have access to it. What is the meaning for me of a meaning outside my condition? I can only understand in human terms. What I touch, what resists me, that is what I understand.]

Admittedly, a lot of people may think this, including Shaw's Joan of Arc and the logical positivists, but Camus's expression of the argument is close to Ivan's and, of course, Camus was composing *Le Mythe de Sisyphe* at the same time as he played the part of Ivan.[46] In any case, an empirically based rational disbelief is a shared characteristic of Ivan and Camus as is a shared antipathy to and rejection of the Christian existentialist leap into faith.

Although Camus uses Ivan's rationalism and empiricism in *Le Mythe de Sisyphe* as ammunition against Christian existentialist apologetics, Ivan also features briefly in another section of the essay, where Camus touches upon the relationship between the absurd and values. If one looks at the various references to Ivan in Camus's works generally, it is manifestly the case that Ivan most interests Camus as an embodiment of and a reflection on the complex problem of moral liberty within the framework of absurd sensibility and thought. It is frequently with reference to Ivan that Camus addresses this problem. This was the case, for example, in 1938, when Camus wrote in the *Carnets*:

La seule liberté possible est une liberté à l'égard de la mort. L'homme vraiment libre est celui qui, acceptant la mort comme telle, en accepte du même coup les conséquences—c'est-à-dire le renversement de toutes les valeurs traditionnelles de la vie. Le 'Tout est permis' d'Ivan Karamazov est la seule expression d'une liberté cohérente. Mais il faut aller au fond de la formule.[47]

[The only possible freedom is a freedom with respect to death. The truly free man is the one who, accepting death as it is, accepts simultaneously the consequences—namely, the overturning of all the traditional notions of values in life. Ivan Karamazov's 'Everything is permitted' is the only coherent expression of freedom. But one has to get to the bottom of the statement.]

Camus's life, in one sense, is dedicated to the exploration of this 'formule' and the presence of Ivan is never far from his thoughts when he approaches the subject of values. The discussion of values in *Le Mythe de Sisyphe* is linked to the formula 'tout est permis' and Camus's quest for a moral imperative, between 1943 and 1951, is paralleled by an increasing preoccupation with Ivan. Ivan's logic is alluded to in the *Remarque sur la révolte* (1945),[48] the article which formed the kernel of *L'Homme révolté*, whilst Ivan's 'tout est permis' also has a very prominent position in the arguments advanced in the important political essays 'Ni Victimes ni bourreaux'.[49] As an expression of his concern with and understanding of moral liberty within the absurd, Camus's preoccupation with Ivan is of paramount significance, allowing the reader to grasp the way Camus conceptualizes his evolving approach to ethical problems between 1938 and 1951, the year of publication of his major work on political philosophy and values. Let us trace Camus's approach in the early period and relate it to his response to the figure of Ivan Karamazov and to Dostoevsky's moral thought in general.

As is evident in the observation in the *Carnets*, quoted above, Camus shared Ivan's belief that without faith in immortality or eternal life, life becomes absurd and moral authority and values are transformed by this awareness. Through the figure of Ivan, Dostoevsky poses the problem which constantly preoccupied him and was eventually to preoccupy Camus in a similarly intense manner: the problem of values outside the domain of religious authority or whether notions of good and evil can be defined coherently in relative human terms. Ivan's ideas on the subject are first presented to the reader by Mioussov, a progressive liberal landowner in *Les Frères Karamazov*. He informs the group assembled at the monastery with Zosime, in the early stages of the novel, of certain propositions put by Ivan to himself and others a few days prior to the gathering. Through Ivan's statement, Dostoevsky advances his conviction that values are rooted in divine authority and that moral anarchy is the harvest of atheism. Mioussov declares:

Il y a cinq jours, dans une société où figuraient surtout des dames, [Ivan] déclara solennellement, au cours d'une discussion, que rien au monde n'obligeait les gens à aimer leurs semblables, qu'il n'existait aucune loi naturelle ordonnant à l'homme d'aimer l'humanité; que si l'amour avait régné jusqu'à présent sur la terre, cela était dû non à la loi naturelle, mais uniquement à la croyance des gens en leur immortalité. Ivan Fiodorovitch ajouta entre parenthèses que c'est là toute la loi naturelle, de sorte que si vous détruisez dans l'homme la foi en son immortalité, non seulement l'amour tarira en lui, mais aussi la force de continuer la vie dans le monde. Bien plus, il n'y aura alors rien d'immoral; tout sera autorisé, même l'anthropophagie. Ce n'est pas tout: il termina en affirmant que pour chaque individu ne croyant ni en Dieu ni en sa propre immortalité, la loi morale de la nature devait immédiatement devenir l'inverse absolu de la précédente loi religieuse; que l'égoïsme, même poussé jusqu'à la scélératesse devait non seulement être autorisé, mais reconnu pour une issue nécessaire, la plus raisonnable et presque la plus noble.[50]

[Five days ago, in a group composed mainly of women, (Ivan) declared solemnly, in the midst of a discussion, that nothing in the world obliged people to love one another, that no natural law existed ordering man to love humanity; that if love had reigned until now on earth, that was not because of any natural law, but exclusively because of people's belief in immortality. Ivan added parenthetically that this belief constituted all the natural law that there was, so that if you destroy man's belief in immortality, love will not only dry up within him, but also the strength to continue living in the world. In addition, there will then be no such thing as immorality; everything will be authorized, even cannibalism. And that isn't all: he ended by claiming that for each and every person believing in neither God nor immortality, the natural moral law should immediately become the absolute opposite of the preceeding religious law; that egotism pushed to knavery must not only be authorized, but recognized as the necessary, most rational and almost the most dignified reaction.]

Thus, for Ivan, without faith in immortality, there can be no authoratitive values ('Il n'y pas de vertu sans immortalité') ['There is no virtue without immortality'][51] and, because of this, immorality becomes the imperative. The argument has Romantic appeal.

Camus was certainly intrigued by Ivan's view of moral liberty within the absurd but he never really accepts Ivan's thinking in all its consequences. Rather, Ivan's 'tout est permis' generates debate in Camus's mind. Even in 1938, when he considers that 'tout est permis' is the only coherent expression of freedom for one who believes that death is final and that traditional values fall down before such considerations, he nonetheless adds that the formula needs further exploration. Camus returns to the problem in *Le Mythe de Sisyphe* and again refers to Ivan.

The thrust of Camus's moral argument in *Le Mythe de Sisyphe* is that *a priori* no morality can be justified if one believes that death is absolute:

> Aucune morale ni aucun effort ne sont *a priori* justifiables devant les sanglantes mathématiques qui ordonnent notre condition.[52]

> [No moral theory or any endeavour are *a priori* justifiable before the gory mathematics which govern our condition.]

If, for both Camus and Ivan, death, when considered final, eats away at the roots of morality, Camus is, at least, prepared to qualify his view with the all important *a priori*. At the same time, Camus is prepared to say, like Ivan, that the absurd man can only respect values when they derive from religious authority, although he does not believe in that authority:

> Il n'est qu'une morale que l'homme absurde puisse admettre, celle qui ne se sépare pas de Dieu: celle qui se dicte. Mais il vit justement hors de ce Dieu.[53]

> [There is only one moral theory that *l'homme absurde* can accept, and that is one which cannot be separated from God: one which is decreed. But, precisely, he lives outside this God.]

This recalls Ivan's idea that morality depends entirely on God for its justification and the fact that Ivan's name appears on the very page where Camus makes this point in *Le Mythe de Sisyphe* is surely indicative of the reality of Ivan's presence in Camus's mind at the time of composition of the moral section of the essay and that the work is evolving in response to Dostoevsky's logic.

A further and important feature of Camus's discussion of values in *Le Mythe de Sisyphe* is that it is linked to a conception of man as innocent. In 1953, referring to his pre-war experience in Algeria, Camus made the following remark which is relevant to this particular aspect of his moral attitudes: 'Au temps de l'innocence j'ignorais que la morale existât' ['In the period of innocence I didn't know that moral philosophy existed'].[54] This feeling of innocence, which seemingly tended to lead Camus away from consideration of formal ethical theories in his early life, is analysed in the essay and Camus links his ideas to those of Ivan. Having stated that the absurd man can only accept as valid a morality rooted in a religious belief which he does not hold, Camus continues:

Quant aux autres morales (j'entends aussi l'immoralisme), l'homme absurde n'y voit que des justifications et il n'a rien à justifier. Je pars ici du principe de son innocence. Cette innocence est redoutable. 'Tout est permis' s'écrie Ivan Karamazov. Cela aussi sent son absurde. Mais à condition de ne pas l'entendre vulgairement. Je ne sais pas si on l'a bien remarqué: il ne s'agit pas d'un cri de délivrance et de joie, mais d'une constation amère. La certitude d'un Dieu qui donnerait son sens à la vie surpasse de beaucoup en attrait le pouvoir impuni de mal faire. Le choix ne serait pas difficile. Mais il n'y a pas de choix et l'amertume commence alors.[55]

[As for the other moral systems (and I include immorality among them), *l'homme absurde* sees in them only justifications and he has nothing to justify. I start here from the principle of his innocence. This innocence is formidable. 'Everything is permitted' cries Ivan Karamazov. That statement smacks of his awareness of absurdity also. But that is provided that we do not interpret it crudely. I do not know if it's been sufficiently recognized: his words are no cry of deliverance and joy but a bitter realization. The certainty of a God who would make life meaningful easily eclipses in appeal the power to do wrong with impunity. The choice would not be difficult. But there is no choice and this is where bitterness begins.]

(Camus is evidently sensitive to the fact that Ivan, like the other rebels, would like to believe but cannot. This is also one of the rare passages in Camus where one is forced to wonder about his own desire for faith.)[56]

Elsewhere in the essay, Camus asserts of *l'homme absurde:* 'A vrai dire, il ne sent que cela, son innocence irréparable. C'est cela qui lui permet tout' ['In truth, he feels only that, his irreversible innocence. This is what allows him to do anything he likes'].[57] The latter part of this quotation again recalls Ivan and, in both quotations given, Ivan's 'tout est permis' appears in this context of innocence. It appears that Camus considered innocence to be an essential part of Ivan's thought but Ivan never actually declares that man is innocent in *Les Frères Karamazov.* It is true that Ivan revolts against God in the name of man's suffering but is it in the name of his innocence? Ivan does consider children innocent and his revolt is intensified by the idea of the innocent child being condemned to suffering. Adults, however, for Ivan are 'repoussants et indignes d'être aimés' ['repellent and unworthy of love'];[58] he cannot understand how one man can love another, since man is an 'animal féroce et méchant' ['savage and nasty animal'],[59] and considered it nothing less than a miracle that Christ managed to love mankind.[60] Ivan sees a child as different from adults because of innocence:

> Je voulais parler [Ivan says to Aliocha] des souffrances de l'humanité en général, mais il vaut mieux se borner aux souffrances des enfants. Mon argumentation sera réduite au dixième, mais c'est mieux ainsi. J'y perds, bien entendu. D'abord, on peut aimer les enfants de près, même sales, même laids (il me semble, pourtant que les enfants ne sont jamais laids). Ensuite, si je ne parle des adultes, c'est que non seulement ils sont repoussants et indignes d'être aimés, mais qu'ils ont une compensation: ils ont mangé le fruit défendu, discerné le bien et le mal, et sont devenus 'semblables à des Dieux'. Ils continuent à le manger. Mais les petits enfants n'ont rien mangé et sont encore innocents.[61]

> [I want to speak of the sufferings of humanity in general but it is better to confine myself to those of children. My argument will lose ninety per cent of its force but it's better like that. Of course, I shall lose by it. First, one is able to love children even when they are near us, even if they are dirty or ugly (however, I do not think that children are ever ugly). Next, if I don't refer to adults, it is not only because they are repellent and unworthy of love but because they have a consolation: they have eaten of the forbidden fruit, have knowledge of good and evil and become 'akin to Gods'. They continue to eat of it. But little children have eaten nothing and remain innocent.]

The implication of this is that Ivan can just about accept God's punishment of adults because they are unworthy but not the punishment of innocent chidren. This reference to Ivan in the context of human innocence is a projection, by Camus, of his own sense of innocence onto the character and indicates how powerfully Camus identified with him.

Starting with this principle of innocence, Camus goes on to argue that although the absurd does not authorize all acts, it does make their consequences of equal value. He writes, in a passage characterized by elusive thinking:

> [L'absurde] n'autorise pas tous les actes. Tout est permis ne signifie pas que rien n'est défendu. L'absurde rend seulement leur équivalence aux conséquences de ces actes. Il ne recommande pas le crime, ce serait puéril. Mais il restitue au remords son inutilité. De même, si toutes les expériences sont indifférentes, celle du devoir est aussi légitime qu'une autre. On peut être vertueux par caprice.[62]

[(The absurd) does not authorize all actions. Everything is permitted does not mean that nothing is forbidden. The absurd only renders equivalence of value to these actions. It doesn't recommend crime, that would be puerile. But it restores to remorse its uselessness. Moreover, if all experiences have the same value, that of duty is as legitimate as any other. One can be virtuous by whim.]

Here again, one can see Camus's reluctance to allow Ivan's formula to pass with his complete approval. When Camus claims that all is permitted does not mean that nothing is forbidden, he appears to wish to impose restrictions on Ivan's freedom, thus questioning the whole validity of the 'tout est permis'. However, Camus does not develop this idea and the only restrictions imposed by him on *l'homme absurde* are those relating to the suppression of awareness of the absurd (*l'homme absurde*, whatever he is doing, must never forget that life is ultimately meaningless and, of course, he does not have the freedom to commit intellectual or physical suicide).

Such remarks as these from Camus's pen have understandably led critics, noticeably J. Cruickshank,[63] to the belief that Camus equated innocence with moral nihilism and, in linking Ivan's argument to the belief in innocence, Camus certainly gives this impression. Indeed, although Camus states that 'tout est permis' is not tantamount to saying nothing is forbidden without developing the reasons why, his assertion to the effect that the consequences of all actions are equivalent seems only another way of saying that all is permitted. However, one must respect both Camus's pronouncement that morality is only *a priori* unjustifiable within the absurd framework and also his statements claiming that a discussion of morality in *Le Mythe de Sisyphe* was beyond his terms of reference.[64] Whatever view one takes of this, the fact is that Camus does approach the question of moral freedom in *Le Mythe de Sisyphe* and Ivan's famous 'tout est permis' appears largely to be intact despite Camus's qualifications of it. Camus's position does, however, constitute a certain 'advance' on Ivan's: Camus does not recommend crime ('on peut être vertueux par caprice' ['one can be virtuous by whim']),[65] but Ivan certainly does.[66]

Camus's moral development does, of course, present some knotty problems to his readers. Although he claimed, in 1951, that he was already thinking about *L'Homme révolté* when he wrote *Le Mythe de Sisyphe*,[67] how is one to reconcile this with his admission that he was a nihilist and professed nihilism[68] (a remark which can only refer to the discussion of morality in *Le Mythe de Sisyphe*, since in his private life Camus never appears to have been a nihilist)?[69] Perhaps Camus was not in a position to break down Ivan's argument in *Le Mythe de Sisyphe*, although it is difficult to tell when Camus was in possession of his concept of revolt which represents his attempt to justify values in an absurd world.[70] It is surely significant that *L'Homme révolté* begins with a critical discussion of *Le Mythe de Sisyphe* and one suspects that Camus was finding it difficult to justify values at the time of the first essay and may even have considered it unnecessary, given his romanticized individualism of innocent pleasure. The fact remains, however, that even in *Le Mythe de Sisyphe*, Camus is reluctant to accept Ivan's nihilism, although without indicating the grounds on which it is to be rejected. Camus's attitude to Ivan's 'tout est permis' in this early essay indicates that future development of the problem of values is possible and, confronted with the moral nihilism of the Nazis during the War, Camus was very quick to root his preoccupations in history, not in romantic posture, and to clarify his position.

It is interesting to recall that, in private life, Camus did follow a simple moral code, although he makes no mention of this in *Le Mythe de Sisyphe*. He used this code, it would seem, before fully developing his concept of revolt, and it seems likely that he opposed this code to Ivan's logic. P. Thody observes that Camus's 'complimentary description of the general morality which prevailed among the working classes of Algeria gives the impression that he himself found it sufficient to most of the problems which confronted him in ordinary life'.[71] The general morality to which P. Thody refers appears in *Noces*, in the *essai* entitled 'L'Été à Alger'. Having described the code, Camus remarks: 'Nous sommes encore beaucoup à observer ce code de la rue, le seul désintéressé que je connaisse' ['There are still many of us who follow this street-code, the only disinterested one that I know'].[72] It seems likely that Camus even opposed this simple 'code de la rue' to Ivan's logic in view of a reference which appears in one of the early formulations of 'L'Été à Alger'. Camus wrote: 'Qu'on n'attende pas ici le "Tout est permis" des *Frères Karamazov*.' ['Do not expect to find here the "Everything is permitted" of *Les Frères Karamazov*'].[73] This reference, removed from the published version of 'L'Été à Alger', seems to lend further support to the view that Camus tended to envisage moral problems within the absurd framework in a dialogue with Ivan's logic and Dostoevsky's thought in general. Until his experience of the Occupation and the Resistance movement, Camus does not seem to have thought it was necessary to possess a more precise and intellectually authoritative morality. During the War, it may well be that Camus actually considered that he was witnessing the logic of Ivan dramatically revealing itself in history. It is tempting to speculate that Camus saw a number of similarities between his situation when faced with the Nazis and that of Ivan confronted with the murder of his father. Ivan's logic demands that he should accept the murder of his father but he finds the murder instinctively unacceptable. Despite his belief in moral nihilism, Ivan cannot tolerate Smerdiakov, his bastard half-brother and double, who puts his ideas into practice and murders old Karamazov.[74] The logic of the mind and the instinctive reactions of the heart are in conflict in Ivan as they are in Raskolnikov and Kirilov. Smerdiakov says to Ivan:

Vous avez tué, c'est vous le principal assassin, je n'ai été que votre auxiliaire, votre fidèle instrument, vous avez suggéré, j'ai accompli.[75]

[You have killed, you are the main murderer, I was only your assistant, your faithful instrument, you made the suggestion, I did the deed.]

A page or so later, Smerdiakov says ' "Tout est permis", disiez-vous, et maintenant vous avez la frousse!' [' "Everything is permitted", you used to say, and now you have got cold feet!'][76]

This conflict finally drives Ivan insane. When Camus speaks in 'La Défense de *L'Homme révolté*' of 'une révolte sûre d'elle-même, mais encore inconsciente de ses raisons' ['a revolt sure of itself but not yet aware of its rational legitimacy'],[77] (referring to his resistance against Nazism), he means that his instinctive revolt against Nazism still awaited an intellectually authoritative justification. Perhaps his mind and his heart were in conflict like Ivan's. In the *Lettres à un ami allemand* and 'La Défense de *L'Homme révolté*', Camus gives the impression that he saw, in retrospect, certain ideas of *Le Mythe de Sisyphe* as a possible justification of Nazism and felt responsible in the same way as Ivan feels responsible for his father's death.[78] Camus had certainly sensed a relationship between the absurd and nihilistic megalomania in 1941[79] and there is a reference in the second volume of the *Carnets* to a projected chapter of *L'Homme révolté* which was to begin: 'Nous autres Nietzschéens' ['We Nietzschians'].[80] There also seems to be a strong element of *mea culpa* in Camus's description of Ivan. In *L'Homme révolté*, as we shall see, he describes Ivan's predicament as that of being 'coincé entre une vertu injustifiable et un crime inacceptable' ['pincered between an unjustifiable value and an unacceptable crime'][81] and this may have been Camus's own dilemma for a short period during the War. This would certainly help to explain Camus's continual preoccupation with Ivan. This remains a speculation, however, and one cannot stretch the comparison too far. As P. Thody remarks, in his consideration of Camus's moral development, Camus never appears as a 'man driven to anguish by a contradiction in his own character'.[82] With his concept of revolt, Camus was able to justify intellectually, at least to his own satisfaction, the logic of the heart. He could thus avoid or extricate himself from the contradiction that was Ivan's fate. Certainly, Camus's philosophy of revolt and political revolution seems to be conceived in a deep spirit of debate with Ivan and his Grand Inquisitor. If Camus's *Le Mythe de Sisyphe* engages Dostoevsky in dialogue in order to refute his Christian existentialist apologetics and proclaim hedonistic individualism as a response to the absurd and an alternative to Christ, so *L'Homme révolté* relaunches the debate in moral and political terms because Camus's first reply has proved inadequate. It has proved inadequate in moral and political terms because history has produced monsters (Nazism and war) which that very hedonism has legitimized inadvertently by preaching ethical equality. Ivan's 'tout est permis' authorized murder in the same way that Camus's 'tout est bien' legitimized the possibility of war. Camus's personal moral world appears to replicate the structures of Ivan's logic and this, in turn, places Dostoevsky at the centre of Camus's moral and political development, providing him with models for analysis and refutation.

Although Camus does not develop his restrictions on Ivan's 'tout est permis' in the early essay, he does present the reader with an ethic of quantity and this too reveals certain affinities between Camus and Ivan which are also worth noting.

In *Le Mythe de Sisyphe*, Camus argues that awareness of the absurd 'revient à remplacer la qualité des expériences par la quantité' ['basically means replacing the quality of experiences by their quantity'].[83] *L'homme absurde* endeavours to live as fully as possible before death:

> Ce qui compte [writes Camus] n'est pas de vivre le mieux mais de vivre le plus. Je n'ai pas à me demander si cela est vulgaire ou écœurant, élégant ou regrettable.[84]

> [What matters is not to live in the best possible way but to live as much as one can. I don't have to ask myself if this is vulgar or disgusting, stylish or unfortunate.]

Through the ethic of quantity, Camus expresses that great love of life which he shared with Dostoevsky. As was seen in Chapter 4, Camus was attracted to Kirilov and Ivan because of this love of life. Ivan, like Camus, is determined to live his life with maximum intensity and he too refuses to heed moralists who condemn excessive love of life as something vulgar.

> Après avoir goûté à la coupe enchantée [Ivan tells Aliocha] je ne la quitterai qu'une fois vidée . . . Cette soif de vivre, certains moralistes morveux et poitrinaires la traitent de vile, surtout les poètes. Il est vrai que c'est un trait caractéristique des Karamazov, cette soif de vivre à tout prix; elle se retrouve en toi, mais pourquoi serait-elle vile?[85]

> [Having drunk from the magic cup, I will not set it down until it is empty . . . This thirst for life is treated by certain po-faced and tub-thumping moralists, especially poets, as vile. It is true that it's a characteristic of the Karamazovs, this thirst to live whatever the cost; you have got it but why should it be vile?]

Both Camus and Ivan lay stress on the enjoyment of life's possibilities and wish to live life to the full; without faith in immortality, both turn to the earth with a passionate determination to enjoy themselves while they can. Camus was very aware of his similarity with Ivan in this respect. He wrote of Ivan in *L'Homme révolté*:

> S'il [Ivan] refuse l'immortalité, que lui reste-t-il? La vie dans ce qu'elle a d'élémentaire. Le sens de la vie supprimé, il reste encore la vie.[86]

> [If he (Ivan) rejects immortality, what does he have left? Life in its basic form. With the meaning of life gone, life itself still remains.]

This is very similar to Camus's position and attitude in *Le Mythe de Sisyphe* and, although the statement was made in 1951, Camus was well acquainted with Ivan's ideas long before this. This joint determination to live life to the full would certainly appear to be a factor in Camus's attraction to Ivan and would explain, in one way, why it was that Camus felt he was expressing himself directly when playing the part of Ivan in 1938. Again one senses that his dialogue with Ivan has a significant role in the formulation of Camus's early ethic of hedonism and sensual gratification, helping to stimulate and crystallize these dimensions of his thought.

It is worth noting, however, that, in one important way, Ivan's attitude to the enjoyment of life is different from Camus's. Ivan bears the stamp of his creator in that he considers it illogical to love life if one does not believe in God. He is unable to reconcile this love with his conception of existence, since, for Ivan, if life is meaningless, pleasure is or should be just as futile as pain. This is why he tells his brother that he loves life 'en dépit de la logique' ['regardless of logic'].[87] As was mentioned before, Camus considered love of life a logical development of the absurd and *Le Mythe de Sisyphe* is, in one sense, an attempt to justify intellectually an instinctive love of life in the same way as *l'Homme révolté* strives to give intellectual authority to instinctive revolt. It may well be that Camus's ethic of quantity was formulated partly as a response to Ivan's belief that logic and love of life were incompatible and this would again strengthen our earlier claim that *Le Mythe de Sisyphe* is a reply to Dostoevsky.

A further, and perhaps the principal similarity between Ivan and Camus is their attitude towards Christianity. Ivan tells Aliocha that even if he did believe in God, he would reject God's creation since it is an order which embraces the suffering of mankind and, in particular, the suffering of innocent children:

> Et si la souffrance des enfants, [observes Ivan] sert à parfaire la somme des douleurs nécessaires à l'acquisition de la vérité, j'affirme d'ores et déjà que cette vérité ne vaut pas un tel prix . . . C'est par amour pour l'humanité que je ne veux pas de cette harmonie.[88]

> [And if the suffering of children serves to make up the total of ills necessary for the acquisition of truth, I declare forthwith that this truth is too expensive at such a price . . . It is because of my love of humanity that I want no part of such harmony.]

Ivan, then, rejects God, gives Him back his ticket, because His creation is premissed on human suffering. Although arguments about theology are not a dominant feature of Camus's early work and a greater emphasis is placed on God as the fear of death and as an obstruction to courageous and lucid hedonism, when moral considerations do start to emerge, they have a distinctly Ivan Karamazovian flavour. For example, Camus reveals his affinity with Ivan in 1943 when he notes in the *Carnets*: 'Ce que je reproche au Christianisme, c'est qu'il est une doctrine de l'injustice' ['What I object to in Christianity is that it is a doctrine of injustice'].[89] This echoes the only statement in *Le Mythe de Sisyphe* to focus on the paradox of Erasmus:

Car devant Dieu, il y a moins un problème de la liberté qu'un problème du mal. On connaît l'alternative: ou nous ne sommes pas libres et Dieu tout-puissant est responsable du mal. Ou nous sommes libres et responsables, mais Dieu n'est pas tout-puissant.[90]

[For in respect of God there is less a problem of freedom than a problem of morality. We know the alternatives: either we are not free and God in his omnipotence is responsible for evil. Or we are free and responsible, but God is not omnipotent.]

In *Le Malentendu*, the old servant is a symbol of a deity indifferent to the suffering of mankind[91] and this symbolic usage also recalls Ivan's notion of God, whilst Martha's cry that Maria's despair will never equal 'l'injustice qu'on a fait à l'homme' ['the injustice done to man'], together with her words about a God who pays no attention to man's distress, appear likewise to contain echoes of Ivan's expression of revolt.[92]

A further example is provided by Caligula who dresses up as Venus in order to show men that the Gods are cruel and deceitful: despite our worship and sacrifice, they condemn us to a wretched condition. For the Emperor, there is only one way to equal the Gods: 'il suffit d'être aussi cruel qu'eux' ['it suffices to be as cruel as they are'].[93] Caligula refuses to serve the Gods for the same reasons that Ivan returns his ticket: 'Les hommes meurent et ils ne sont pas heureux.' ['Men die and they are not happy'].[94] In a similar vein, the Emperor, who lists immortality together with happiness and the moon as part of his 'besoin d'impossible' ['need for the impossible'], condemns the Gods in the name of justice and it is possible, as Strem has plausibly suggested, that his way of judging the Gods morally in terms of the suffering inherent in their creation was a yardstick that Camus inherited from Ivan.[95]

If there are convergences between Camus and Ivan on matters of theodicy when they do surface in Camus's early work, they are very much more in evidence in what Camus called his most anti-Christian novel, *La Peste*. The anti-Christian arguments of *La Peste* all develop the idea that Christianity is a doctrine of injustice. Although Rieux, like his creator, is able to accept that suffering on occasions can be positive and redemptive (as was the case, for Camus, of Oscar Wilde's period of imprisonment), Rieux refuses to share the Christian Paneloux's attitude to the suffering of Othon's child, whom the doctor sees as an innocent victim: 'Ah! celui-là [says Rieux, talking of the child], au moins était innocent, vous le savez bien!' ['Ah! That one there, at least was innocent, and you know it'] and when Paneloux tells him that it is perhaps necessary to love suffering, although it is hard to accept, Rieux replies: 'Non, mon frère . . . Je me fais une autre idée de l'amour. Et je refuserai, jusqu'à la mort, d'aimer cette création où des enfants sont torturés' ['No, my brother . . . I have a different idea of love. And, until I die, I shall refuse to love this order of creation where children suffer and die'].[96] Rieux was certainly expressing Camus's own opinion on this point since, in his speech to the Dominicans at *La Tour Maubourg* in 1948 Camus observes:

> Je partage avec vous la même horreur du mal. Mais je ne partage pas votre espoir et je continue à lutter contre cet univers où des enfants souffrent et meurent . . . Nous ne pouvons pas empêcher peut-être que cette création soit celle où des enfants sont torturés mais nous pouvons diminuer le nombre des enfants torturés.[97]

> [I share with you the same horror of evil. But I do not share your hope and I shall continue to fight against this world where children suffer and die . . . We cannot perhaps stop this order of creation from being one where children are tortured but we can reduce the number of children tortured.]

In the *Lettres à un ami allemand*, the same sensibility manifests itself when Camus tells his friend that he and the Nazis sided with the Gods when they chose the path of injustice: 'Pour tout dire, vous avez choisi l'injustice, vous vous êtes mis avec les dieux' ['Finally, you have opted for injustice, you have put yourself with the gods'].[98]

These various observations from the *Carnets, La Peste, L'Incroyant et les Chrétiens*, the *Lettres à un ami allemand, Caligula* and *Le Malentendu* reveal that Camus, in his approach to theodicy, as in his general discussion of moral values, is very close to Ivan's persuasions and responses. Does this indicate that Camus's sensibility was contingently similar, to a remarkable degree, to Ivan's or did Dostoevsky's character have a positive effect upon Camus's development in this respect? Resemblance does not prove influence, and, in any case, to attack Christianity as a philosophy which embraces and justifies man's suffering and the suffering of innocent children is certainly not an uncommon view. J. Marek, for example, remarks of Ivan's revolt against God:

> Ivan était uniquement guidé par un souci de justice. Dans cette perspective, il reprenait les protestations les plus banales de la sensibilité humaine depuis l'Antiquité, il n'est pas *juste* que l'inno-

cence soit opprimée, il n'est pas *juste*, que les petits enfants meurent.[99]

[Ivan was guided exclusively by a concern for justice. From this point of view, he rearticulates the most common complaints of humanity from the ancient world onwards, it is not *just* that innocence be oppressed, it is not *right* that little children should die.]

The socialist critic, Noël Lafon, writing in the *Revue Socialiste*, also reminds us of both the German philosophical and political roots of such anti-Christian sensibility:

Camus a peut-être conservé sa vision du christianisme de la fréquentation de la philosophie allemande ou encore de ses rapports antérieurs avec le parti communiste qui reproche à la religion catholique d'être une superstructure chargée de justifier des infrastructures où règne l'injustice.[100]

[Camus perhaps took his view of Christianity from his reading of German philosophy or else from his earlier links with the Communist Party which reproaches Catholicism for being a superstructure charged with justifying infrastructures of injustice.]

The formation and development of Camus's anti-Christian sensibility is evidently a complex issue. Moreover, when Camus says that he was expressing himself directly when playing Ivan in 1938, the implication appears to be that he had found a fictional character who resembled him by chance rather than one who had helped to shape his sensibility. Despite this, it is tempting to believe that *Les Frères Karamazov* and Ivan in particular helped to crystallize Camus's anti-Christian ideas in respect of suffering and innocent children. One cannot confine the question here to Ivan, since Dmitri too is preoccupied with the suffering of children, and Camus was aware of this,[101] although Ivan undoubtedly made a greater impression on Camus than any other character in the novel. Garret Green has suggested, in his very interesting essay, that Camus may well have borrowed the symbol of the suffering child in *La Peste* from Dostoevsky[102] and this seems a perfectly reasonable suggestion except that man is in part responsible for this suffering in *Les Frères Karamazov*, whereas, in *La Peste*, the death of Othon's child appears to be God's responsibility.[103] *La Peste* generally as a novel also appears to be specifically designed to refute the idea of divine justice so powerfully expressed in Dostoevsky's world. Paneloux, the abstracted, intellectual Jesuit, is depicted as having to accept the suffering of man and innocent children in the name of God's love. Rieux's non-Christian humanism is formulated in contrast, and, antithetically, to Paneloux's views and is depicted as more energetically and authentically morally engaged on the side of justice, real human love and values and defence of the innocent. Once again, Camus takes Dostoevsky's logic and turns it on its head by arguing that the lay humanism represented by Rieux and the *formations sanitaires* [health teams] is the only coherent expression of authentic revolt, whilst Christianity in essence is unjust to man.[104]

Yet another illustration of convergence, affinity and identity between Ivan and Camus is to be found in their opposition to capital punishment. Ivan sees capital punishment as a symbol of God's creation. He relates to Aliocha the execution of Richard, a murderer and a thief, who was guillotined for his crimes. Before his death, Richard repents and becomes a Christian and this is how Ivan describes his death:

> 'Meurs, frère,' crie-t-on à Richard, 'meurs dans le Seigneur; sa grâce t'accompagne.' Et, couvert de baisers, le frère Richard monte à l'échafaud, on l'étend sur la bascule et sa tête tombe au nom de la grâce divine.[105]

> ['Die brother,' they cry out to Richard, 'die in the Lord; may the grace of God be with you.' And, smothered in kisses, Richard climbs the scaffold, they place him on the block and his head is cut off in the name of God's grace.]

The connection between Ivan's attitude to God and his opposition to capital punishment is not difficult to see. Ivan considers grace conditional on mankind's suffering and death, in other words his crucifixion or execution, and this is something he cannot accept. Although Camus does not use the image of the *condamné* in the same way that Ivan does as a symbol of man's relationship to God and of God's brutal condemnation of man, when Camus speaks of 'les sanglantes mathématiques', ['gory mathematics'] there is enough romantic protest in the statement to make one think of Ivan and Richard. It has already been argued that Camus uses Dostoevsky's image of the *condamné* in *L'Idiot* as a paradigm of *l'homme absurde* in order to promote hedonism as a reply to Dostoevsky. Ivan's *condamné* is more expressive of Camus's view of capital punishment as an injustice perpetrated by man against man and relates to the deep compassion for others felt by both Camus, Dostoevsky himself, and the Russian fictional character. Later, Camus will see Ivan's image of the *condamné* as a fundamental image of revolt and symbolically he will link it to 1789 and to the execution of the King of France in 1793. Then, for the first time in human history, Divinity is executed in the name of human justice, reversing the polarities of power between man and God bricked into Ivan's view. Socialism will then be conceived by Camus as the quest for a transparent human justice in this world, undertaken in opposition to the injustices and mystifications of divine authority. However, these are later developments, as Camus uses Ivan to explore the link between metaphysical and political revolt.[106] For the moment, it is enough to note that opposition to capital punishment is powerfully voiced by both Camus and Ivan and constitutes another notable example of an affinity between the two individuals, favouring the process of identification and dialogue and helping to account for the impression of familiarity experienced by Camus when reading and playing the part of Ivan Karamazov.

Further traces of Ivan's presence in Camus's early work lend added support to the idea that Camus's inner world is conceived in a spirit of debate and dialogue with Ivan. For example, Ivan asks at Dmitri's trial: 'Qui ne désire pas la mort de son père?' ['Who does not wish for his father's death?'][107] In *L'Étranger* which, like *Les Frères Karamazov*, contains the court trial of a murderer, Meursault observes: 'Tous les êtres sains avaient plus ou moins souhaité la mort de ceux qu'ils aimaient' ['All normal people have more or less wished for the death of persons they love'].[108] This appears to be a clear and conscious intertextual reference to Ivan, on Camus's part as, indeed, could Cherea's point to Caligula: 'je souhaite parfois la mort de ceux que j'aime' ['I sometimes wish for the death of persons I love'].[109] Moreover, the man who is to be tried in court after Meursault is to face a charge of patricide, the charge morally haunting Ivan and actually facing Dmitri. This could, therefore, also be a reference to Dostoevsky which could imply that Camus had *Les Frères Karamazov* partly in mind when writing the trial scenes of *L'Étranger*. Certainly, Dostoevsky's powerful probing of psychology as a double-edged weapon in *Les Frères Karamazov* and his equally powerful exposition of the unreliability of judgements, readily link up with corresponding themes in *L'Étranger* which examines the inappropriateness of the certainties of capital punishment given the subjective failings and imperfections of human judgement.[110] These echoes of Dostoevsky in *L'Étranger* also serve as a defining context for Camus to launch Meursault's philosophy as an answer to Dostoevsky; in other words, the text of *L'Étranger* engages

Dostoevsky in dialogue or flags these allusions to his work in order to prepare for the last scene, where Meursault emerges as a new and alternative Christ.[111]

Ivan's presence also seems to haunt Camus's *Caligula* and provides an early insight into the way Camus's moral evolution and concept of inauthentic revolt is tied to his understanding of Ivan. It has already been noted how Caligula's reaction to death and the Gods echoes Ivan's revolt. However, Ivan and Caligula are identical in that their revolt against an unjust condition leads them both to moral nihilism. They both come to believe that all is permitted and both move from a revolt undertaken in the name of justice to the legitimization of murder and to the reversal of the traditional moral law, although Caligula's nihilism is, admittedly, much more determined and 'pedagogical' than Ivan's. Ivan becomes an 'objective' murderer through the agency of Smerdiakov, whereas Caligula puts his logic into practice himself. Eventually, both characters feel guilty and responsible for their 'crimes' despite their belief that no values are justified.[112] Their bold proclamations of freedom lead to disaster for themselves and others and both characters find themselves in contradiction to the original impetus of their revolt.

Caligula explains the logical nature of his nihilism to Cherea in Act II, Scene 6. Cherea here concedes that moral nihilism is a logical consequence of the absurd but tells the Emperor that one should refuse to heed such logic in the name of simple happiness and a life of common decency.[113] The scene is a condensed expression of Camus's moral dilemmas at the time. It is very tempting to see Caligula's logic as a restatement of Ivan's 'tout est permis', whilst Cherea's reply is clearly an embodiment of the 'code de la rue' of 'L'Été à Alger'. The whole scene reflects Camus's feelings of responsibility for Nazism and throws into perspective the inadequacy of Cherea's code and, by extension, the whole of Camus's early philosophy and its cogency as a reply to Dostoevsky. Camus also uses Scipion to restate his early views and to underscore both their dangers (ethical indifference) and their temptations (serenity because 'tout est bien'). Scipion can understand the monster that is inside Caligula because it is *also* inside him (Camus's friendship with the German of *Lettres à un ami allemand* is premissed on the same basis). It is because of this understanding that Scipion wins the poetry competition organized by the Emperor with a poem lyricizing lucidity and serene joy before death.[114] It is also because of this understanding that he withdraws from the conspiracy against Caligula: he refuses to resist in the name of those features which he shares with the Emperor, despite the fact that Caligula has committed the

Dostoevskian crime *par excellence* and killed the poet's father. He tells Cherea, when deserting the conspiracy: 'Quelque chose en moi lui ressemble pourtant. La même flamme nous brûle le cœur' ['Something in me is like him, however. The same flame burns in our hearts'].[115] Camus's whole moral experience at the time of the War is articulated within the Caligula/Scipion/Cherea triangle which is the moral heart of the play. Ivan's logic and guilt are central to these deliberations as Camus reassesses his early work and his early reply to Dostoevsky in the light of European history and Nazism.[116]

The subsequent and final scenes of the play show Caligula's logic negating itself and illustrate Camus's notion of a revolt which falls into contradiction and implodes, 'une révolte qui se retourne contre elle-même' ['a revolt which contradicts its own internal logic']. The logic of authentic revolt is not, however, stated, so no philosophical reply to Ivan/Caligula is revealed in the play. This will come in both the *Remarque sur la révolte* and *L'Homme révolté* and in both works Ivan will figure significantly. As these developments occur in Camus, so the central significance of Ivan changes: from a hero of the absurd and of moral equivalence, he becomes a pivotal expression of a metaphysical revolt which falls into contradiction, nihilism and madness, legitimizing murder and the oppression of the Grand Inquisitorial regime. The Second World War and its aftermath produced in Camus a far deeper understanding of metaphysical rebellion and political nihilism and this, in turn, initiates an evolution in his reading of Dostoevsky, particularly of *Les Frères Karamazov* and *Les Possédés*. If the evidence suggests that Ivan is of paramount significance in the development of the early Camus as a kindred spirit and crystallizing force, there is no question that Ivan's presence makes itself felt just as powerfully and perhaps even more so during the years when Camus tries to redress the moral nihilism of *Le Mythe de Sisyphe* and formulate an ethic of humanist persuasion capable of answering simultaneously Ivan's 'tout est permis', Dostoevsky's general Christian challenge and his warning that socialism is doomed to nihilism through atheism. This will be the subject of our next chapter.

7

Ivan and Metaphysical Revolt
The Shadow of The Grand Inquisitor

As the historical circumstances of Occupation, Resistance and War propel Camus beyond the hedonistic and individualistic imperatives of *Le Mythe de Sisyphe*, and as the Cold War develops and intensifies, so his perspectives on Dostoevsky widen and deepen. The brilliant analyst of human psychology and of the world of the absurd acquires, in Camus's eyes, a new status as a prophet of twentieth-century nihilism and totalitarian oppression. Once again, it is principally *Les Possédés* and *Les Frères Karamazov* which attract Camus's attention, but his interest centres on the analysis they contain of the links between disbelief, moral nihilism, socialism, revolution and violence. Dostoevsky becomes for Camus, in the second phase of his interest, the person who, more lucidly than either Marx or Nietzsche, could see how Western atheism and the death of God could generate twentieth-century totalitarian paternalism, dictatorship and historical messianism with its emphasis on the ends justifying the means. The same author who appears to have played such an essential role in the crystallization of his conception of the absurd now begins to be an equally important element in the conceptualization of his moral and political philosophy. As was the case for the arguments of *Le Mythe de Sisyphe*, it seems that the ideas and substance of the principal works of Camus's moral philosophy, *Remarque sur la révolte* and *L'Homme révolté*, are conceived in a spirit of debate and dialogue with the Russian writer, involving areas of convergence and divergence. The terms of this new debate between the two authors are clearly defined and concern the possibility of constructing a non-religious humanism. It was one of Dostoevsky's most cherished beliefs that not only was moral nihilism an inevitable consequence of the absurd and disbelief, but that socialism and any form of humanism cannot be successfully constructed in history outside of Christian parameters. Love of other people, so essential to the socialist and humanist enterprise, is impossible for Dostoevsky if one is not convinced of the immortality of the human soul. Without such a conviction, love turns to hatred and nihilism. To build the Kingdom of Man without God is a doomed aspiration, for the human kingdom, without the law of God, will quickly degenerate into murder, tyranny and oppression. Western atheism was, for Dostoevsky, infecting the Russian intelligentsia, particularly its so-called liberals, and its ultimate harvest, if Russia abandoned God, would be political chaos and oppression. If Ivan's revolt against God can be used to legitimize murder, so the reign of the Grand Inquisitor can use the same nihilistic logic to legitimize itself through *Realpolitik* and Verkhovensky can use Chigalev's Hegelian philosophy to justify anything in the name of some future state, where all will be well. These are, of course, the major themes of both *Les Possédés* and *Les Frères Karamazov* but Dostoevsky clearly states his personal view-point in the *Journal d'un écrivain*:

J'énonce . . . que l'amour de l'humanité est inconcevable, in-compréhensible et même impossible sans la foi en l'immortalité de l'âme humaine. Ceux qui, après avoir arraché à l'homme sa foi en l'immortalité, cherchent à remplacer cette foi par cet autre idéal qui est 'l'amour de l'humanité,' ceux-là, dis-je, attentent contre eux-mêmes, car au lieu de l'amour de l'humanité, ce n'est que le germe de la haine de l'humanité qu'ils plantent au cœur de ceux qui ont perdu la foi . . . Je soutiens même et j'ose énoncer que l'amour de l'humanité *en général* est, en tant qu'idée, une des idées les plus inaccessibles à l'esprit humain. Précisément sous forme d'idée. Il n'y a que le sentiment qui puisse en justifier. Mais ce sentiment n'est possible qu'autant que l'on est convaincu de l'existence de l'âme humaine.[1]

[I declare . . . that love of humanity is inconceivable, in-comprehensible and even impossible without a belief in the immortality of the soul. Those who, having ripped to pieces our belief in the immortality of the soul, seek to replace this belief with that other ideal which is love of humanity, these people, I say, trespass against themselves, for instead of love of humanity it is nothing but the seed of hatred of humanity that they sow in the heart of those who have ceased to believe . . . I maintain and dare to declare that love of humanity *in general* is, as an idea, one of the most inaccessible to the human mind. Precisely as an idea. Only sentiment can provide it with justification. But sentiment is only possible if one is convinced of the existence of the soul.]

This extract, taken from the December 1876 issue of the *Journal* which contains 'Moralité un peu tardive' and which Camus, as we have seen, knew very well indeed, formulates explicitly those challenges to non-Christian ethics and lay political philosophy which underpin *Les Frères Karamazov* and *Les Possédés*: Russia without God, Christ and the Tzar, is heading towards moral relativism and political chaos in the form of the Grand Inquisitor and Chigalevism.

If the face of twentieth-century history appeared, in Camus's view, to be providing confirmation of Dostoevsky's prophetic powers, did this indicate that a return to Christian absolutism was the only answer to nihilism? The germ of Camus's answer, which is fully developed in *L'Homme révolté*, is expressed in the *Carnets* in an entry for 1947, among a series of reflections on Russia and politics which he will later feed into *Les Justes* and *L'Homme révolté* itself:

> Si, pour dépasser le nihilisme, il faut revenir au christianisme, on peut bien suivre alors le mouvement et dépasser le christianisme dans l'hellénisme.[2]

> [If, in order to go beyond nihilism, we have to return to Christianity, it is indeed possible to continue in the same direction and go beyond Christianity into Hellenism.]

If Camus's concept of revolt is his answer to Ivan's 'tout est permis', so 'la pensée de midi' and the Hellenic, Mediterranean politics of *mesura* is his answer to *Les Possédés* and Chigalev. If *Le Mythe de Sisyphe* replies to Dostoevsky's views on suicide and the absurd, *L'Homme révolté* points to a pathway outside Dostoevsky's contention that socialism without Christ must be oppressive. It tries to build 'le socialisme de liberté' ['the socialism of freedom'] as against 'le socialisme césarien' ['caesarian socialism'], to rescue humanism from nihilism and value from history. To see how this debate is fully developed in Camus's moral and political philosophy, as was the case for *Le Mythe de Sisyphe*, an analysis will be made of Camus's use of Dostoevsky in *L'Homme révolté*. This will begin with the exploration of Camus's use of Ivan in the essay and concentrate on Ivan's place in the evolution of metaphysical revolt. The following chapter will deal with Camus's reading of *Les Possédés* as a prophetic expression of historical revolt that has fallen into nihilism.

Camus's analysis of Ivan is placed within the first part of the essay dealing with metaphysical revolt in a subsection entitled 'Le Refus du salut'. It seems possible that the whole intellectual architecture of *L'Homme révolté*, with its major divisions between 'la révolte métaphysique' and 'la révolte historique', is linked to Camus's reading of *Les Frères Karamazov* and his dialogue with Dostoevsky and Ivan. Camus was fond of quoting Dostoevsky's conviction, voiced through Ivan, that 'Les questions de Dieu et de l'immortalité sont les mêmes que les questions du socialisme mais sous un autre angle' ['The questions of God and of immortality are the same as the questions of socialism but seen from a different angle'].[3] Both in *L'Homme révolté*[4] and 'Pour Dostoïevski',[5] Camus dwells on the relationship in Dostoevsky between metaphysical rebellion, revolt against God and socialist historical endeavours, which are likened to movements to build the transparently just Kingdom of Man on Earth in opposition to the unjust Kingdom of God. Socialism is seen as an attempt to construct a world of Christian solidarity but expressed in lay terms, with God excluded, in the name of justice, because He condemns mankind to suffering and death. Camus shares with Dostoevsky a marked tendency to see history as metaphysical ideas in action and to see faith and rebellion against God as the central questions of European intellectual, political and social history. Although Dostoevsky firmly believed that socialism without God would fall into murder and tyranny, he saw an essential link between social protest and theodicy. Camus also believed that social protest was the historical expression of metaphysical revolt. This is one reason why it is Dostoevsky, and not Marx with his emphasis on the economic infrastructure, who is, for Camus, the true prophet of the twentieth century. It is tempting to believe that Camus's predilection for Dostoevsky's metaphysics and for his analysis of nihilism played a significant part in shaping the intellectual and political perspectives which he uses to structure the arguments in *L'Homme révolté* and that Camus's responses to the world of history and politics, with their characteristic metaphysical flavour, are partly inherited from his dialogue with Dostoevsky. His analysis of Ivan in *L'Homme révolté* is certainly indicative of a great depth of involvement in the whole Dostoevskian question of revolt against God and the legitimization of murder, the central problem of *L'Homme révolté*.[6]

Dostoevsky's Ivan Karamazov, in Camus's analysis, widens, deepens and intensifies Western European expressions of revolt in several pivotal ways. Ivan's revolt is deeper than that of the Romantic movement generally, of which it is nonetheless a part, because it emphasizes, in its initial movements, solidarity and love, whereas Romantic revolt was individualistic and blaspheming against a cruel

God, cultivating 'le mal' as an ostentatious rejection of divine values. Ivan 'prend le parti des hommes . . . Il affirme que la condamnation à mort qui pèse sur eux est injuste. Dans son premier mouvement, au moins, il plaide pour la justice qu'il met au-dessus de la divinité' ['is on the side of men . . . He affirms that the death penalty which hangs over them is unjust. In his initial reactions, at least, he pleads for justice which he places above divinity'].[7] Like the Romantics, Ivan does not deny God's existence, but his rejection of God goes beyond Romantic posturing because it is done in the name of a high moral value, justice. God is not moral enough for Ivan, says Camus, because His creation involves the suffering of innocence. Romantic sensibility, before Dostoevsky, aspired to be God's equal, to rival His cruelty with evil, pride and blasphemy. Ivan changes the tone and texture of revolt. If suffering is necessary to creation, then God's creation is unacceptable. Ivan will put his faith in transparent justice, not in a mysterious Divinity. Justice, as a value, is higher than grace or God: '[Ivan] inaugure l'enterprise essentielle de la révolte qui est de substituer au royaume de la grâce celui de la justice' ['inaugurates the essential endeavour of revolt which is to replace the kingdom of grace with the kingdom of justice'].[8] If the Romantics rebelled against God because of his cruelty, Ivan's revolt is more extensive because he also rejects the God of love: suffering is too high a price to pay for the truth of God's love. Ivan's revolt specifically targets the Christian God of the New Testament because acceptance of suffering in the name of divine mercy is rejected without qualification as an injustice bricked into God's creation. Not only this, Ivan claims that he would persist in his indignation and revolt *even if* it could be proved that he was wrong, that suffering were to be redeemed unconditionally and ultimately by divine love. What Camus refers to as Ivan's 'même si', ['even if'] his rejection of salvation uncon-ditionally because God is unjust, even if some ultimate legitimization could be demonstrated as true, is, for Camus, a highly significant moment in the history of revolt; he calls it 'le moment capital de la révolte métaphysique' ['the pivotal moment of metaphysical revolt'][9] and later 'le cri le plus profond d'Ivan, celui qui ouvre les abîmes les plus bouleversants sous les pas du révolté' ['Ivan's most profound protest, the one which opens up the most disturbing chasms beneath the rebel's pathway'].[10] Ivan will only accept grace unconditionally and he repudiates any *marché* which will grant him eternal life in exchange for accepting God's creation. Neither will his revolt be 'bought off' by any privileged status: he will not accept salvation for himself. Ivan believes in a logic which includes 'tous ou personne' ['all or none'] in the same way that he believes, when it comes to notions of divine justice, in the logic of 'tout ou rien' ['all or nothing'].[11] Ivan's initial solidarity with his fellow men against divine injustice, his refusal to be saved alone, his tenacious adherence to transparent notions of human love, compared to divine mystification, constitute for Camus 'le mouvement le plus pur de la révolte' ['the purest expression of revolt'] making Ivan, for Camus, what Dunwoodie calls:

> la plus grande figure révoltée du xixème siècle, sorte d'Archange du bien poussé inexorablement vers le Mal par la force de sa propre logique, esprit rigoureux imbu de rationalisme mais miné par le doute, celui qui rejette la vision religieuse du monde parce qu'elle ne peut répondre à son exigence de justice.[12]

> [the greatest rebel of the nineteenth century, a sort of Archangel of good pushed inexorably towards evil by the force of his own logic, a rigorous mind imbued with rationalism but undermined by doubt, a person who rejects the religious view of life because it doesn't satisfy his demand for justice.]

This rejection of a future possible happiness in the name of an immediate love of other human beings becomes a crucial determinant in Camus's notion of authentic revolt and fuels his opposition to those political philosophies which justify present tyrannies in the name of some future good which will redeem the deaths of their victims. Ivan's revolt involves 'une généreuse complicité' ['an altruistic complicity with his fellow human beings'][13] and is not based on Scheler's notion of resentment or utilitarian calculations of self-interest.[14] The love that Ivan refuses God is initially turned towards others to create the community of victims of God's tyranny and injustice. However, with God and immortality rejected, Ivan's moral sense implodes and the primal murder of the father ensues as revolt collapses into nihilism.

Again in opposition to other expressions of Romantic revolt which would, according to Camus, have been satisfied with an ostentatious display or parade of disaffected feelings about God, Ivan wishes to pursue his logic to its absolute conclusion. If immortality is gone, what is left for Ivan? asks Camus, as though restating the opening of the *Mythe de Sisyphe*. Quoting Ivan's statement to Aliocha: 'Je vis en dépit de la logique' ['I live despite logic'], Camus points out that Ivan can find no value in the name of which he can justify his own pleasures in life. Without immortality, for Ivan, as for Dostoevsky, 'il n'y a pas de vertu. Tout est permis' ['there is no virtue. Everything is permitted'].[15] Camus's response to Ivan at this moment is important. He designates the 'tout est permis' as the true beginning of twentieth-century nihilism:

A ce 'tout est permis' commence vraiment l'histoire du nihilisme contemporain.[16]

[With this 'everything is permitted' the history of contemporary nihilism truly begins.]

No longer then, is Ivan, as he was in 1942, a tzar of the mind and an embodiment of the sovereign freedom available to the absurd man but an individual, a rebel, who is 'déchiré' ['torn apart'] by the negative and positive charges of his revolt which generate a tension which is difficult to sustain. Romantic revolt, in its earlier manifestations, was not nihilistic, but a blasphemous challenge to divine law. With Ivan, states Camus: 'la logique de l'indignation va retourner la révolte contre elle-même et la jeter dans une contradiction désespérée' ['the logic of indignation will turn revolt against itself and catapault it into a desperate contradiction'].[17] Evidently, Camus finds in Ivan a perfect paradigm of a revolt which fails to maintain its internal moral dynamic and essential no/yes polarities in equilibrium and falls into nihilism. Thus Camus can argue:

Le même homme qui prenait si farouchement le parti de l'inno-cence, qui tremblait devant la souffrance de l'enfant, qui voulait voir 'de ses yeux' la biche dormir près du lion, la victime embrasser le meurtrier, à partir du moment où il refuse la cohérence divine et tente de trouver sa propre règle, reconnaît la légitimité du meurtre.[18]

[The same man who so fiercely defended innocence, who shook before the suffering of children, who wanted 'with his own eyes' to see the lamb sleep with the lion, the murdered man embrace the murderer, this same man, once he refuses to accept that the divine order is morally coherent and tries to establish his own rules, accepts the legitimacy of murder.]

Although Ivan does not commit murder, he legitimizes it as part of the logic of his revolt against God; his attitude is one of *laissez-faire* and forms, for Camus, the vital bridge between the postures of Romanticism and modern revolutionary extremist action, infected with nihilism, undertaken to build the Kingdom of Man in this world now that God is dethroned.[19] Ivan's metaphysical rebellion, initially positive and premissed on justice, topples into the contradictions of nihilism and justifies murder of the father and, by extension, any action.

Camus describes Ivan's dilemma as having to be 'vertueux et illogique, ou logique et criminel' ['virtuous and illogical or logical and criminal'].[20] This was precisely Camus's own private dilemma, at least in philosophical terms, in the 1940s: Le Mythe de Sisyphe not only legitimized crime and thus, theoretically, Nazism but it could not, in addition, provide any moral authority for resistance. Ivan himself becomes haunted because of the intensity of the lived contradiction between not wishing to acknowledge moral distinctions intellectually and feeling morally responsible for patricide. Ivan's dilemma in this way represents for Camus a decisive moment in the history of metaphysical revolt as he understands it:

> La question que se pose enfin Ivan, celle qui constitue le vrai progrès que Dostoïevski fait accomplir à l'esprit de révolte est la seule qui nous intéresse ici: peut-on vivre et se maintenir dans la révolte?[21]

> [The question posed by Ivan, the one which demonstrates the real progress which Dostoevsky achieved for the spirit of revolt is the only one which interests me here: can one continue to live and maintain the attitude of revolt?]

Camus is thus able to pose, through Ivan's revolt, the very question which dominates his political and literary production between 1943 and 1951: does absurdity lead to nihilism? It might be thought that Camus is most fortunate to find in Ivan and Les Frères Karamazov generally such a precise and felicitous model of a revolt which turns against itself and one which lends itself so readily to the perspectives of the essay and to his own personal quest for a moral value capable of legitimizing resistance to Nazism. A more convincing argument is to see Dostoevsky as a very real presence in the evolution of Camus's moral and political philosophy with Ivan as the character who most challengingly questions the possibility of values in an absurd world. Camus, by 1951, reads Ivan as a literary and philosophical expression and exploration of his own difficulties in redesigning the quantative ethic of Le Mythe de Sisyphe to fit the circumstances of Occupation and Resistance.

Camus, it should be noted, so arranges his analysis of Ivan to focus attention on an idea of contradiction which is inherent in his *own* philosophy of revolt but quite separate from Dostoevsky's. Although Camus is keen to point out, as he did in Le Mythe de Sisyphe, that

Dostoevsky gives the impression that he is 'plus à l'aise' ['more at ease'][22] with Ivan than with Aliocha, the contradiction brought to light by Dostoevsky in the characterization of Ivan is the one indicated by the devil in the novel and which Camus quotes: 'Tu vas accomplir une action vertueuse et pourtant tu ne crois pas à la vertu, voilà ce qui t'irrite et te tourmente' ['You are going to commit a virtuous act and yet you don't believe in virtue, that is what is annoying and tormenting you'].[23] Dostoevsky is, of course, focusing attention on what was for him the reality of moral conscience as an element of the Divine. Whatever Ivan may deduce in intellectual terms from his reason and revolt, he *feels* responsible for the murder of his father. The hypothetical superman, liberated from the constraints of conventional values, so effectively evoked by the devil who haunts Ivan, fails to materialize because the divine part of man will not be denied. This is also the fate of Raskolnikov who moves from murder to resurrection through Christ. Camus, however, wants to use Ivan, not as Dostoevsky intended, but as an example of revolt which denies its positive content and falls into nihilism and murder. By interpreting Ivan's contradiction in this way, Camus hopes to define the parameters of a consistent lay humanism within the terms set by Ivan and by Dosteovsky himself. Camus's argument is that the *real* logic of Ivan's revolt, undertaken against God on behalf of man in the name of justice, should be to establish not murder and nihilism but the just Kingdom of Man in opposition to the unjust Kingdom of God. Ivan, however, has no concept of the logic of authentic revolt, as conceptualized by Camus, because he is the creation of Dostoevsky who saw no possibility of justifying values outside of divine authority. For this reason, Ivan 'allows' the murder of old Karamazov to be committed by Smerdiakov and eventually goes insane, because he cannot reconcile the logic of his heart with that of his reason. Camus tries to create a life-line for Ivan with his theory of revolt in order to rescue him from this impasse. He describes Ivan's dilemma thus:

> Coincé entre une vertu injustifiable et un crime inacceptable, dévoré de pitié et incapable d'amour, solitaire privé du secourable cynisme, la contradiction tuera cette intelligence souveraine.[24]

> [Pincered between an unjustifiable value and an unacceptable crime, devoured by pity and incapable of love, a solitary man without the support of cynicism, this sovereign mind will be destroyed by contradiction.]

Camus is clearly moved by Ivan's intense conflicts and madness and full of deep admiration for Dostoevsky's creative genius in being able to construct such a powerful character so close to his world. However, it is unlikely that either creator or character would have accepted the life-line or would have yielded to Camus's view that Ivan's revolt against God produces an autonomous value independent of God, in the name of which socialist humanism can build the Kingdom of Man without God.

Whatever the views of Ivan and Dostoevsky themselves on the logic of revolt, Camus is able to claim that Ivan's logic and example initiate social and political action in the real world of history. Ivan's madness does not preclude the possibility of his providing a political progeny. Camus writes: 'Ce naufrage [Ivan's madness] n'empêche pas, du reste que le problème posé, la conséquence devait suivre: la révolte est désormais en marche vers l'action' ['This disaster does not however prevent that, once the problem is posed, the consequence should follow: revolt is henceforth mobilized for action'].[25] This is a supremely important moment for Camus in the intellectual and political history of European metaphysical revolt. The logic of Ivan, whatever the character's personal fate, legitimizes the ultimate metaphysical rebellion: to murder God the Father in the name of human justice and solidarity and to begin the work of building man's Kingdom on Earth. However, the enterprise is fatally infected with Ivan's 'tout est permis' and, in consequence, produces political nihilism. This in turn becomes an all too readily available instrument in the rationalization of *Realpolitik*. Ivan's revolt is moral and intellectual but, for Camus, its practical and political consequences are far-reaching:

> Son projet d'usurpation [Ivan's revolt against God] reste donc tout moral. Il ne veut rien réformer dans la création. Mais la création étant ce qu'elle est, il en tire le droit de s'affranchir moralement et les autres hommes avec lui. A partir du moment, au contraire, où l'esprit de révolte, acceptant le 'tout est permis' et le 'tous ou personne', visera à refaire la création pour assurer la royauté et la divinité des hommes, à partir du moment où la révolution métaphysique s'étendra du moral au politique, une nouvelle entreprise, de portée incalculable, commencera, née elle aussi, il faut le remarquer, du même nihilisme.[26]

> [His project to usurp God's authority thus remains moral. He doesn't wish to reform any element of creation. But creation being what it is, he claims from it the right to transcend moral values for himself and all others. However, from the moment that revolt, accepting the 'everything is permitted' and the 'all or nobody',

strives to refashion creation to secure the royalty and divinity of man, from the moment that metaphysical revolt spreads from morals to politics, then a new enterprise will begin, one of immeasurable importance and born also, one must note, of the self-same nihilism.]

Ivan is thus, for Camus, a seminal moment in the evolution of metaphysical revolt because he is at that particular junction where metaphysical insurrection against God begins to justify political nihilism in the name of a greater good. It is for this reason that Dostoevsky has such a profound importance for Camus in the post-war period: he is the nineteenth-century writer who understood, more comprehensively than any other, the relationship between revolt against the God of love and a humanism infected with nihilism. More precisely, Dostoevsky understood, in Camus's eyes, how the socialist movement in Europe emerged from Western European atheism and metaphysical rebellion and how that movement became permeated with paternalism and nihilism. Dostoevsky, he argues, 'avec une intensité prophétique' ['with prophetic intensity'] and as a 'prophète de la nouvelle religion' ['prophet of the new religion'][27] articulates, through Ivan and 'The Legend of the Grand Inquisitor', the political consequences of 'tout est permis'. To understand Camus's response to this legend and assess his use of the idea of the Grand Inquisitor in the expression of his political philosophy, a number of details from Ivan's parable must be established.

What Ivan describes to Aliocha as his 'poème' about the Grand Inquisitor is a philosophical and moral tale about Christ and the Tower of Babel, voicing some of Dostoevsky's deepest thoughts on the subject of Christian freedom and fellowship. The same subject matter is approached directly and in an almost identical language by Dostoevsky himself in his celebrated 'Discours sur Pouchkine' in June 1880 and published in the *Journal d'un écrivain*.[28] Camus knew this text very well and described it as 'admirable',[29] no doubt partly because he was moved by Dostoevsky's great sense of the public responsibility of the writer, so evident in the speech, but possibly in greater measure for reasons related to the profound moral vision of solidarity that it contains. This expresses itself most forcefully when Dostoevsky analyses *Eugène Oniéguine* and, more specifically, the encounter between Tatiana and Oniéguine which, for the Russian author, poses the fundamental questions of human happiness: is happiness possible if it is built on sin or the suffering of others? Should Tatiana betray her husband and will she find happiness if she does? Dostoevsky writes:

Est-ce que l'homme peut fonder son bonheur sur le malheur d'autrui? Le bonheur n'est pas tout dans les plaisirs de l'amour, il est aussi dans l'harmonie supérieure de l'esprit. Où l'esprit trouvera-t-il le repos s'il a par devers lui une action malhonnête, méchante et inhumaine . . . Permettez, imaginez que vous soyez vous-même chargé de construire l'édifice des destinées humaines dans le but final de rendre les hommes heureux, de leur donner enfin la paix et le repos. Et là-dessus, imaginez-vous aussi que pour cela il soit nécessaire et indispensable de torturer une seule créature humaine, une seule, pas davantage, et même fort peu intéressante, un être qui pourrait passer pour grotesque, non pas un Shakespeare quelconque, mais simplement un honnête vieillard . . . Or c'est celui-ci uniquement qu'il s'agit de bafouer, de déshonorer et de torturer, c'est sur les larmes de ce vieillard sans défense que doit se fonder notre bonheur. Consentiriez-vous à ce prix à être l'architecte d'un pareil édifice? Telle est la question. Et pouvez- vous admettre, fût-ce une minute, l'idée que ceux pour qui l'on a construit cet édifice consentiraient eux-mêmes à recevoir de vous un tel bonheur, si dans ces fondations se trouve la souffrance du plus infime des êtres, impitoyablement et injustement torturé à cette fin; et pensez-vous en acceptant ce bonheur, rester à jamais heureux?[30]

[Can man build his happiness on the misfortune of others? Happiness is not all a question of love's pleasures, it is also linked to the superior harmony of the mind. How will the mind be able to find peace if it has in its history an action which is dishonest, wicked or inhuman . . . ? Let me make this point, imagine that you yourself are charged with constructing the edifice of human destiny in order to make all men happy, to give them at long last peace and tranquillity. And then, imagine also that to do this it is necessary and unavoidable to torture one living being, only one, no more, and even one of very little interest, a being who could be seen as grotesque, not some sort of Shakespeare but just an honest old man . . . Now he is the only person you've got to taunt, dishonour and torture, it is upon the cries of this defenceless old man that you must build our happiness. Would you agree to be the architect of the building at such a price? That is the question. And can you concede, even for just a minute, that those for whom the edifice was built would agree to receive such happiness from you, if at its foundations can be found the sufferings of this most weak of beings, pitilessly and unjustly tortured to this end; and do you think you will stay forever happy accepting that kind of happiness?]

What Camus liked to call elsewhere 'le communisme spirituel de Dostoïevski . . . la responsabilité morale de tous' ['the spiritual communism of Dostoevsky . . . the moral responsibility of all'][31] is contained in the 'Discours sur Pouchkine' which ends up with a vision of Russian genius spearheading the idea of 'la grande, universelle harmonie, de l'accord définitif et fraternel de toutes les races de la terre sous la loi évangélique du Christ'['the great, universal harmony, of the definitive brotherly accord of all races of the Earth under the evangelical laws of Christ'].[32]

This Dostoevskian vision of universal Christian solidarity is embodied in the pronouncements of the terminally ill Staretz Zosime of *Les Frères Karamazov* who tells Aliocha that each of us is 'coupable de tout envers tous' ['guilty of everything before everybody'].[33] Later, Zosime warns that all attempts to build the universal human community without Christ 'finiront par inonder le monde de sang' ['will end up by creating rivers of blood in the world'][34] even if they are undertaken in the name of justice and that self-destructive pride and deracination will be the lot of those who reject the divine part of the ideal of Christian love or try to divorce love from its base in Christ.[35] Zosime's idea of intersubjective Christian harmony replies both to Ivan's 'tout est permis' and to the arguments of the legend, for the Grand Inquisitor himself probes the thematic of the Tower of Babel but in a way which is specifically designed to refute the ideals of Christ and those notions of love which take their inspiration from His view of freedom.

Ivan's story is set in the period of the Inquisition. Ivan imagines that Christ has returned to Earth and is arrested by the Inquisitor who subjects him to a lengthy disquisition on the inadequacies and overdemanding expectations of his vision of humanity, especially as evidenced by his responses to 'l'Esprit terrible et profond, l'Esprit de la destruction et du néant' ['the deep and terrible Spirit, the Spirit of destruction and nothingness'],[36] in other words, to the devil at the time of the great temptations in the desert. Essential to the meaning of Ivan's story is the Roman Catholic framework, since Christ's authority is now vested in an infallible Pope, and Christ, for this reason, is not allowed to say anything new. Christ's answer to the Inquisitor's charges is to kiss him on the lips and depart, an act which Aliocha believes to be a proof of the goodness of Christ and the power of divine love but which the Inquisitor interprets as a recognition of defeat. It is not necessary to go into great detail on this subject but the Inquisitor tells Christ that His greatest error was to offer people 'le pain du ciel' and not 'le pain de la terre' ['the bread of heaven' and not 'the bread of earth'].[37] The reason why

Christ made this choice, says the Inquisitor, was because Christ preferred to give man moral freedom to pursue spiritual needs and realities. However, the larger part of mankind, according to the Inquisitor, finds such freedom a burden and a source of unhappiness and would gladly exchange it for the satisfaction of material needs. Christ should rather have transformed the deserts into bread and accepted to be Caesar. He would then have been worshipped as a protective authority, rather than seen as a spiritual challenge. Luckily, however, according to the Inquisitor, the Church and papal authority have been able to see the error of Christ's demands: the Inquisitors have undertaken to build human happiness by satisfying people's material needs and removing from them the burden of their freedom. The new Tower of Babel will be headed by papal Caesars who will run the world for the benefit of all. A benevolent, paternalistic dictatorship, worshipped by a contented but enslaved mass of people, will assume the burden of freedom for all and will do whatever is necessary to keep humanity on course towards a better tomorrow. Through 'The Legend of the Grand Inquisitor', the spiritual challenges of Christ's message are seemingly pushed aside in favour of a usurping, worldly orthodoxy of power politics with its eyes set on global domination. Aliocha is quick to express the view that Ivan's poem is really about atheism, political power and the displacement of divine love by a fraudulant humanism which transforms most people into obedient animals and slaves in the name of their happiness.[38]

In *L'Homme révolté*, Camus interprets 'The Legend of the Grand Inquisitor' as a prophetic prefiguration of Stalinism, degenerate socialism and totalitarian philanthrophy.[39] Ivan's revolt is experienced by himself, Camus argues, only in terms of 'maîtrise de soi' ['self-mastery'] and Aliocha is right to treat his brother as 'un vrai blanc-bec' ['a true fledgling'] because he does not envisage clearly the heavy social and political consequences which will ensue from his nihilistic revolt.[40] Using Dostoevsky's figure of the Grand Inquisitor, Camus creates a political category of his own, 'les Grands Inquisiteurs' and 'les Césars' who haunt Western manifestations of political revolt:

De Paul à Staline, les papes qui ont choisi César ont préparé la voie aux Césars qui ne choisissent qu'eux-mêmes. L'unité du monde qui ne s'est pas faite avec Dieu tentera désormais de se faire contre Dieu.[41]

[From Saint Paul to Stalin, the popes who have chosen Caesar have prepared the way for Caesars who chose only themselves. The unity of the world which was not realized with God will henceforth seek to realize itself against Him.]

Camus thus sees in the legend how Ivan's revolt in the name of justice against the God of love can generate totalitarian paternalism. The Grand Inquisitors who eventually appear on the European political stage 'refusent fièrement le pain du ciel et la liberté et offrent le pain de la terre sans la liberté' ['proudly refuse the bread of heaven with freedom and offer the bread of earth without it'].[42] Their ideology is based on the view that universal happiness is incompatible with individual moral freedom. Christ's method is unreliable for the collective good and unity can only be achieved by authority and Caesarism. In this way, the essentially noble aspirations of revolt have been usurped and betrayed by a self-appointed power elite who rely on human laziness and the desire for peace and satisfaction of basic appetites to settle for what the Caesars offer rather than face the stiffer tests of individual freedom. Since Christ refuses to legitimize the Inquisitor's grand design (he listens in silence) history itself, Camus argues, will be the Inquisitor's authority:

Le Grand Inquisiteur est vieux et las, car sa science est amère. Il sait que les hommes sont plus paresseux que lâches et qu'ils préfèrent la paix et la mort à la liberté de discerner le bien et le mal. Il a pitié, une pitié froide, de ce prisonnier silencieux [Christ] que l'histoire dément sans trêve. Il le presse de parler, de reconnaître ses torts et de légitimer, en un sens, l'entreprise des Inquisiteurs et des Césars. Mais le prisonnier se tait. L'entreprise se poursuivra donc sans lui; on le tuera. La légitimité viendra à la fin des temps quand le royaume des hommes sera assuré.[43]

[The Grand Inquisitor is old and tired, because his knowledge is bitter. He knows that men are lazy rather than cowardly and that they prefer peace and death to moral freedom. He coldly pities this silent prisoner (Christ) whom history ceaselessly refutes. He urges him to speak, to admit his errors and to legitimize, in a sense, the work of the Inquisitors and the Caesars. But the prisoner says nothing. The work will then go on without him: he will be killed. Legitimacy will come at the end of history when the kingdom of man is assured.]

The Inquisitor, for Camus, thus becomes an expression of the divinization of man and history, of that historical messianism which he felt to be at the centre of the bankrupt revolutions and self-serving ideologies of the twentieth century. Objective crimes and the show trials of the Stalinist revolution, the police state, the Inquisitorial regime, Big Brother, they are all prefigured in the story:

> Dans l'univers du procès, enfin conquis et achevé, un peuple de coupables cheminera sans trêve vers une impossible innocence, sous le regard amer des grands Inquisiteurs. Au xxème siècle, la puissance est triste.[44]

> [In a world of trials, finally subjugated and complete, a guilty people will advance relentlessly towards an impossible innocence beneath the bitter look of the Grand Inquisitors. In the twentieth century, power is sad.]

Camus's analysis of *Les Frères Karamazov* in *L'Homme révolté*, of Ivan's revolt and the Grand Inquisitor's philosophy, reveals that his moral and political philosophy develop in the context of a deep debate with the novel. If 'la pensée de midi' is an Hellenic response to Ivan's 'tout est permis' and to Dostoevsky's Christianity, the concept of authentic revolt throws down a democratic challenge both to the Grand Inquisitor's power politics and to Dostoevsky's thesis that socialism without Christ and God must necessarily fall into nihilism. The human community which Dostoevsky believed could only be founded in God and which the Grand Inquisitor claimed to be incompatible with Christ's freedom provide an important focus and perspective in Camus's mind when he elaborates his own notion of humanism and of the collective. To Ivan's question: 'peut-on vivre révolté?' ['can one live as a rebel?'][45] Camus replies: 'Je me révolte donc nous sommes' ['I revolt therefore we are']. This Camusian moral paradigm endeavours to establish the human community neither on divine authority nor on Caesarian notions of power and totality as envisaged by the Grand Inquisitor. The community of free individuals, as conceptualized by Camus, discovers its values and its source of unity in the negative and positive movements of revolt itself. Whereas inauthentic revolt is characterized by a dialectic which kills God in order to build a church or, in other words, destroys transcendence in order to create political or historical orthodoxies under the control of Caesars, authentic revolt will promote dialogue and pluralist democracy: 'le socialisme de liberté' ['the socialism of freedom'] will be Camus's answer to 'le socialisme césarien' ['Caesarian socialism'].

The significance of the impact of Ivan and the Grand Inquisitor on the development of Camus's moral and political philosophy can be measured not only in terms of the ideas in *L'Homme révolté* but also in other political writings by Camus. For example, in 1953, in an important speech given to *La Bourse du Travail de Saint-Etienne*,[46] Camus uses the Grand Inquisitor's language to define his opposition to the police state. He calls the article 'Le Pain et la liberté', placing it in a clear relationship with the Grand Inquisitor's charge against Christ that he should have given the people bread not freedom. The substance of the article is to claim that economic and political feeedom must go hand in hand, that freedom from hunger without freedom from political oppression is a slavery which diminishes us all:

> Si quelqu'un vous retire votre pain, il supprime en même temps votre liberté. Mais si quelqu'un vous ravit votre liberté, soyez tranquille, votre pain est menacé, car il ne dépend plus de vous et de votre lutte, mais du bon plaisir d'un maître . . . Les opprimés ne veulent pas seulement être libérés de leur faim, ils veulent l'être aussi de leurs maîtres.[47]

> [If somebody takes your bread away, he also takes your freedom. But if somebody steals your freedom, rest assured, your bread is threatened, for it no longer depends on you and your strength but on the whims of a master . . . The oppressed do not only want to be free from hunger, they also want to be free of their masters.]

This statement replies very precisely to the Grand Inquisitor's arguments about bread and freedom. It is important also to note that it is a *socialist* economic argument that Camus is advancing here. He is not saying that collectivist economics (bread) is incompatible with freedom, as the Grand Inquisitor claims, or that in order to have political freedom, we must avoid the collectivist economy, as Western liberalism claims. Camus is trying to reconcile, in the article, liberal politics and the collectivist economy; he is not justifying private capital as the guarantee of individual freedom.[48] Camus is between Tocqueville and Marx in 'Le Pain et la Liberté, trying to ground the former's notion of political freedom in the latter's concept of economic emancipation. Political freedom and economic justice can be reconciled, in Camus's eyes, by the politics of authentic revolt which must distance itself from revolutionary orthodoxies but not from collective economics.

The second part of this article also echoes the Grand Inquisitor's argument about Caesar and power. Camus writes:

Et si, aujourd'hui, sur une si grande part du monde, elle [la liberté] est en recul, c'est sans doute parce que jamais les entreprises d'asservissement n'ont été plus cyniques et mieux armées . . . Oui, le grand événement du xx siècle a été l'abandon des valeurs de liberté par le mouvement révolutionnaire, le recul progressif du socialisme de liberté devant le socialisme césarien et militaire. Dès cet instant, un certain espoir a disparu du monde, une solitude a commencé pour chacun des hommes libres.[49]

[And if, today, in so many parts of the world, liberty is in retreat, it is undoubtedly because never before have the enterprises of servitude been more cynical and better armed . . . Yes, the great event of the twentieth century has been the abandonment of the values of freedom by the revolutionary movement, the cumulative retreat of the socialism of freedom before Caesarian and militaristic socialism. From that moment, a certain hope disappeared from the world, loneliness began for every free man.]

Here Caesarian socialism, which Camus detested, is clearly related to the following utterances from the Grand Inquisitor about Caesar and human happiness:

Nous avons accepté Rome et le glaive de César, et nous nous sommes déclarés les seuls rois de la terre, bien que jusqu'à présent nous n'ayons pas encore eu le temps de parachever notre œuvre . . . Oh! l'affaire n'est qu'au début, elle est loin d'être terminée [the construction of the new Babel], et la terre aura encore beaucoup à souffrir, mais nous atteindrons notre but, nous serons Césars, alors nous songerons au bonheur universel.[50]

[We have accepted Rome and the sword of Caesar and we have declared ouselves the only kings of the Earth, although so far we have not had time to complete our work . . . Oh! the work has only just begun, it is far from finished, and the Earth will still have to suffer a great deal but we shall achieve our aim, we shall be Caesars, then we shall think of the happiness of all.]

This passage, quoted by Camus in L'Homme révolté, provides a key to his understanding of state terror and oppression in the name of some vague historical state of future human happiness, as well as providing him with a model of an elite and oppressive minority claiming to know what's best for everyone.

Further echoes of Les Frères Karamazov, in Camus's political journalism, underline the fact that Dostoevsky's presence haunts his political perspectives. In 'Épuration des purs', written in 1952 in defence of *L'Homme révolté*, Camus writes, in a passage questioning the role of the Church in the Albigensian heresy: 'comment donc expliquer qu'à l'occasion de l'hérésie albigeoise, justement, ce soit l'Église . . . qui ait créé de toutes pièces *l'Inquisition, modèle des polices terroristes?*' ['how then are we to explain that, during the time of the Albigensian heresy, it was precisely the Church . . . which created in all respects *the Inquisition, the model of police states?*'][51]

Further traces of Ivan's political parable can be found in the 1952 article, 'Révolte et romantisme' where Camus again reflects on Bakunin, nihilism and authoritarianism;[52] in 'Révolte et servitude' (Camus's famous letter to Sartre), where he makes reference to 'les maîtres insolents de notre temps . . . [et] leurs esclaves' ['the insolent masters of our times . . . and their slaves'];[53] in 'Défense de la Liberté' where Camus's intervention on behalf of Henri Martin is expressed in terms of individual freedom and authority, especially Stalinist authority, which are imbued with the thinking behind the legend;[54] and finally in the 'Discours de Suède' in which Camus speaks of the world as 'un monde menacé de désintégration, où nos grands inquisiteurs risquent d'établir pour toujours les royaumes de la mort' ['a world threatened with disintegration where our Grand Inquisitors are on the point of establishing forever the kingdoms of death'].[55] In his creative writing, the parable has a special resonance in the key 1948 troubled meditation on beauty entitled 'L'Exil d'Hélène'. Here, Camus, clearly weary of political life, envisages history as a long struggle between 'la création et l'Inquisition' ['creativity and the Inquisition'] as he tries simultaneously to define the artist's responsibility to beauty and to the world of politics and history. Significantly, because it demonstrates that Camus is thinking of Dostoevsky in this essay, he comments on how 'les paysages' or scenes of natural beauty have been disappearing from European literature since Dostoevsky. Later in the same essay, when defining the limits of revolt and political engagement, he again refers to Dostoevsky, this time to his 'bouffons', likening modern man to 'ces bouffons de Dostoïevski qui se vantent de tout, montent aux étoiles et finissent par étaler leur honte dans le premier lieu public' ['those buffoons of Dostoevsky who boast about everything, climb to the stars and end up displaying their shame in the first public place they can find'].[56]

It seems fair to deduce that Camus's dialogue with Dostoevsky and especially with Dostoevsky's *Les Frères Karamazov* is of very considerable importance in the evolution and shaping of Camus's moral and political philosophy. The novel provides Camus with a model of revolt which moves from justice and love to nihilism and murder and a political parable perfectly able to articulate his fears about authoritarian socialism and the police state. However, the scale of Camus's dialogue with Dostoevsky's political world does not become fully apparent until one reaches the second part of *L'Homme révolté* which deals with historical revolt and gives a place of great prominence to *Les Possédés*. A proper assessment of Dostoevsky's role in the crystallization of Camus's moral and political ideas can only be conducted after Camus's continuing preoccupation with *Les Possédés* in the post-war period has been analysed and explained.

8

Camus and *Les Possédés*
Nihilism and Historical Revolt

This chapter will first examine the ways in which Camus integrates Dostoevsky's novel *Les Possédés* into the body of arguments presented in the second major section of *L'Homme révolté*, 'La Révolte historique'. Camus's purpose, in this part of his book, is to explore history as the expression and enactment of the ideas and themes expounded in the genesis and evolution of metaphysical revolt as a philosophical construct. The metaphysical rebel says 'no' intellectually to God's Kingdom, in the name of justice, and defines thus the human community of love and value in opposition to the rejected, unethical order of the Divine. Historical revolt is the concrete attempt to build this new order and to create the socialist and humanist state as the fulfilment of human possibility.

Just as Ivan Karamazov represented a crucial and pivotal moment in the development of the sensibility of the metaphysical rebel, so *Les Possédés*, in Camus's eyes, provides a highly significant novelistic representation of some of the key elements and problems in the actual history of revolt. Dostoevsky's novel can be said to offer Camus a powerful and unique lens for reading history, enabling him, in his own mind at least, to see the profound relationship between socialist aspiration and nihilism at the moment when revolt becomes absolutized or messianic and is characterized by an all or nothing attitude, empowering it to justify today in the name of tomorrow. A second aim of the chapter will be to assess the impact of *Les Possédés* on Camus's general formulation of the problem of nihilism and political revolution, both in terms of the overall perspectives of *L'Homme révolté* and of his other writings of the period. This will involve some comment on the ideological dimensions and objectives of his 1959 adaptation of *Les Possédés* and especially on the critical responses to it. Our aim here will be to raise the question of whether Dostoevsky's novel so coloured Camus's political perceptions that he begins to see the political complexity of his own period though the lens of *Les Possédés*; that is to say, in terms of demons like Verkhovensky and Chigalev.

It is worth recalling now some of the general points that Camus made about *Les Possédés* at the time of the Radio Europe tribute to Dostoevsky in 1955 and in the context of the adaptation in 1959. First, in 1955, he observed:

Je mets *Les Possédés* à côté de trois ou quatre grandes œuvres, telles *l'Odyssée*, *La Guerre et la paix*, *Don Quichotte* et le théâtre de Shakespeare, qui couronnent l'énorme entassement des créations de l'esprit.[1] [Later, in the same tribute, Camus refers to Dostoevsky as] celui qui a vécu et exprimé le plus profondément notre destin historique [and as] l'écrivain qui, bien avant Nietzsche, a su discerner le nihilisme contemporain, le définir, prédire ses suites monstrueuses et tenter d'indiquer les voies du salut.[2]

[I rate *Les Possédés* with three or four works, like *The Odyssey*, *War and Peace*, *Don Quixote* and Shakespearian theatre, which crown the enormous range of human creativity . . . the person who lived and expressed most profoundly our historical destiny . . . the writer who, long before Nietzsche, understood contemporary nihilism, defined it, predicted its horrendous consequences and attempted to show pathways out of it.]

In the 'Prière d'insérer *des Possédés*,' written for the adaptation of 1959, Camus further comments on his admiration for the novel:

Les Possédés sont une des quatre ou cinq œuvres que je mets au-dessus de toutes les autres. A plus d'un titre, je peux dire que je m'en suis nourri et que je m'y suis formé . . . Et si *Les Possédés* sont un livre prophétique, ce n'est pas seulement parce qu'ils annoncent notre nihilisme, c'est aussi qu'ils mettent en scène des âmes déchirées ou mortes, incapables d'aimer et souffrant de ne pouvoir le faire, voulant et ne pouvant croire, qui sont celles mêmes qui peuplent aujourd'hui notre société et notre monde spirituel . . . Ce n'est donc pas seulement un des chefs-d'œuvre de la littérature universelle qui est, aujourd'hui, porté sur notre scène, mais une œuvre d'actualité.[3]

[*Les Possédés* is one of the four or five works that I rank above all others. In more ways than one, I can say that it has enriched and shaped me . . . And if *Les Possédés* is a prophetic text, it is not only because it heralds the nihilism of our age, but also because it shows us torn and dead souls, incapable of loving, and suffering because of it, wanting and not being able to believe, and these are the very souls who populate our own society and spiritual world . . . This is then not only one of the masterpieces of world literature which is staged today but a work of immediate relevance to our times.]

To these comments should be added Camus's answers to some of the questions in the 'Questionnaire pour *Spectacles*' (1958). Here Camus is asked: 'Par rapport à *L'Homme révolté*, comment, dans la ligne de votre œuvre, situer la pièce que vous tirez du roman de Dostoïevski?' ['With reference to *L'Homme révolté*, how in the general direction of your work, do you situate the play you have created from Dostoevsky's novel?'] He replies: 'Un chapitre de *L'Homme révolté* s'appelle *Les Possédés* [sic]. Grâce à cette adaptation, le voilà illustré sur la scène' ['A chapter of *L'Homme révolté* is called *Les Possédés* (sic). Thanks to this adaptation, it can be seen on the stage'].[4] In the same interview, he refers once again to Dostoevsky and not Marx as being the true prophet of the twentieth-century, because he announced the reign of the Grand Inquisitors and the advent of power politics.[5]

It has already been suggested how such glowing tributes to *Les Possédés* find concrete expression and validation in *Le Mythe de Sisyphe*, principally through Kirilov. It is now time to turn to *L'Homme révolté*. Two sections of 'La Révolte historique' refer specifically to *Les Possédés*, one entitled 'Trois Possédés'[6] and the second, 'Le Chigalevisme'.[7] Neither section amounts to anything like an extensive analysis of the novel but this is not Camus's purpose. His aim is to situate *Les Possédés* in the evolving patterns of historical revolt and, more precisely, in the framework of nineteeth-century Russian liberalism as it hardens and radicalizes under the impact of Hegel and moves gradually closer to nihilistic and messianic *Realpolitik* via Pisarev, Bakunin and Nechaev, whom Camus chooses to refer to as 'trois possédés'. Camus is not so much analysing Dostoevsky's novel here as endeavouring to demonstrate the Russian writer's prophetic powers of historical analysis and understanding. To grasp fully why Camus feels able to claim that Pisarev, Bakunin and Nechaev can be described in terms of perspectives derived from *Les Possédés*, it is necessary to examine the general patterns of Dostoevsky's thought in the novel and Camus's assimilation and use of them in the composition of *L'Homme révolté*. This will enable us to see why it is that Camus is inclined to see twentieth-century history as foreshadowed prophetically in Dostoevsky.

Notwithstanding its aesthetic autonomy and its transhistorical novelistic invention, *Les Possédés* has to be seen as part of Dostoevsky's continuing struggle against the Russian revolutionary left. At the centre of his preoccupations in the novel, which was originally conceived as a pamphlet, is the question of the paternity of the Russian radical movement of the 1860s and, more specifically, of the transformation, as Dostoevsky saw it, of the Enlightenment-inspired moral idealism of 1840s liberalism (Herzen, Belinski, Turgenev) into the nihilistic pragmatism of Pisarev, Bakunin and Nechaev. In *Crime et châtiment*, Dostoevsky had already created a fiction to probe Pisarev's thesis that moral categories are merely relative, social constructs which must be transcended by radical supermen, disaffected from the society in which they live: one can bludgeon to death one's mother to show contempt for existing social power relationships and to open up revolutionary possibility in the future.[8] In *Le Sous-Sol*, Dostoevsky had also used the Underground Man to explore the link between inertia and self-consciousness and to advance the idea that doing nothing is a sign of intellectual distinction, whilst action is always driven by mediocrity. The protagonist simultaneously mocks the belief in the 'crystal palace' view of human reality and the idea that there will be some future state of universal communion when all individual self-interests will be reconciled in a collective.[9] These earlier works, however, are much more philosophically based than *Les Possédés* which is rooted in the history of anti-Tzarist radical militancy and the trial of the most notorious of the Russian nihilists, Nechaev. As Nechaev and the 'Nechaev affair', as it became known, are so pertinent to Dostoevsky's political thematic in *Les Possédés*, it will be useful to recall here some details about the case.[10]

Sergey Nechaev was an extreme radical, a militant disciple of Bakunin and, originally at least, he enjoyed the friendship of the master, until Bakunin recognized that there were no limits to his militancy. Together, they composed the *Catechism of a Revolutionary*, which was intended to serve as a kind of manual of revolutionary strategy to aspiring Nechaevists. Nechaev and his followers had no time for revolutionary chatterers; their goal was radical nihilist action to destroy the existing social order of Europe, including Russian Tzarism. The catechism advocated internationally organized, cell-based subversion, in clandestinity, as the most effective form of political action. It also claimed 'the right to infamy' ('le droit au déshonneur' or 'pravo na beschest'e' as Dostoevsky calls it),[11] stating that members of the revolutionary cell should have no sense of honour or moral obligation towards the world which they hate and want to destroy. All means are good if they work. Effectiveness in the struggle is the only principle of power.

In accordance with his views, Nechaev set up a Moscow group, called 'Popular Vengeance', in the Petrovsky Academy of Agriculture. In November 1869, a member of the group, an agricultural student named Ivanov, was murdered, seemingly because he was alienated by the group's authoritarian and elitist leadership. I say 'seemingly' because this was never clearly established nor was it certain that there was any real cause for the murder, except to bind the group in culpability: murder of the faint-hearted, whether the faint-heartedness was proven, assumed or strategically designed, was seen by Nechaev, and recommended in the *Catechism*, as a reliable way of binding people authentically to the group's political objectives. Ivanov's murder led to the arrest of Nechaev and sixty-three other members of the group. These events and the public trial, which took place throughout the summer of 1871, in Moscow, aroused a great deal of interest. Dostoevsky, exiled in Dresden, but in communication with his brother-in-law about the affair, avidly read the press reports of the murder and the trial.

At some moment in these developments, between December 1869 and February 1870, Dostoevsky decided to abandon *La Vie d'un grand pécheur* and to take up arms against nihilism by writing 'une chose tendancieuse' ['a tendentious thing'], based on the murder of Ivanov and the ideological practices of Nechaev.[12] However, this historical and political base is soon broadened and deepened, by Dostoevsky's celebrated 'fantastic realism', to become part of the demonic vision, articulated in *Les Possédés*, of revolutionary radicalism threatening to poison Mother Russia and European civilization. Because of the great importance accorded by Camus to this novel as a prophetically decisive moment in the history of revolt, it is essential to sketch in the main lines of Dostoevsky's attempt to weave together history and fiction in the composition of his novel.

Nechaev and Popular Vengeance figure in *Les Possédés* as Piotr Verkhovensky and the group, sarcastically referred to as 'les nôtres', which meets at Virguinsky's house, situated symbolically in the *Rue de la Fourmi* [literally 'Ant Street']. Whatever one thinks of Dostoevsky's representation of the Russian radical movement in the novel, Frank has shown that almost every detail of Piotr's behaviour is based on some detail or other of the *Catechism* or on press reports of the trial. Nechaev, in real life, paraded bogus credentials, stating that he was representative 2771 of the World Revolutionary Alliance and personally approved by Bakunin and the Cultural Committee of the European Revolutionary Alliance. These quasi Pythonesque details were all fantasy but they were designed to make potential recruits feel part of a vast international conspiracy. Piotr asks Stavroguine, at the Virguinsky gathering, to pretend to be part of the international organization and to be introduced to the group as a founding member of the global revolutionary project. Under Dostoevsky's handling, however, Piotr is, at one and the same time, the son of Stéphane Trophimovitch, the liberal idealist of the 1840s (linked in Dostoevsky's mind to Herzen and Belinski),[13] and the disciple of Stavroguine, himself a former pupil of Piotr's father and the embodiment, in the text, of an all-pervasive, sterilizing atheism. In weaving together in this way generational themes and themes of spiritual paternity, Dostoevsky is able to suggest that the younger Verkhovensky's political nihilism and demonic proclivities are directly descended from the liberal idealism of the 40s. Moreover, since this idealism took its inspiration from the anti-theist rationalism of the European Enlightenment and from the French radical movement with its epicentre in the Revolution, Dostoevsky is also able to develop the argument that Stéphane's generation of liberals had been responsible for importing into Russia the Western radicalist thinking and atheism which are threatening to poison Russian indigenous culture. They are the real progenitors of the nihilism and the spiritual atrophy of Piotr and Stavroguine.

Into this general patterning of themes, Dostoevsky introduces an enormous range of related preoccupations, some of which need mentioning to provide a context for Camus's reading of the text in *L'Homme révolté*. Turgenev finds a place in *Les Possédés*, thinly disguised as Karmazinov, a writer divorced from the Russian people, spending most of his time in Paris, the centre of Enlightenment atheism. It is Karmazinov who is responsible, in the novel, for the transmission of liberal Western thinking into Russian society and his work thus bears a major responsibility for nihilism. He is also the character who speaks of 'le droit au déshonneur' ['the right to infamy'][14] eagerly adopted by Piotr as a political weapon. In this way, Dostoevsky can charge Turgenev with the responsibility of giving the nihilists a certain prestige: he had written *Fathers and Sons* and made Bazarov so famous that the nihilists adopted him as their hero and model. Although Bazarov never actually uses the phrase 'le droit au déshonneur', his statements contain many echoes of the idea.[15] Piotr can thus be projected as the spiritual son of Turgenev/ Karmazinov as well as the disciple of Stavroguine and the actual heir of Stéphane: such a powerful cocktail of forces in his making was bound to produce a demon!

An antithetical response to this 'droit au déshonneur' is embodied in Chatov (a wavering member of Piotr's group), who plays, in the novel, the part of the murdered Ivanov. With characteristic brilliance, Dostoevsky credits Chatov with humanity, decency and honour. He is also a disciple of Stavroguine, however, and his faith in God, if not in Christ, is not certain.[16] Chatov delights in the birth of his baby, despite the problems he faces in his marriage (Stavroguine has slept with his wife), and introduces a positive perspective about the future into the novel. Chatov is a character who has emerged from the people and is on the way to recovering from his flirtation with the West and atheist socialism. His murder can, therefore, be dramatized as a profound threat to the future integrity and decency of Russian society. Chatov detests Piotr as the embodiment of all that is perverse and foreign to the Russian people: he refers to him as 'Cette punaise, cet ignorant, cet imbécile qui ne comprend rien à la Russie' ['This louse, this ignoramus, this idiot who understands nothing about Russia'].[17] As it is Kirilov who decides that he will accept responsibility for Chatov's murder and allow the group to use his suicide as a cloak for their crime, Dostoevsky is able to bring into focus, through this character, the relationship between philosophies which deify man and provoke premeditated murder, a restatement on a wider political canvas of the themes of *Crime et châtiment*.

A further string to Dostoevsky's bow in the depiction of the nihilists is the bizarre character Chigalev, who comes to play a pivotal role in Camus's political argument in *L'Homme révolté*. Chigalev is the philanthropic philosopher in the group, well-versed in Rousseau, Proudhon, Fourier and Cabet (like Dostoevsky!) and familiar with the works of Herzen and Belinski. He has written, in draft form, a book with ten chapters on democratic freedom and equality but his extensive studies bring him to make the following statement, which leaves him 'acculé au désespoir' ['trapped in despair'].[18]

> M'étant consacré entièrement à l'étude de l'organisation de la société de l'avenir qui doit remplacer la nôtre . . . je suis arrivé à cette conviction que tous les créateurs de systèmes sociaux, depuis les temps les plus reculés jusqu'à nos jours, ont été des rêveurs, des conteurs de sornettes, des sots, qui se contredisaient eux-mêmes et ne comprenaient rien aux sciences naturelles et à cet étrange animal qu'on appelle l'homme. Platon, Rousseau, Fourier ne sont que des colonnes d'aluminium; ils sont bons, tout au plus, pour les moineaux et non pour les hommes. Or comme les formes

sociales de l'avenir doivent être fixées précisément maintenant, quand enfin nous sommes tous décidés à passer à l'action sans plus hésiter, je propose mon système d'organisation du monde. Le voici, déclara-t-il en frappant son cahier. Je voulais vous exposer mon livre aussi succinctement que possible; mais je vois qu'il me faudra y joindre encore quantité d'explications verbales. Mon exposé exigera donc au moins dix soirées d'après le nombre des chapitres de mon livre . . . De plus, je dois vous prévenir que mon système n'est pas complètement achevé . . . Je me suis embrouillé dans mes propres données et ma conclusion se trouve en contradiction directe avec l'idée fondamentale du système. Partant de la liberté illimitée, j'aboutis au despotisme illimité. J'ajoute à cela cependant, qu'il ne peut y avoir d'autre solution du problème social que la mienne.[19]

[Having devoted myself totally to the study of the future forms of social organization which will replace our own . . . I have reached the conclusion that all previous philosphers of social systems, from the beginning of time until now, have been dreamers, tellers of fairy stories, idiots who contradicted themselves and understood nothing about natural sciences or the strange animal called man. Plato, Rousseau, Fourier are lightweight figures, fit only for the study of sparrows and not men. Now that we have all at last decided to move to action without further dithering, because the social forms of the future need immediate definition, I propose my system of world organization. Here it is, he said, striking his exercise-book. I wanted to explain my book as succinctly as possible; but I see that I shall have to add to it lots of explanatory details. My analysis will thus need at least ten sessions, one for each chapter of my book . . . Furthermore, I must tell you in advance that my system is not entirely finished . . . I became caught up in my own premises and my conclusion flatly contradicts the basic principle of my system. Beginning with unlimited freedom, I end up with unlimited despotism. I would add, however, that there can be no other solution to the social problem than the one I propose.]

Chigalev's statement produces quite a lot of laughter among the members of the group, despite his confession of despair, but he is defended by the 'professeur boiteux' ['lame professor'] who has read the draft and argues that Chigalev has indeed resolved all his difficulties in the book, using science and erudition:

Non, messieurs, il ne s'agit pas de cela. M. Chigaliov s'est voué trop entièrement à sa tâche, et, en plus, il est trop modeste. Je connais son livre. Pour résoudre définitivement la question sociale, il propose de partager l'humanité en deux parts inégales. Un dixième obtiendra la liberté absolue et une autorité illimitée sur les neuf autres dixièmes qui devront perdre leur personnalité et devenir en quelque sorte un troupeau; maintenus dans une soumission sans bornes, ils atteindront, en passant par une série de transformations, à l'état d'innocence primitive, quelque chose comme l'Éden primitif, tout en étant astreints au travail. Les mesures préconisées par l'auteur pour dépouiller les neuf dixièmes de l'humanité de leur volonté et les transformer en troupeau au moyen de l'éducation, sont extrêmement remarquables; basées sur les données des sciences naturelles, elles sont parfaitement logiques. On peut ne pas accepter certaines de ses conclusions, mais il est impossible de nier l'intelligence et les connaissances de l'auteur. Il est regrettable que, vu les circonstances, nous ne puissions pas lui accorder les dix soirées qu'il réclame, car nous entendrions certainement bien des choses intéressantes.[20]

[No, gentlemen, this is not the point. Mr Chigalev has more than committed himself fully to his objective, and, indeed, is too modest. I have read his book. To resolve once and for all the question of society, he proposes to divide humanity into two unequal parts. One-tenth of people will possess absolute freedom and unlimited power over the other nine-tenths who will lose all their individual personalities and become like sheep; maintained in unrestricted passivity, they will reach, through a series of transformations, a state of primitive innocence, like the original Eden, although they will be obliged to work. The measures advocated by the author to strip the nine-tenths of their individual wills and change them into sheep are very remarkable indeed; based on the data of the natural sciences, they are perfectly logical. One might not be able to accept some of his conclusions, but it is impossible to deny the intelligence and knowledge of the author. It is regrettable that, under the circumstances, we cannot give him the ten sessions he needs, for we would certainly hear some interesting things.]

This whole scene in the novel is highly entertaining and members of the group find it difficult to know whether to take 'le chigalevisme' seriously or to laugh at it. Dostoevsky is careful, in order at least to try to avoid accusations of distortion and prejudice, not to 'demonize' all the members of the group or make them total objects of ridicule. Several of the people who speak at Virguinsky's are committed socialists. Even Piotr is not completely pathologized for he is sensitive to beauty and moved by the state of the poor in Russia and wishes for a better future for them.[21] However, beneath the laughter provoked by Chigalev and his system is a real threat: Chigalev is very concise, confident and audacious and his paradigm of a democratic philosophy of freedom and equality, derived from scientific principles, and producing, finally, the enslavement of the mass of the people to a radical elite, certainly has the power to haunt. Frank locates the source of Chigalev both in the Social Darwinism of V. Zaitsev and in the essays of P. N. Tkachev who formulated a *Programme of Revolutionary Activities* which included a plan to create Paradise on Earth by selective socialist breeding.[22] Camus, as we shall see, views the novel and the character in a wider frame of reference which includes Rousseau, Hegel and Marx.[23]

Camus begins his analysis of 'La Révolte historique' with the following quotation, which, as Dunwoodie underlines, demonstrates how very significantly in this essay 'le lexique retenu par Camus est proche de l'imaginaire dostoïevskien' ['the lexicon retained by Camus is close to Dostoevsky's fictional world'].[24]

Comme le mouvement de révolte débouchait dans le *Tout ou Rien*, comme la révolte métaphysique voulait l'unité du monde, le mouvement révolutionnaire du xxème siècle, arrivé aux conséquences les plus claires de sa logique, exige, les armes à la main, la totalité historique. La révolte est alors sommée, sous peine d'être futile ou périmée, de devenir révolutionnaire. Il ne s'agit plus pour le révolté de se déifier lui-même comme Stirner ou de se sauver seul par l'attitude. Il s'agit de déifier l'espèce comme Nietzsche et de prendre en charge son idéal de surhumanité afin d'assurer le salut de tous, selon le vœu d'Ivan Karamazov. *Les Possédés* entrent en scène pour la première fois et illustrent alors l'un des secrets de l'époque: l'identité de la raison et de la volonté de puissance. Dieu mort, il faut changer et organiser le monde par les forces de l'homme. La seule force de l'imprécation n'y suffisant plus, il faut des armes et la conquête de la totalité. La révolution, même et surtout celle qui prétend être matérialiste, n'est qu'une croisade métaphysique démesurée.[25]

[In the same way that the movement of revolt ends up by asking for *All or Nothing*, just as metaphysical revolt wanted the unity of the world, so the revolutionary movement of the twentieth-century, in reaching the most obvious consequences of its logic, demands, with guns in its hands, historical totality. Revolt is then called upon, in order to avoid being called futile or outmoded, to become revolutionary. It is no longer a question for the rebel of self-deification as it was for Stirner or of saving oneself alone by an attitude. It is a question of deification of the human species like Nietzsche wanted and of taking on board his ideal of the superman in order to secure salvation for all, as Ivan Karamazov wanted. *Les Possédés* appears on stage for the first time and then reveals one of the secrets of the period: the convergence between reason and the will to power. With God dead, it is necessary to change and organize the world in human terms. The force of words alone being inadequate to create change, arms are needed to conquer totality. The revolution, above all the one claiming to be materialistic, is nothing but an excessive metaphysical crusade.]

Ivan, Kirilov and *Les Possédés* are thus linked together, in Camus's argument, as decisive moments in the quest for totality (the human Kingdom of Justice in opposition to the injustices of the Divine order), a quest which, according to Camus, underpins ninteenth-century radicalism. It must be quite puzzling for political analysts and historians, possibly not familiar with Dostoevsky, to find such statements and couplings in a central position in a work of political philosophy. Later, in the section on 'Le Terrorisme individuel', Camus again uses Dostoevsky, when he entitles a subsection on Russian radicalism 'Trois Possédés' without explaining how and why such a nomenclature could be justified and without even explicitly linking it to the novel. Finally, at the end of the section on individual terrorism, a final part is called 'Le Chigalevisme' as though this was an historically identified system of thought rather than one derived from Dostoevsky's fiction. At all times throughout this section of *L'Homme révolté* Camus's intentions are quite clear to anyone familiar with this Russian novel and its history, but it is doubtful that the bringing together of history, politics and fiction in this way would make much sense to the non-initiated.

Be that as it may, Camus's 'Trois Possédés' are Pisarev, Bakunin and Nechaev himself. They represent, for Camus, three moments in the history of individual terrorist revolt, each one increasingly radicalized and nihilistic. They are people who are 'possessed' in the sense that their political views become increasingly colonized by the demons of nihilism in such a way that the positive content of their revolts against the existing social order are displaced by negativity, destruction and murder. All three radicals suffer from contradictions; they want change and thus must want it in the name of a value but values become a restrictive limit to their aims. Therefore, they must transcend values but when this happens revolt degenerates and loses itself in the perversions of murder and revolutionary power politics. From Pisarev to Nechaev, in Camus's eyes, revolt becomes increasingly violent, cynical and abstracted from its creative roots. The society of love and fraternity is not, in consequence, founded in the present and protected but projected towards a mythical future. What Camus calls 'l'avènement du règne des possédés' ['the coming of the reign of the possessed'] represents precisely the moment when the revolution becomes the only value, and friendship and solidarity must wait to the end of history for their fulfilment.[26] With the advent of the reign of the possessed, real human love and brotherhood become lost in the abstractions of history. Nechaev is the culminating point of this process of nihilistic radicalization. Camus refers to him as '[une] figure moins connue que celle de Bakounine, plus mystérieuse encore, mais plus significative pour notre propos' ['a figure less known than Bakunin, even more shadowy, but more significant for our purposes'].[27] Nechaev's significance for Camus is that he pushed 'la cohérence du nihilisme aussi loin qu'il se pouvait' ['nihilistic coherence as far as it could go'] and that he is 'presque sans contradiction' ['almost without contradiction'] in that he claimed total freedom to pursue revolutionary objectives.[28] Furthermore, Nechaev, Camus tells us, applied absolute religious zeal to his political aims, making politics a new religion of man and becoming 'le moine cruel d'une révolution désespérée' ['the cruel monk of a desperate revolution']. He founds 'l'ordre meurtrier' ['the order of murder'] which turns all revolutionary endeavour into prehistory and calls for universal destruction.[29] His greatest originality, for Camus, was to 'revendiquer froidement pour ceux qui se donnent à la révolution, le "Tout est permis", et de se permettre tout en effet' ['to claim coldly for those who serve the revolution, the "all is permitted", and to permit themselves everything in fact'].[30] With Nechaev, crucially, for Camus 'pour la première fois . . . la révolution va se séparer explicitement de l'amour et de l'amitié' ['for the first time ever . . . the revolution will distance itself from love and friendship'].[31] The revolution of love gives way to the revolution of hate; all measure is transcended in the quest for total power and revolt heads towards totalitarianism.

Nechaev, then, for Camus, is fully 'possessed'. No revolutionary, so Camus thinks, before Nechaev, had justified violence against one's own allies or brothers to secure revolutionary advance. His tactics legitimized mystification, deceit, oppression, murder. With him, revolutionary ideology produces a monster of megalomania and ruthlessness beyond anything that preceded him because he is not just prepared to act on his views but to justify them philosophically. Camus then tells us that 'ces belles pensées . . . [ont] pris tout leurs sens aujourd'hui' ['these fine thoughts . . . [have] acquired their full meaning today'] in order to identify Nechaev not only as the demon of fanaticism haunting modern revolutionary politics (and, no doubt, Stalinism by implication) but also to suggest that all revolutionary movements set in motion strategies of radicalization which can go on to claim the 'Tout est permis' or 'le droit au déshonneur' and these movements will negate and destroy the positive views which generated the original protest. In Camus's political journalism, it will be Nechaev who figures as an embodiment of the excessive pride triumphing in twentieth-century Marxism and perverting the quest for justice.[32]

Nechaev, then, becomes a person of fundamental and pivotal importance in Camus's analysis of historical revolt. When Ivanov is murdered, Bakunin, Camus tells us, protests against 'cette répugnante tactique' ['this repellent technique'][33] but repugnance points to a value which Nechaev has already eliminated in the name of the revolution:

> Mais au nom de quoi décider que cette tactique est répugnante si la révolution, comme le voulait Bakounine, est le seul bien?[34]
>
> [But in the name of what value can one decide that this technique is repellent if, as Bakunin argued, the revolution is the only good?]

The elevation of Nechaev to a seminal role in the development of revolutionary terrorism, comparable to the crucial position allotted to Ivan Karamazov in the development of metaphysical revolt, must surely indicate that Camus's whole understanding of Russian radicalism and his entire way of analysing historical revolt in *L'Homme révolté* is filtered through the perspectives of *Les Possédés*. N. Gourfinkel has rightly suggested that Nechaev, although an unusual person in history and cetainly important, was perhaps 'un personnage magnifié' ['a character of magnified stature'] in Camus's thought because of his reading of *Les Possédés*.[35] However, the suggestion does not probe adequately the deep penetration of Camus's political thinking by the imaginative structures of *Les Possédés*. This appears to be so extensive that Camus is able to borrow categories and titles from the Russian novel and to use them in an analytical/historical context as though they constituted some agreed category of truth, a point which is further emphasized in the final part of 'Le Terrorisme individuel' section of *L'Homme révolté*, called 'Le Chigalevisme'.

If Camus is able to pay homage to Dostoevsky for seizing the signifiance of Nechaev and Ivanov's murder and for capturing, in a fictional work, the enormous historical and political significance of 'l'avènement des *Possédés*', ['the coming of *Les Possédés*'] he further underscores his deep admiration for the Russian novelist's prophetic powers by giving a separate section of 'La Révolte historique' to 'Le

Chigalevisme'. Between this part and the earlier pages on 'Trois Possédés', comes Camus's analysis of 'Les Meurtriers délicats' ['the delicate murderers'], the 1905 revolutionaries whom he sees as providing a temporary escape from radical nihilism, before it develops into state terrorism and the totalitarian regimes of which Chigalev is, for Camus, a prophetic prefiguration. Nechaev's radical nihilism is claimed, by Camus, to infect the scientific socialism of the 1880s in Russia: 'L'héritage conjugué de Netchaiev et de Marx donnera naissance à la révolution totalitaire de xxème siècle' ['The combined heritage of Nechaev and Marx will give birth to the totalitarian revolution of the twentieth-century'].[36] Leninism, drawing its inspiration from Marx, Nechaev and his spiritual brother, Tkatchev, will go on, in Camus's mind, to give birth to 'le socialisme césarien' or state terror legitimized in the name of the construction of some future historical state of human happiness[37] This is a capital moment in history for Camus:

> Une boucle s'achève ici et la révolte, coupée de ses vraies racines, infidèle à l'homme parce que soumise à l'histoire, médite maintenant d'asservir l'univers entier. Alors commence l'ère du chigalevisme, exaltée dans *les Possédés* par Verkhovensky, le nihiliste qui réclame le droit au déshonneur.[38]

> [A circuit is completed here and revolt, cut off from its true origins, disloyal to humanity because subjected to history, contemplates the enslavement of everybody and everything. Then begins the age of Chigalevism which Verkhovensky, the nihilist who claims the right to infamy, enthusiastically endorses in *Les Possédés*.]

What Camus is claiming is that individual terrorism, practised in absolute terms by Nechaev, eventually leads to totalitarian state repression. This means that the positive content of revolt can be dispersed by revolutionary extremism. Democratic aspirations for a legitimate justice can produce Caesarian socialism. *Les Possédés* can produce 'Les Grands Inquisiteurs'. It is Chigalevism which provides the philosophical legitimization of these political transformations which pervert the true aims of authentic revolt. Chigalev's philosophy, for Camus, announces 'les théocraties totalitaires du xxème siècle, la terreur d'État' ['the totalitarian theocracies of the twentieth-century, state terror'].[39] His philosophy, born of a profound desire for equality, desperately succumbs to nihilism in its revolt against oppression, and creates a new elite class of Caesars (or lords or Grand Inquisitors, as Camus variously calls them). Their reign will be cruel and oppressive but they will create the Kingdom of Man on Earth (what Dostoevsky, in differing moods of antagonism, referred to as the ant-hill, the Crystal Palace or the Tower of Babel!). In the interim, victims and murderers will both live in desperation; the masters will be morose in their creation of equality, for, if man is to become God, he will have to suffer torments first in order to build the new Jerusalem.

Chigalev, for Camus, is also the 'garant' for Verkhovensky (this means his philosophical guarantor). Describing Piotr as an 'esprit malheureux et implacable' ['an unhappy and implacable person'] who claims 'le droit au déshonneur' and chooses 'la volonté de puissance' ['the will to power'][40] to give history meaning exclusively in human terms, Camus is able to use the Dostoevsky character as a prefigurative model of all totalitarian potentates. In a similar way, Chigalev and Chigalevism encompass, for Camus, all those philosophies which preach freedom but can be used to justify destruction, tyranny and authoritarianism in the present by reference to a future state of common good. Although Camus does not specifically state it in this section of text, it is clear from arguments elsewhere in *L'Homme révolté* that these philosophies embrace the works of Rousseau, Hegel and Marx in particular.[41]

Given these preceding comments, it is not difficult to see why Camus saw *Les Possédés* as 'une œuvre d'actualité' ['a work of relevance'] or 'un livre prophétique' ['a prophetic book'], and Dostoevsky as 'celui qui a vécu et exprimé le plus profondément notre destin historique' ['the person who lived and expressed most profoundly our historical destiny']. The difficult question to resolve is whether Dostoevsky and his novel do have such prophetic dimensions and such contemporary relevance or whether Camus himself is so steeped in the novel's powerful world that he sees history and politics through its perspectives. Of course, Dostoevsky is a novelist using concrete particulars as free-floating signifiers, capable of diverse interpretations. These particulars can be divorced from his own antipathy to nihilism, Russian radicalism or to Slavophobia. In this sense, Camus is well entitled to read the novel in the way that he does. However, there is a difference between doing this and writing an essay in political philosophy and the history of ideas which gives a highly controversial attack on Russian radicalism such a crucial and decisive importance. When Camus states of *Les Possédés*: 'A plus d'un titre, je peux dire que je m'en suis nourri et que je m'y suis formé' ['In more ways than one, I can say that it has enriched and shaped me'], he appears to be inviting his critics to identify the possible parameters of his apprenticeship in the Russian novel. One such parameter must surely include the suggestion that the whole conceptual architecture of the historical revolt section of *L'Homme révolté* appears to resonate with Dostoevsky's preoccupations in *Les Possédés*. The welding together of elements drawn from the novel with Camus's more general analytical framework in the essay (for example, using the words 'Trois Possédés' and 'Le Chigalevisme' as section headings) further reinforces the impression of an extensive Dostoevskian underpinning of Camus's view of political history. Combined with the references to Ivan Karamazov, the 'Tout est permis' and 'le Grand Inquisiteur' in the metaphysical part of the essay, it is very clear that Dostoevsky's voice is certainly a major presence as Camus tries to assemble his moral and political philosophy in *L'Homme révolté*. Once again, it is possible to advance the claim that Camus is trying consciously to formulate a reply to the novelist and that the work is conceived in a wide-ranging intertextual debate with him. A number of points need to be made to clarify this more precisely.

Moral nihilism, for Dostoevsky, such as that professed by Ivan Karamazov or practised by Raskolnikov or Smerdiakov, is rooted, as we have seen, in atheism. Thus the political nihilism of Piotr or Nechaev and its moral prerogative, 'le droit au déshonneur', derive intellectually from the same source. Socialism, for him, was a laicised form of Christianity which is bound to degenerate into murder and authoritarian duplicity; the demons of Nechaev, Piotr, Chigalevism and the Grand Inquisitors will be the political harvest of atheism, as madness, suicide and Stavroguinism will be its psychological harvest. Christ teaches us to love one another and to honour our mother and father. Socialism, as Karmazinov points out in *Les Possédés*, in its Russian Revolutionary form 'consiste essentiellement dans la néga-tion de l'honneur' ['basically consists in the negation of honour'].[42] Socialism is thus conceived by Dostoevsky as basically hostile to the Christian view of life and incapable of guaranteeing values to stop itself falling into murder, especially patricide, nihilism and power politics.

It is with his concept of revolt that Camus hopes to reintroduce value into the world of power politics and thereby triumph over nihilism and at the same time provide a reply to Dostoevsky. Revolt is always undertaken in the name of something positive or yet to be created. The rebel must never forget these positive origins of his revolt and to do this he must recognize limits in the conduct of revolt. By divorcing revolt from nihilistic revolution, Camus is hoping to rescue political advance from totalitarian absolutism. He thus produces 'la pensée de midi', his Hellenic philosophy of measure and limits, at the end of *L'Homme révolté*, as an answer to Ivan's

'Tout est permis', and to the perversions and mutations, in history, of revolt into totalitarianism, fascism and nihilism. No such limits or balances could possibly survive in the world of Dostoevsky without a God or Christ to guarantee them. We have already seen in the previous chapter how Camus tries to expose and refute the all or nothing polarities of Ivan's metaphysical revolt and to reply to his nihilism. A parallel line of argument is developed by Camus in the historical section of the essay in order to rescue the positive content of political revolt from absolutism and extremism. Symbolically placed between the sections of the essay called 'Trois Possédés' and 'Le Chigalevisme' is Camus's analysis of the 1905 revolutionaries whom he chooses to call 'Les Meurtriers délicats' ['The delicate murderers']. These are the revolutionaries who triumph momentarily in history over Nechaev's limitless realism and resist Chigalevism and Hegelian historicism.[43] Their brief moment of existence, for Camus, also signified a triumph over historical messianism. After them, he says: 'La provocation remet en place le "Tout est permis" et identifie encore l'histoire et la valeur absolue' ['Revolutionary provocation puts the 'all is permitted' back into place and once again identifies history and absolute value'].[44] These 1905 terrorists, then, are presented by Camus in a clear intertextual relationship with the Russian writer's ideas (and thus with Ivan, Piotr, Chigalev and le Grand Inquisiteur) and they also carry the total force of Camus's thesis that 'la vraie révolte est créatrice de valeurs' ['True revolt creates values'].[45] The delicate murderers accept, in Camus's eyes, that violence and murder are in contradiction with the positive content and values of revolt. If they do transcend the limit, they will acknowledge the contradiction and pay for it with their own lives (although, to the impartial critic, this does seem a rather speedy way of eliminating your terrorist group and its historical effectiveness).

Confirmation that Camus's 'meurtriers délicats' and, by extension, the whole philosophy of revolt are used by him to formulate a Hellenic reply to Dostoevsky's Christian mysticism or demonic socialism is provided by *Les Justes*, a play which dramatizes the dilemmas and actions of these 1905 revolutionaries. Although a substantial part of the action of the play is drawn from Boris Savinkov's *Les Mémoires d'un terroriste*, as is the section of *L'Homme révolté* called 'Les Meurtriers délicats', the extreme radical nihilist, Stépan, is not in Savinkov and is very much a Nechaevist/Piotr character, derived from the demons of Dostoevsky. His statements and exchanges with other members of his group pick up many of the ideological arguments of the section of *L'Homme révolté* called 'Trois Possédés' and combine Dostoevskian nihilist language with

Camusian notions of limits. It is Annenkov, the terrorist leader, who tells Stépan:

> quelles que soient tes raisons, je ne puis te laisser dire que tout est permis. Des centaines de nos frères sont morts pour qu'on sache que tout n'est pas permis.[46]

> [whatever your reasons may be, I cannot let you say that everything is permitted. Hundreds of our brothers died so that we know that everything is not permitted.]

A discussion is thus engaged in the play about value in basic Dostoevskyian terms. The point at issue in the play is whether Kaliayev, who articulates the Camusian philosophy of authentic revolt, should have blown up 'le grand-duc' when there were children in his carriage, (we have already seen that the suffering of innocent children is central to Camus's dialogue with Ivan Karamazov). Stépan dismisses these scruples as 'niaiseries' ['inanities'] and adds, in language that recalls Nechaev/Piotr:

> Quand nous nous déciderons à oublier les enfants, ce jour-là, nous serons les maîtres du monde et la révolution triomphera.[47]

> [When we decide to forget about children, then we will be masters of the world and the revolution will triumph.]

When Dora tells Stépan that if that day comes, the whole of humanity will hate the revolution, he replies, in a language echoing Chigalev:

> Qu'importe si nous l'aimons assez fort pour l'imposer à l'humanité entière et la sauver d'elle-même et de son esclavage?[48]

> [What does it matter, if you love it sufficiently to impose it on humanity and rescue it from itself and servitude?]

Stépan is a bureaucratic terrorist attached to *L'Organisation*, like Nechaev. He has no time for the limits which Dora places on revolutionary action and declares: 'Il n'y a pas de limites' ['There are no limits'], pointing to the future liberation of mankind as the justification for present murder.[49] In his exchanges with Kaliayev, Stépan appears as the tormented soul, humiliated and injured, who wishes to hurt others because he has been hurt himself. His is not the creative socialism of love and solidarity with its emphasis on present happiness but an abstracted quest for domination and totality, rooted in hatred. He tells Dora: 'Mais, moi, je n'aime rien et je hais, oui, je hais mes semblables. Qu'ai-je à faire avec leur amour?' ['But, I myself love nothing and I hate, yes, I hate my fellow men. What is their love to me?']⁵⁰ His is the socialism of the Inquisitors, the Caesars and the Chigalevs, a sombre menace to the world of true and authentic fellowship⁵¹ These exchanges between Stépan, Kaliayev, Dora and the terrorist group in general, dramatize, in a way that some will find too abstracted and systematic for the stage, the principal ideological perspectives on revolt and value in *L'Homme révolté*. However, they also do show very clearly how Camus tries to find a way out of Dostoevsky's demonic representation of socialism with his concept of revolt. The Christian love and divine authority which Dostoevsky places at the centre of his universe are replaced by Camus with the purely human notion of love guaranteed by a philosophy of limits: 'Je me révolte, donc nous sommes' ['I revolt, therefore we are']. This love is much more than the pure love of life which both writers shared and which was at the centre of Camus's earlier hedonism and first major dialogue with Dostoevsky. Such a hedonistic love proved to be an inadequate base for the guarantee of civilized life and allowed for 'insensibilité' ['ethical insensitivity'] and the growth of Nazism. Now Camus hopes to reply to Dostoevsky both by endorsing his view of Russian radicalism and by suggesting what he considered to be a new pathway out of its nihilism. The moderation of authentic revolt was Camus's answer and alternative to Dostoevsky's Christian Tzarism. Such a reply, it hardly needs to be said, would not satisfy Dostoevsky: no lay or civic value could exist, for him, in a moral vacuum, since authority, in order to be recognized, must be absolute and that meant rooted in divine mystery. Lay morality, according to the Russian writer, only ends up by saying: 'Chacun pour soi et Dieu pour tous' ['Everybody for himself and God for everybody'], producing a 'save your own skin' individualism.⁵²

Be that as it may, *Les Possédés* haunts Camus as a work with magnetic powers of prophecy. For him, it prefigured our history by providing models of the police state, totalitarianism, Stalinism and *Realpolitik*. Given Camus's profound desire to reshape the politics of his period and to redefine socialism in terms of moderation and limits, it is hardly surprising that a major dimension of that project included both a restatement of Dostoevsky's 'le procès même de l'anarchie' ['the trial of anarchy itself'], as Gide once described *Les Possédés*,⁵³ and some reworking of its elements to provide an answer to its challenges.

No study of Camus's life-long preoccupation with *Les Possédés* would be complete without reference to his January 1959 adaptation of the novel to the stage. The dramatization of this work, which had made such a lasting impression on him, had been one of the ambitions of his youth.[54] Although it is not our purpose to analyse the complexities of the adaptation and comment on its theatrical merits,[55] it is certainly worth considering the motives behind Camus's desire to stage the novel in the late 50s and thus relaunch his dialogue with Dostoevsky. It is surely significant also that some eight years after the publication of *L'Homme révolté*, notwithstanding the split with Sartre and the turmoil of Algeria, Camus should still wish to restate his attachment to Dostoevsky's description of revolutionary nihilism in *Les Possédés*.

Camus's decision to adapt *Les Possédés* was motivated by two considerations. First, he wanted to repeat some of the main political theses of *L'Homme révolté*, particularly those dealing with nihilism, in a more accessible form than a philosophical essay. Secondly, the adaptation can be seen as a further attempt by Camus, after his adaptation of Calderón and Faulkner, to create a modern stage tragedy, one of his prime aims as a dramatist. Dostoevsky had already provided him with dramatic material in *Caligula* and *Le Malentendu*.[56] In 1959, he was to give him the means to write a full-blown play with contemporary political relevance and tragic potentiality. Let us look at each aim in turn.

In his 'Questionnaire pour *Spectacles*', Camus emphatically underlines the relationship between his adaptation and his political philosophy: 'Un chapitre de *L'Homme révolté* s'appelle *Les Possédés* [sic]. Grâce à cette adaptation, le voilà illustré sur la scène' ['A chapter of *L'Homme révolté* is called *Les Possédés* (sic). Thanks to this adaptation, it can now be seen on the stage'].[57] At the same time, he tells a critic, in *Les Nouvelles Littéraires*: 'En tout cas ce qui dans son œuvre [Dostoevsky's] est un pamphlet contre la révolution nihiliste, je le signe des deux mains' ['In any case, everything in his book (Dostoevsky's) which is a pamphlet against nihilistic revolution, I unreservedly endorse'].[58] Camus, it should be noted, does not try to hijack what he refers to as Dostoevsky's 'communisme évangelique' ['evangelical communism'][59] and reroute it through his own humanist notion of revolt but, from the opening scene, Camus inscribes the play into contemporary political debate. The narrator tells the audience, when speaking of Stéphane Trophimovitch's dead wives: 'Mais on ne peut pas aimer sa femme et la justice' ['But you cannot simultaneously love your wife and justice'], evidently echoing Camus's own remark about the relationship between justice and his mother during the Algerian crisis and opening up further discreet perspectives on the debate already engaged with Ivan Karamazov about love and justice[60] Thereafter, on several occasions in the play, Camus suggestively links his adaptation to the thematics and preoccupations of his own work, thus giving the text of the play a sense of intertextual resonance and dialogue with his own original work. For example, Stavroguine's farewell speech to Dacha, where he tells her, 'Tout m'est étranger' ['I am a complete outsider'], recalls not only *L'Étranger* itself but signals the relationship between death, social alienation, and ethical insensibility in the early Camus.[61] Kirilov's suicide is also linked to the same idea: at the very moment when he allows young Verkhovensky to dictate to him a suicide letter which he will sign, thus accepting responsibility for the murder of Chatov, he says: 'Je ne crains personne, tout est indifférent' ['I fear nobody, everything is indifferent'].[62] Is it implausible to suggest that this moment recalls the one where Meursault pens the famous letter for Raymond and initiates the cycle of events that will lead to the murder of the Arab? Both acts originate in a state of alienated indifference in the protagonists to the ethical values of their society. In another scene, Pierre's exchanges with his father are used by Camus to underline the split between love and revolutionary extremism so central to his own concept of revolt. In fact, Camus demonizes Verkhovensky junior even more powerfully than Dostoevsky himself: Camus's megalomaniacal monster has no redemptive human features at all. He is utterly, inhumanly ruthless in his response to Chatov and arranges and carries out the murder with total cynicism.[63] Significantly, he rejects the word 'honour' in his exchanges with Chatov, describing it as 'un mot vague, très vague' ['a vague word, a very vague word'],[64] picking up the main arguments of *Les Justes*. His goal is destruction and domination. Crucially too, he has no time for liberal reformism or meliorism of any kind. Building is for the future: destruction and terror are the agenda of today. He says to his father, whom he certainly does not honour:

> Je détruirai tout et d'autres bâtiront. Pas de réforme. Pas d'amélioration. Plus on améliore et on réforme et pire c'est . . . Détruire d'abord . . . Le reste est sornettes, sornettes, sornettes.[65]

> [I shall destroy everything and others will build. No reformism. No meliorism. The more one improves or reforms things the worse it is . . . First destroy . . . All the rest is rubbish, rubbish, rubbish.]

Pierre's attitude towards his father is pointedly expressed in a language which recalls Sartre's and Jeanson's critique of *L'Homme révolté*, as though Camus wishes to use *Les Possédés* to discredit the French residual revolutionary left. Pierre's statement: 'Pas besoin de s'aimer! Il y aura la science' ['No need to love your neighbour! Science will do it for you'],[66] sarcastically rejects the idealistic humanism of his father with an allegiance to 'la science'. This remark appears to tilt at the so-called scientific Marxism of a Jeanson and, by implication, all advocates of authoritarian, messianic socialism with their alleged contempt for 'les belles âmes' ['the well-intentioned'] and 'la morale de Croix-Rouge'['Red Cross moral philosophy'].

Such resonances are all successfully integrated into the adaptation of Dostoevsky's novel without distorting the transposition which is very faithfully executed. Indeed, Camus's dramatization belatedly reduces and corrects the importance and ascendancy given by him to Kirilov over Stavroguine in *Le Mythe de Sisyphe* in 1942. Without destroying Kirilov's Man-God project as a positive force, Camus clearly places the engineer in a subordinate relationship to Stavroguine who is presented as the central force of the play: all the other main characters, including Pierre and Chatov, are seen as fragments of Stavroguine's personality, whilst the inclusion in the adaptation of the censored episode, 'Chez Tikhone', further emphazises his crucial or pivotal role in the events of the novel.[67]

Camus's purpose in giving his adaptation these intertextual references to his own work is obviously to validate his claim that *Les Possédés* is a prophetic work about twentieth-century nihilism, that it is an 'œuvre d'actualité' ['work of relevance'] and that its imaginative world mirrors our own. Few critics, however, responded to the adaptation in this way. The majority of reviews concentrated on the techniques and talents of Camus as an adaptor, discussing his production in purely aesthetic terms.[68] Such reviews, in the main, complimented Camus on his virtuosity in having made a difficult novel much more comprehensible, without sacrificing either the mystery, atmosphere or power of the original. Those critics who did discuss the political and philosophical significance of the play, generally did so in a hostile fashion. Thus, R. Poulet, writing in *Carrefour*, expressed regret that a mind as fine as Camus's should adapt the works of reactionary writers of the purest sort, mentioning not only Dostoevsky, a supporter of Tzarism and the Church, but Faulkner, an American representative of the 'patriciat sudiste' ['southern patricianism'] and Calderón, a Spanish defender of theocratic monarchy.[69] Guy Leclerc, in *L'Humanité*, was generous enough about the aesthetic merits of Camus's adaptation but was totally scathing about its political relevance: 'Quant à cette peinture d'un nihilisme si profondément désuet, comment le prendre au sérieux?' ['As for this picture of nihilism which is so profoundly moribund, how can you treat it seriously?'][70] Paul Morelle, in *Libération*, could find nothing favourable to say about the play in any way: its ideas were outmoded and irrelevant; it would weaken the French left of which Camus was supposed to be a part; it tediously favoured Dostoevsky over Marx in a propagandist manner.[71] An article by Renée Saurel in *Les Temps modernes* favourably reviewed the adaptation but expressed regret that Camus did not write an original play about nihilism and that he also admired the reactionary politics of Dostoevsky.[72]

The range of responses to the play serves as a timely reminder to us, in 1997, that in 1959, using the words of Olivier Todd, 'l'adaptation de Camus est prise dans les remous de la guerre froide. Tout passe au prisme politique' ['Camus's adaptation is caught up in the currents of the Cold War. Everything passes through this political prism'].[73] If the left consensus at the time was that Camus was shifting to the right and that his reformist politics of revolt objectively served reaction and even imperialism, how different a picture prevails today. Thus, Jeanyves Guérin is able to declare in a recent article designed to underscore the 'actualité' ['relevance'] of Camusian political analysis:

La fortune politique de Camus va de pair avec la déconfiture de Sartre. Ceux qui ont adoré le gourou des *Deux-Magots* se hâtent aujourd'hui de le brûler. Quarante ans après, il est difficile de comprendre pourquoi le lynchage de *L'Homme révolté* n'a pas soulevé alors plus d'indignation. Les puristes qui ont prétendu juger Camus se sont jugés eux-mêmes. C'est que, de Gdansk à Moscou et d'Alger à Sarajevo, l'événement a balayé les certitudes marmoréennes des progressistes et donné raison au paria de *Saint-Germain des prés*. Ses analyses qui ont essuyé tant de sarcasmes lui valent aujourd'hui un brevet de clairvoyance . . . Plus question non plus de dauber sur sa belle âme et sa morale de Croix-Rouge . . . La débâcle du marxisme, l'effondrement du mythe communiste, la faillite du socialisme tropical, la redécouverte de l'idée démocratique ont donné un coup de vieux à la doxa progressiste dont Camus s'était nettement désolidarisé dès la fin des années 1940. L'on a l'embarras du choix pour montrer sa clairvoyance.[74]

[Camus's political good fortune is matched by Sartre's demise. Those who once worshipped the guru of the *Deux Magots* today line up to burn him. Forty years on, it is difficult to understand why the lynching of *L'Homme révolté* didn't arouse, at the time, greater indignation. The purists who dared to judge Camus have judged themselves alone. For, from Gdansk to Moscow and from Algeria to Sarajevo, events have swept away the antidiluvian certainties of the so-called progressives and legitimized the pariah of *Saint-Germain des prés*. His views, which were subjected to so much sarcasm then, now deserve a medal for clearsightedness . . . It is no longer a question of going on about his good intentions or Red Cross moral philosophy . . . The failure of Marxism, the collapse of the communist myth, the bankruptcy of third-world socialism, the rebirth of social democracy, have made the so-called progressive orthodoxies, from which Camus distanced himself very clearly in the late 1940s, look like dinosaurs. We are spoilt for choice when seeking examples of Camus's clearsightedness.]

Clearly, in certain circles, if not all, Camus's political views enjoy a much higher level of support and a much stronger reputation for acuity and relevance than they did in 1959, at the time of the adaptation of *Les Possédés*. Political history is indeed a fickle animal.

In terms of his purely theatrical project to write a modern tragedy, Camus's adaptation has to be classed a success. Several critics point out that Camus's fairly unsuccessful attempts to create a modern tragedy of his own led him to adaptations of good tragic novels and that Camus owes a further debt to Dostoevsky in providing him with the material for the realization of this ambition. Camus fully acknowledged his debt to Dostoevsky in respect of this play. He tells us, in his 'Prière d'insérer des *Possédés*', that, for twenty years, he had visualized *Les Possédés* 'sur la scène' ['on stage']. Dostoevsky's characters possess not only 'la stature des personnages dramatiques' ['the stature of dramatic characters'] but they also have 'la conduite, les explosions, l'allure rapide et déconcertante' ['the conduct, the explosions, the swift and unpredictable movement']. Dostoevsky as a novelist, he tells us, uses:

> une technique de théâtre: il procède par dialogues, avec quelques indications de lieux et de mouvements. L'homme de théâtre, qu'il soit acteur, metteur en scène ou auteur, trouve toujours auprès de lui tous les renseignements dont il a besoin.[75]

> [a theatrical technique: he uses dialogue in his developments with various hints about pace and movement. Anybody interested in theatre, whether as actor, director or author, always finds in his work all the information needed.]

Les Possédés, then, in Camus's view, was simply crying out for theatrical adaptation and provided him with all the material that he could possibly want to get his tragedy off the ground.

Following the success of *Les Possédés*, at least in aesthetic if not in political terms, it is possible to think that, had Camus lived, he might have gone on to create an original tragedy because he had derived much from his apprenticeship with Faulkner and Dostoevsky. This, however, remains a speculation and *Les Possédés* was to be Camus's last play. Yet had Camus not died, one feels that the adaptation of *Les Possédés* is the culminating point of his life-long interest in Dostoevsky. In his 1955 preface to the works of Roger Martin du Gard, Camus had already expressed the wish that French literature should go beyond Dostoevsky (and, by this, he surely meant that his own literature should do this) and he dreamt of a novel that would combine the French sobriety of Martin du Gard with the density and form of Tolstoy.[76] *Le Premier Homme*, as we shall see in our final chapter, appears in one sense to address these aesthetic demands for a post-Dostoevskian world.[77] Perhaps the adaptation of *Les Possédés* was to be Camus's final tribute to a writer who had been a constant companion to him from the early 1930s and to a work that had interested him so profoundly for its philosophy, its politics, and its tragic potentialities on the stage. However, between 1951, the publication date of *L'Homme révolté*, and the 1959 adaptation, which can be read as a farewell to Dostoevsky, Camus's work continues to engage the Russian writer in dialogue, especially through the voice of Clamence in *La Chute*.

9

From the Last to the First Man
The Challenge of the Underground

Couvert de cendres, m'arrachant lentement les cheveux, le visage
labouré par les ongles, mais le regard perçant, je me tiens devant
l'humanité entière, récapitulant mes hontes, sans perdre de vue
l'effet que je produis, et disant: 'J'étais le dernier des derniers.'[1]

[Covered in ashes, slowly tearing at my hair, my face furrowed by
my fingernails, but with a piercing look, I stand before the whole
human race, recapitulating my shameful acts, never losing sight of
the effect I am producing and saying: 'I was the last of the last.']

La Chute must unquestionably be seen as Camus's most
Dostoevskian work, both in formal and thematic terms. Camus
appears to borrow, as it were, a canvas from the Russian writer.
Formally the technique of monological/dialogical confession used
in *La Chute* echoes parts of *Crime et châtiment* and *Le Sous-Sol*.
Thematically, the canvas presents the familiar paradigms of
Dostoevsky's universe: tormented and oppressed self-awareness,
duplicity, culpability, judgement, cynicism and calculated confession.
Here is a world of lost innocence and despair, clamouring for
forgiveness. Camus takes this Dostoevskian picture of our fallen state
to rework it and to colour it with his own preoccupations, conceptual
detail and lexicon. In this sense *La Chute* is engaged very self-
consciously in an extensive intertextual dialogue with Dostoevsky's
world and work, and our first aim, in this chapter, will be to identify
the sources and substance of these intertextual relationships, using
existing scholarship as appropriate. At the same time, the chapter
will endeavour to place *La Chute* in the context of the suggested
debate between the two writers concerning Christianity, nihilism and

Hellenic humanism. No reader of *La Chute*, with its mocking and cynical description of socialism and liberal humanism alike, can avoid the question: how much of Camus's own humanism is targeted in Clamence's analysis and how secure are the foundations of Camus's political philosophy against the charges of his own protagonist? In other words, how confident is the Camus of 1956 that his philosophy of revolt is an adequate reply to Dostevsky's vision of atheistic, socialist nihilism and underground despair? Has the Camus of *La Chute* lost confidence in his own ethic and does his use of a Dostoevskian canvas indicate a critical loss, on Camus's part, of the negative/positive equilibrium of authentic revolt and a decisive move in the direction of Dostoevsky's vision of atheism? Has Camus any suggested way out of the underground for those who live without grace or is it claiming him as a victim, in accordance with Dostoevskian logic? Certainly, no Orphic pathway out of the underground is suggested in *La Chute*, where Clamence ends up in a real impasse and where redemption through Christ is pointedly designated as a desperate illusion. However, as we shall see, the posthumous *Le Premier Homme*, which appears, through the personage of Jacques Corméry, the first man, to be in an antithetical relationship to Clamence, the last of the last, opens up new perspectives on Camus's dialogue with Dostoevsky.

A first point of interest about the Dostoevskian dimensions of *La Chute* is related to Camus's dramatic switch in the choice of decor for this particular *récit*: the Mediterranean luminosity of Algeria, which framed *L'Étranger* and *La Peste*, gives way to the dark, sepulchral, concentric canals of Amsterdam, linked in the text to the circles of Hell in Dante. The oppressive, fog-engulfed streets of the town express, metaphorically, Clamence's fallen state and are the very antithesis of the world of self-confident pagan innocence evoked in *Noces*, with its emphasis on ecstatic moments of communion with the expanses of nature, comparable to moments of grace without God. A key to this change of decor and a strong indication that the thinking behind it is associated, in Camus's mind, to his dialogue with Dostoevsky, is provided by his essay in *L'Été* called 'L'Exil d'Hélène'.

In 'L'Exil d'Hélène', which explores the alienated state of modern man, itself the subject of *La Chute*,[2] Camus argues that the quest for political freedom for the artist cannot be separated from the quest for beauty. However, what he calls 'l'esprit historique' or Hegelian-inspired political historicism, dominates modern sensibility. Quoting Hegel, who once observed: 'Seule la ville moderne offre à l'esprit le terrain où il peut prendre conscience de lui-même' ['The modern town alone provides the mind with a space where it can recognize itself'],[3] Camus claims that we, in the twentieth century, live in 'le temps des grandes villes' ['the time of the big towns'], that '[i]l n'y a plus de conscience que dans les rues' ['now, consciousness is only in the streets'] and that we are, in consequence, exiled from Helen or the world of natural beauty.[4] He then goes on to state, with a key reference to Dostoevsky:

> On cherche en vain les paysages dans la grande littérature européenne depuis Dostoïevski. L'histoire n'explique ni l'univers naturel qui était avant elle, ni la beauté qui est au-dessus d'elle. Elle a donc choisi de les ignorer. Alors que Platon contenait tout, le non-sens, la raison et le mythe, nos philosophes ne contiennent rien que le non-sens de la raison, parce qu'ils ont fermé les yeux sur le reste. La taupe médite.[5]

> [We look in vain for landscapes in great European literature since Dostoevsky. History explains neither the world of nature that existed before it nor beauty which transcends it. It thus chooses to pay no attention to either. Whereas Plato's work contained everything, the irrational, the rational and myth, our philosophers speak only of the irrationality of reason because they have closed their minds to everything else. The mole cogitates.]

Dostoevsky, then, is clearly for Camus, in one sense, an 'Hegelian' novelist of the town and modern in that he uses the decor of St Petersburg to construct a material correlative to an oppressed and deracinated state of mind. Camus's reference to the meditating mole must surely thus be seen as having some degree of convergence with Dostoevsky's notion of the 'underground' or that area of acute consciousness which can plunge us into sterile solipsism and paralysis of will which, invariably in Dostoevsky, is linked to isolation in some confined and restricted habitation of the town.[6]

It seems possible to deduce from these statements in 'L'Exil d'Hélène', that Camus's Amsterdam consciously engages in dialogue with Dostoevsky's underground and the Russian writer's symbolic use of St Petersburg. Confirmation of this idea can certainly be supported by parallels in the text but, before discussing this, it is necessary to bring into focus another aspect of 'L'Exil d'Hélène' which makes further reference to Dostoevsky. Speaking of twentieth-century man's desire for absolutes and empire and our lack of humility, he says:

Pareils à ces bouffons de Dostoïevski qui se vantent de tout, montent aux étoiles et finissent par étaler leur honte dans le premier lieu public, nous manquons seulement de la fierté de l'homme qui est fidélité à ses limites, amour clairvoyant de sa condition.[7]

[Similar to those buffoons of Dostoevsky who boast about everything, climb to the stars and end up displaying their shame in the first public place they can find, we simply lack the pride of being human which is fidelity to limits and lucid love of our condition.]

Insofar as it is precisely Clamence who makes the journey from self-glorification to self-abasing confession in the Mexico-City bar in Amsterdam, Camus is, by implication, inviting his readers to see his penitent judge in terms of Dostoevsky's 'bouffons', thus further emphasizing the dialogue between *La Chute* and Dostoevsky's world.[8]

The Dostoevskian character who is most likely to provide the key to Camus's remark about 'ces bouffons', as I have argued elsewhere,[9] is Marmeladov of *Crime et châtiment*. Raskolnikov meets Marmeladov in a St Petersburg *cabaret* and begins a conversation thus:

Oserai-je, Monsieur, m'adresser à vous pour engager une conversation des plus convenables? Car malgré la simplicité de votre mise mon expérience devine en vous un homme instruit et non un pilier de cabaret. Personnellement j'ai toujours respecté l'instruction unie aux qualités du cœur. Je suis d'ailleurs conseiller titulaire: Marmeladov, tel est mon nom, conseiller titulaire: puis-je vous demander si vous faites partie de l'administration?[10]

[Dare I, sir, turn to you to engage you in friendly conversation? For, despite the simplicity of your dress, my experience of life tells me that you are an educated person and not a pillar of *cabarets*. I myself have always respected education when it is coupled with qualities of the heart. I am, moreover, a titular councillor. Marmeladov, titular councillor, for such is my title. Can I ask you if you are part of the administration?]

Marmeladov speaks with 'aisance et vivacité' ['ease and animation'] and Raskolnikov is surprised by his 'langage ampoulé' ['stilted language'].[11] Marmeladov's speech is remarkably similar in tone and rhythm to Clamence's opening lines in *La Chute*:

Puis-je, monsieur, vous proposer mes services, sans risquer d'être importun. Je crains que vous ne sachiez vous faire entendre de l'estimable gorille qui préside aux destinées de cet établissement.

Il ne parle, en effet, que le hollandais. A moins que vous ne m'autorisiez à plaider votre cause, il ne devinera pas que vous désirez du genièvre.[12]

[Can I, sir, offer you my services without risk of being inopportune? I fear that you will not manage to make yourself understood by the worthy gorilla who is in charge of destinies in this establishment. He only speaks Dutch, in fact. Unless you authorize me to plead your cause, he will not divine that you want some gin.]

Although Marmeladov does not maintain his high level of fluency and becomes increasingly incoherent as he continues to talk, it does seem possible that these opening words provide a model for Clamence's discourse. Camus could then be said to be flagging his general use of the Dostoevskian canvas at the beginning of *La Chute* for the purpose of engaging in further dialogue with his Russian companion of so many years.

Further aspects of the canvas have been identified over the years by various scholars and it is worth recalling them here before discussing what may be the reasons for these parallels, or appropriations, as Dunwoodie prefers to call them. In purely formal terms, it is Dostoevsky's *Le Sous-Sol*, a work Camus first refers to explicitly in 1948,[13] which most critics identify as a possible model for *La Chute*.[14] Both works feature a protagonist seemingly engaged in a dialogue which is, in reality, a monologue. Admittedly, there are differences in the use of this technique: Dostoevsky's protagonist speaks directly to his readers, endlessly teasing and challenging them intellectually and psychologically and posing questions which he proceeds to answer. Clamence, however, engages in dialogue with a seemingly real, single interlocutor but one whose actual presence in the text is only indicated through Clamence's own statements. The technique allows both writers to range freely over their chosen themes and to hit their satirical targets at will. Myrna Magnan-Shardt has argued, with the support of Jean Onimus, that this technique derives from the Russian *skaz*, a name given to a first-person narrative in popular style.[15] Such a view is rightly rejected by Dunwoodie, who in turn is supported by Sturm, when they use Bakhtin's view of the *skaz* as essentially monological, to argue that both *La Chute* and *Le Sous-Sol* are really works which, despite the self-obsession of the protagonists, foreground 'la nature dialogique des techniques utilisées' ['the dialogical nature of the techniques used'], whereas 'le skaz n'est pas nécessairement orienté vers le discours d'autrui' ['the *skaz* is not of necessity directed at the language of other people'].[16]

Again using Bakhtin, Dunwoodie prefers to view the techniques of *La Chute* as a reworking, by both Dostoevsky and Camus in their different ways, of the modes of 'la satire Ménippée' or what he calls 'cette lignée de la ménippée où est tracée la dystopie qui confronte l'homme contemporain' ['this tradition of "satire Ménippée" where the dystopia of contemporary man is mapped out'].[17] Thus, in the same way that Dostoevsky's *Le Sous-Sol* attacks the utopian socialism of Chernyshevsky's *What is to be done?* (targeted by Dostoevsky in the text as the Crystal Palace, two plus two logic and the rational pursuit of self-interest),[18] Camus satirizes the naïveté and well-intentioned inadequacies of right and left-wing progressives.[19]

Moving beyond formal considerations, it is worth noting that a number of critics believe that Camus's general notion of the 'juge-pénitent' ['judge-penitent'] is also borrowed from Dostoevsky. Here, the designated text, or intertext, as some would prefer, is *Jugement* whose importance in Camus's *Le Mythe de Sisyphe* was discussed earlier.[20] The protagonist of *Jugement* says, in the final paragraph of his suicide letter:

> Puisque enfin, dans cet ordre de choses, j'assume à la fois le rôle du plaignant et celui du répondant, de l'accusé et du juge, et puisque je trouve cette comédie de la part de la nature tout à fait stupide, et que même j'estime humiliant de ma part d'accepter de la jouer: En ma qualité indiscutable de plaignant et de répondant, de juge et d'accusé, je condamne cette nature qui avec un si impudent sans-gêne m'a fait naître pour souffrir—je la condamne à être anéantie avec moi . . .[21]

> [Because finally, in this order of things, I assume simultaneously the role of petitioner and respondent, of accused and judge, and because I find this cruelty on the part of nature utterly stupid, and indeed humiliating for me to agree to take part in it: in my indisputable capacity as petitioner and respondent, judge and accused, I condemn this nature which, with such impudent casualness, has caused me to be born in order to suffer—I condemn it to be destroyed with me . . .]

This passage, quoted by Camus in *Le Mythe de Sisyphe*,[22] clearly embodies the dialectic of judge/accused, petitioner/respondent, agressor/victim which informs the psychological acrobatics of Clamence, the penitent-judge turned confessor. Of course, Clamence is not about to kill himself but he is just as much trapped in the self-destructive circles of his own logic as the protagonist of *Jugement*.

Other oppositions in the body of the text of *La Chute* also have a distinctly Dostoevskian ring to them. We have already referred to the general semiotic town/street/solipsism/exile versus country/expanse/beauty analysed by Camus in *L'Été*. *La Chute* develops this patterning extensively and does so seemingly in a dialogue with Dostoevsky.[23] Thus, Clamence's bedroom, in *La Chute*, reduced to its bare essentials, is 'comme un cercueil' ['like a coffin'] and appears to echo, in several respects, the stifling space ('le tout petit réduit' ['the tiny cubby-hole']) of Raskolnikov's room, described by his mother as 'un cercueil' ['a coffin'].[24] The reference to coffins brings into play associations with burial, confinement and, crucially, the underground prison of those alienated, self-introverted practitioners of confessions, like Clamence and the Underground Man. Of course, Camus's use of images of confinement is not restricted to *La Chute*: everywhere in his work, confined space is apparent (Meursault's room and cell or the old people's home at Marengo in *L'Étranger*; the closed gates of *La Peste*; land-locked Czechoslovakia and the hotel room in *Le Malentendu*; the hotel room in Prague of 'La Mort dans l'âme' in *L'Envers et l'endroit*, etc.). However, it is certainly in *La Chute* that Camus's use of this particular semiotic is closest to Dostoevsky's exploration of the same idea. Dunwoodie emphatically confirms this by also showing how Camus, in *La Chute*, reworks a number of oppositions between the small room, untidiness, poverty, squalor as against neatness, cleanliness, purity and innocence, borrowed mainly from *Crime et châtiment*, to create, in Clamence's discourse, a world of uncomfortable ambiguity where all reassuring distinctions between culpability and innocence are destabilized.[25]

Developing these space parallels and assorted oppositions further, it is possible to argue that the bridges and quays of Paris, in *La Chute*, also relate intertextually to Dostoevsky. For example, the episode in *Crime et châtiment* where a young mother attempts suicide by drowning and throws herself from a bridge, observed by the immobile Raskolnikov, consciously mirrors the pivotal *Pont-Royal* episode in *La Chute*.[26] Also, the 'rire' ['laughter'] which Clamence hears on the *Pont des Arts*, which gave rise to his sense of being 'double' and a veritable Janus, certainly seems to relate to the actual 'dédoublement' ['the splitting of personality'] of Goliadkine on the bridge in *Le Double* and to Ivan's encounter, in *Les Frères Karamazov*, with the jocular devil who is his alter ego.[27] In a similar way to these bridges, which fracture the ego structures of the protagonists, the quay of St Petersburg, in *Les Nuits blanches*, segments into two contrasting zones of black and white the psychological life of the isolated protagonist. A parallel psychological/spatial schism is visible in Clamence, who loves the Edenic light but forces himself to like the canals of Amsterdam because they capture the dark, funereal side of existence.[28]

The parallels and dialogues between the work of Dostoevsky and *La Chute*, which we have seen expressed in formal and general semiotic terms are also evident, as one might expect, in the domain of ideas where convergences and oppositions proliferate. First, it should be pointed out that Clamence is very much '[un] Français cartésien' ['(a) Cartesian Frenchman'],[29] as he describes himself, and thus given to rational analysis, although he also informs us later that one of the houses that provided shelter to Descartes in Amsterdam, during his expulsion from France, is now 'un asile d'aliénés' ['a madhouse']. This change of use, according to him, means Cartesianism has given way to 'le délire général et la persécution' ['general madness and persecution mania'] and we are all in the madhouse.[30] With analytical truth set aside and knowledge in a crisis of uncertainty, Clamence is able to speak, seemingly randomly, about his life and views, without our knowing whether he is speaking sincerely or ironically, or simply lying. We never know what he truly thinks nor are we sure that *he* knows. Be that as it may, Clamence's stream of ideas frequently flows into Dostoevsky's tormented world.

Central to Clamence's 'philosophy' is the idea of individual guilt. It is impossible to establish truth and innocence but of guilt we can be certain because we are all judges: 'puisque nous sommes tous juges, nous sommes tous coupables les uns devant les autres' ['because we are all judges, we are all guilty each before everyone'], says Clamence, who earlier declares: 'nous ne pouvons affirmer l'innocence de personne, tandis que nous pouvons affirmer à coup sûr la culpabilité de tous. Chaque homme témoigne du crime de tous les autres, voilà ma foi, et mon espérance' ['we cannot establish with certainty anybody's innocence, whereas we can declare with total confidence everybody's culpability. Each man bears witness to the crime of everyone else, that is my faith and hope'].[31] These statements both echo *and pervert* the basic propositions of what Camus called elsewhere 'le communisme spirituel de Dostoïevski . . . la responsabilité morale de tous' ['the spiritual communism of Dostoevsky . . . the moral responsibility of everybody'].[32] These reciprocal, moral propositions, which underpin Dostoevsky's faith, find expression in the pronouncements of Zosime: 'chacun de nous est coupable devant tous pour tous et pour tout . . . souviens-toi que tu ne peux être le juge de personne . . . Crois fermement à cela, c'est là-dessus que reposent l'espérance et la foi des saints' ['each of us is guilty before everybody for everyone and everything . . . remember that you can be nobody's judge . . . Hold firmly to this belief, for it is upon this that rest the hope and faith of saints'].[33] It is also worth noting that this same theme of universal solidarity surfaces, in *Les Frères Karamazov*, during the first 'réunion' ['meeting'] between other characters and Zosime. This takes place in 'la cellule du starets' ['the staretz's cell'][34] and is prefaced by Aliocha's reflections on Zosime as a saint. Aliocha cogitates in the following terms:

> Il a dans son cœur le mystère de la rénovation pour tous, cette puissance qui instaurera enfin la justice sur la terre; alors tous seront saints, tous s'aimeront les uns les autres; il n'y aura plus ni riches, ni pauvres, ni élévés, ni humiliés; tous seront comme les enfants de Dieu et ce sera l'avènement du règne du Christ.[35]

> [His heart holds the mystery which renews all of us, the power which will finally instil justice on earth; then we shall all be saints, we shall love one another; the divide between rich and poor will end; there will be no exalted and no humiliated people; we shall all be the children of God and this will be the coming of the reign of Christ.]

Clamence too makes reference to 'le lyrisme cellulaire' ['cellular lyricism'] of modern man but it is not, of course, a lyricism of Christian love and justice as represented by Zosime and Aliocha but its antithesis, a lyricism of conflict and rootless solitude, where we are 'tous christs à notre vilaine manière, un à un crucifiés' ['all Christs in our base way, crucified one by one'].[36] Whereas Zosime tells us that, if we have sinned, we should rejoice in the existence of one who is righteous and goes on to define Hell as 'la souffrance de ne pouvoir plus aimer' ['the pain of no longer being able to love'],[37] Clamence uses his own 'sin' to create the kingdom of universal guilt with its defining power structure: the master/slave relationship. In this structure, we shall be 'tous réunis, enfin, mais à genoux, et la tête courbée' ['all together again at last, but on our knees with our heads buried'].[38] Clamence's kingdom of non-redemptive guilt in effect uses Zosime's language in order to poison its content in a cynical perversion of Christian hope. This also appears to be the case when it comes to the question of lying.

Zosime tells old Karamazov, who has asked him about how to merit eternal life:

> Mais surtout, avant tout, ne mentez pas . . . Surtout ne vous mentez pas à vous-même. Celui qui se ment à soi-même et écoute son propre mensonge va jusqu'à ne plus distinguer la vérité ni en soi

ni autour de soi; il perd donc le respect de soi et des autres. Ne respectant personne, il cesse d'aimer, et pour s'occuper et se distraire, en l'absence d'amour, il s'adonne aux passions et aux grossières jouissances; il va jusqu'à la bestialité dans ses vices, et tout cela provient du mensonge continuel à soi-même et aux autres.[39]

[But above all and before everything, do not lie . . . And more than anything else, do not lie to yourself. The person who lies to himself and listens to his own lies ends up by being unable to see the truth either in himself or about him; he thus loses the respect of others and his own self-respect. Respecting nobody at all, he ceases to love, and in order to occupy and distance himself, to compensate for this absence of love, he becomes addicted to passions and vulgar pleasures; he will reach the point of bestiality in vice, and all this comes from lying to oneself and to others.]

Clamence, whose psychological evolution is well captured in Zosime's pronouncements, dismisses the distinction between truth and falsehood and advocates the superior half-light of lies as an alternative to the blinding light of truth: 'La vérité', he says, 'comme la lumière, aveugle. Le mensonge, au contraire, est un beau crépuscule, qui met chaque objet en valeur' ['Truth, like the light, blinds. Lying, on the other hand, is a beautiful twilight which gives everything value'].[40] Clamence, predictably, loses the power to love, because of the distrust of others generated by his own lies.

Other parts of *Les Frères Karamazov* seem equally engaged in dialogue by Clamence's pronouncements in *La Chute*, especially those relating to freedom and slavery, which echo the logic of the Grand Inquisitor. Clamence, for example, argues that freedom is basically solitude in 'une salle morose'['a dreary room'], a terrible burden which leads us inexorably towards a willing state of servitude in order to escape its exigencies:

La liberté n'est pas une récompense, ni une décoration qu'on fête dans le champagne . . . Oh! non, c'est une corvée, au contraire, et une course de fond, bien solitaire, bien exténuante. Pas de champagne, point d'amis qui lèvent leur verre en vous regardant avec tendresse. Seul dans une salle morose, seul dans le box, devant les juges, et seul pour décider, devant soi-même ou devant le jugement des autres. Au bout de toute liberté, il y a une sentence; voilà pourquoi la liberté est trop lourde à porter, surtout lorsqu'on souffre de fièvre, ou qu'on a de la peine, ou qu'on n'aime personne.

Ah! mon cher, pour qui est seul, sans dieu et sans maître, le poids des jours est terrible. Il faut donc se choisir un maître . . .[41]

[Freedom is not a reward nor an honour celebrated with champagne . . . Oh, no, it is, on the contrary, a burden, a real trial, a very lonely and exhausting experience. No champagne, no friends to toast you or to give you loving looks. Alone, in a dreary room, alone in the box, before the judges, alone with a decision to make before oneself or before the judgement of others. At the end of every freedom, there is a sentence to be pronounced; that is why freedom is too heavy a burden to carry, especially when you are suffering from fever or are in pain or you don't love anybody. Ah, my dear friend, when you are alone, without a God or a master, the weight of the days is frightful. You must, therefore get a master . . .]

The Grand Inquisitor pursues an identical train of thought when he rejects Christ's message. Whilst admitting that he can understand how Christ finds the idea of human freedom so 'séduisant' ['seductive'], he proclaims, to Christ, in a speech which clearly made a major impact on Camus and is indeed one which Clamence himself could, in many respects, be making, that freedom is 'un fardeau terrible' ['a terrible burden'] and adds:

Tu n'as pas voulu priver l'homme de la liberté, et tu as refusé, [to turn the desert stones into bread] estimant qu'elle était incompatible avec l'obéissance achetée par les pains. Tu as répliqué que l'homme ne vit pas seulement de pain, mais sais-tu qu'au nom de ce pain terrestre, l'Esprit de la terre s'insurgera contre toi, luttera et te vaincra, que tous le suivront en s'écriant: 'Qui est semblable à cette bête, elle nous a donné le feu du ciel?' Des siècles passeront et l'humanité proclamera par la bouche de ses savants et de ses sages qu'il n'y a pas de crimes, et, par conséquent, pas de péché; qu'il n'y a que des affamés. 'Nourris-les, et alors exige d'eux qu'ils soient "vertueux" '! Voilà ce qu'on inscrira sur l'étendard de la révolte qui abattra ton temple. A sa place un nouvel édifice s'élèvera, une seconde tour de Babel, qui restera sans doute inachevée, comme la première; mais tu aurais pu épargner aux hommes cette nouvelle tentative et mille ans de souffrance. Car ils viendront nous trouver, après avoir peiné mille ans à bâtir leur tour. Ils nous chercheront sous terre comme jadis, dans les catacombes où nous serons cachés (on nous persécutera de nouveau) et ils clameront: 'Donnez-nous à manger, car ceux qui nous avaient promis le feu du ciel ne nous l'ont pas donné.' Alors, nous achèverons leur tour, car il ne faut pour cela que la nourriture, et nous les nourrirons, soi- disant en ton nom, nous le ferons accroire. Sans nous, ils seront toujours affamés. Aucune science ne leur donnera du pain, tant qu'ils demeureront libres, mais ils finiront par la déposer à nos pieds, cette liberté, en disant: 'Réduisez-nous plutôt en servitude, mais nourrissez-nous.' Ils comprendont enfin que la liberté est inconciliable avec le pain de la terre à discrétion, parce que jamais ils ne sauront le répartir entre eux! Ils se convaincront aussi de leur impuissance à se faire libres, étant faibles, dépravés, nuls et révoltés. Tu leur promettais le pain du ciel; encore un coup, est-il comparable à celui de la terre aux yeux de la faible race humaine, éternellement ingrate et dépravée? Des milliers et des dizaines de milliers d'âmes te suivront à cause de ce pain, mais que deviendront les millions et les milliards qui n'auront pas le courage de préférer le pain du ciel à celui de la terre? Ne chérirais-tu que les grands et les forts, à qui les autres, la multitude innombrable, qui est faible mais qui t'aime, ne servirait que de matière exploitable? Ils nous sont chers aussi, les êtres faibles. Quoique dépravés et révoltés, ils deviendront finalement dociles. Ils s'étonneront et nous croiront des dieux pour avoir consenti, en nous mettant à leur tête, à assurer la liberté qui les effrayait et à régner sur eux, tellement à la fin ils auront peur d'être libres. Mais nous leur dirons que nous sommes tes disciples, que nous régnons en ton nom. Nous les tromperons de nouveau, car alors nous ne te laisserons pas approcher de nous. Et c'est cette imposture qui constituera notre souffrance, car il nous faudra mentir . . . Car il n'y a pas pour l'homme, demeuré libre, de souci plus constant . . . que de chercher un être devant qui s'incliner.[42]

[You did not want to deprive man of his freedom and you refused, (to turn the desert stones into bread) believing that freedom was incompatible with obedience purchased with bread. You replied that man does not live by bread alone but do you realize that in the name of this terrestrial bread, the Spirit of the Earth will rise up against you, fight you and defeat you, that everybody will follow the Spirit and cry: 'Who is like unto the beast who maketh fire come down from heaven?' Ages will pass and humanity will claim through its learned men and its sages that there are no crimes and thus no sins; there are only hungry people. 'Feed them, and then ask them to be "virtuous"!' This is what will be written on the banner they will raise against you which will destroy your temple. In its place, a new edifice will rise, a second tower of Babel which will also, no doubt, remain unfinished, like the first. But you could have spared man this new endeavour and a thousand years of suffering. For they will come to us, after a thousand years of labouring to build their tower. They will seek us underground as before in the catacombs where we shall be hiding (they will persecute us again) and they will clamour: 'Give us food, for those who promised us the fire of heaven have not given it to us.' Then, we shall be the ones to finish the tower, for we need only food to do it and we shall feed them in your name and we shall convince them of it. Without us, they will remain hungry. No science will provide them with bread as long as they are free but they will finally place this freedom at our feet, saying: 'Rather make us slaves but feed us.' They will understand at last that freedom and bread when you want it are incompatible because they could never learn to share it out among themselves. They will become convinced too that they are incapable of being free because they are weak, depraved, worthless and rebellious. You promised them the bread of heaven; but, once again, can that be compared to earthly bread in the eyes of the weak, eternally unfaithful and depraved creatures who make up the human race? Thousands and tens of thousands of souls will follow you for this bread of heaven, but what will become of the millions, the billions who will not have the courage to prefer the bread of heaven to earthly bread? Will you have a care only for the great and the strong for whom the rest, the huge multitude who love you in their weakness, are nothing but matter for exploitation? They are dear to us, these weak beings. Although depraved and rebellious, they will finally become docile. They will be astonished and take us for gods because we will consent, in becoming their masters, to take over the freedom which frightened them and to rule over them to the point where they will fear reasserting their freedom. But we shall tell them that we are your followers and that we rule in your name. We shall lie to them again, but we shall not let you near us then. And this deception will be the cross we bear for we shall have to lie . . . For in the eyes of the man who is free there is no more constant preoccupation . . . than to seek a being before whom to bow.]

The essential components of Clamence's vision of a master-race assuming the burden of freedom and guilt for the enslaved are all clearly in evidence here.

Later statements by Clamence on the subject of freedom incorporate elements drawn from 'le Chigalevisme' which, as was seen earlier, is linked, in Camus's mind, to the logic of the Grand Inquisitor. For example, Clamence declares to his interlocutor, when explaining the logic of his master-slave society:

Sur les ponts de Paris, j'ai appris moi aussi que j'avais peur de la liberté. Vive donc le maître, quel qu'il soit, pour remplacer la loi du ciel . . . Voilà pourquoi, très cher, après avoir salué solennelle-ment la liberté, je décidai en catimini qu'il fallait la remettre sans délai à n'importe qui. Et chaque fois que je le peux, je prêche dans mon église de *Mexico-City*, j'invite le bon peuple à se soumettre et à briguer humblement les conforts de la servitude, quitte à la présenter comme la vraie liberté.

Mais je ne suis pas fou, je me rends bien compte que l'esclavage n'est pas pour demain. Ce sera un des bienfaits de l'avenir.[43]

[On the bridges of Paris, I learnt that I too was afraid of freedom. Long live the master, then, whoever it may be, to replace the law of heaven . . . That is why, my dear friend, after having solemnly saluted freedom, I decided secretly that you had to off-load it immediately onto somebody else. And whenever I can, I preach my message in my Mexico-City church, I invite the people to surrender and to seek humbly the comforts of servitude, always ready to present this as true freedom. But I am not mad, I realize that slavery is not for tomorrow. It will be one of the benefits of the future.]

Further confirmation, if it were needed, that *La Chute* is extensively intertextually entwined with Dostoevsky's work is provided by *Le Sous-Sol*, the text most frequently identified by critics as a generic model for Camus's book. In addition to the formal parallels already discussed, mention should be made of the following thematic overlaps: the protagonist of *Le Sous-Sol* refers to the impossibility of self-love for the person who is really self-aware or fully conscious. Consciousness, for this type of person, is basically a terrible sickness: 'Une conscience trop clairvoyante, je vous assure, messieurs, c'est une maladie, une maladie très réelle' ['Too much conscious awareness, I can tell you, gentlemen, is an illness, a real illness'].[44] This sickness undermines self- respect: 'Tout cela provient de ce que je ne m'estime pas: mais celui qui se connaît peut-il s'estimer, ne fût-ce qu'un peu?' ['All this comes from the fact that I have no self-respect: but if a person knows himself, can he respect himself, even a little bit?'][45] Camus, who singles out this statement for inclusion in the *Carnets*,[46] infects Clamence with a similar self-alienation, born of self-knowledge. Indeed, *La Chute*, in one sense, pursues relentlessly this theme of a lost paradise of the mind and stability of consciousness destroyed by the discomforts of self-knowledge. Looking in the mirror to see ourselves fractures the spontaneity and the innocence of non self-conscious existence, enjoyed by animals or people like animals!

Such discomfort in both protagonists breeds, simultaneously, cynicism and a curious determination to enjoy one's humiliation in the underground of life. Hence, Dostoevsky's character defines man, when seeking the best description of him, as 'un être à deux pieds et ingrat' ['an ungrateful biped'].[47] Clamence, restricting his definition to modern man says gleefully: 'Une phrase . . . suffira pour l'homme moderne: il forniquait et lisait des journaux' ['One sentence . . . will suffice to describe modern man: he fornicated and read the papers'].[48] The Underground Man develops his cynical description by asking whether civilization is improving people morally, in a speech about killing which could be part of *L'Homme révolté* or of Clamence's general description of twentieth-century man:

Avez-vous déjà remarqué que les sanguinaires les plus raffinés furent toujours des messieurs très civilisés, auprès desquels tous ces Attila, tous ces Stenka Razine feraient très piètre figure? Si ces messieurs se font moins remarquer, cela tient à ce qu'ils se rencontrent plus souvent et que nous y sommes habitués. Mais si la civilisation n'a pas rendu l'homme plus sanguinaire, elle l'a certainement rendu plus vilainement, plus lâchement sanguinaire. Dans le temps, l'homme considérait qu'il avait le droit de répandre le sang et c'est la conscience bien tranquille qu'il détruisait qui bon lui semblait. Aujourd'hui, tout en considérant l'effusion de sang comme une mauvaise action, nous tuons quand même, et plus souvent encore qu'auparavant. Cela vaut-il mieux? Décidez-en vous-mêmes. On dit que Cléopâtre (excusez cet exemple tiré de l'histoire romaine) s'amusait à enfoncer des aiguilles dans le sein de ses esclaves et prenait grand plaisir à leurs cris et à leurs contorsions. Vous me direz que cela se passait à une époque relativement barbare, que notre siècle est barbare, lui aussi, car on continue à enforcer des aiguilles dans les chairs.[49]

[Have you noticed that the most sophisticated and blood-thirsty individuals have always been very civilized people beside whom all these Attilas and Stenka Razines are very feeble figures. If such people are less well known, it is because there are so many of them and we are used to them. But if civilization has not rendered people more blood-thirsty, it has certainly rendered them blood-thirsty in a base and more cowardly way. In the past, man considered that he had the right to spill blood and destroyed whoever he pleased with a clear conscience. Nowadays, whilst considering the shedding of blood as bad, we kill all the same and more tranquilly than before. Is this better? Decide for yourself. It is claimed that Cleopatra (and pardon my use of an example from Roman history) enjoyed sticking needles into the chests of her slaves and took great delight in their screams and contortions. You will say that this happened in a period of relative barbarism but our period is also equally barbaric for we continue to stick needles in flesh.]

Such cynicism does not preclude, and is, in fact, intensified, in both characters, by a sense of their own superiority and insight, despite their knowledge of their own imperfections (cf. *Le Sous-Sol*: 'J'ai un amour-propre terrible' ['I have an incredibly high opinion of myself']. *La Chute*: 'J'ai contracté dans ma vie au moins un grand amour, dont j'ai toujours été l'objet' ['I did in my life engage in at least one great love affair, with myself as the other person']).[50] In both characters, guilt fractures this narcissism but can produce a masochistic encirclement in self-abasement and humiliation: in *Le Sous-Sol*, the protagonist insists defensively on his 'volupté dans l'humiliation' ['voluptuous pleasure in humiliation'], whilst Clamence insists on the happiness he finds in confessing his imperfections and does so with lyrical effusions whose very intensity subverts their power to convince.[51] Both protagonists practise their confessions, whilst fully admitting that confession is specious and frequently duplicitous, especially when it is a question of literary confessions: the Underground Man prefaces his confession with the following remark:

> Moi, en tout cas, il n'y a pas très longtemps que je me suis décidé à me ressouvenir de certaines de mes anciennes aventures; jusqu'ici je les évitais, et non sans une certaine inquiétude. Or, maintenant, lorsque je les évoque et veux même les noter, maintenant je tente l'épreuve: est-il possible d'être franc et sincère, au moins vis-à-vis de soi-même, et peut-on se dire toute la vérité? J'observerai à ce propos que Heine assure qu'il ne peut exister d'autobiographies exactes et que l'homme ment toujours lorsqu'il parle de lui-même. Rousseau, à son avis, nous a certainement trompés dans ces *Confessions*, et même délibérément, par vanité.

> [As for myself, not long ago, I resolved to recall some of the episodes of my past; until then, I avoided them and not without a certain anxiety. Now, whenever I think about them and want to detail them, I put myself to the test: is it possible to be frank and sincere, at least to oneself, and can one be completely truthful to oneself? I shall observe, in this respect, that Heine maintains that exact autobiographies cannot exist, that people always lie when they speak of themselves. Rousseau, in his view, certainly lied to us in his *Confessions* and did so deliberately, out of vanity.]

Clamence declares, in turn:

> D'ailleurs, je n'aime plus que les confessions, et les auteurs de confession écrivent surtout pour ne pas se confesser, pour ne rien dire de ce qu'ils savent. Quand ils prétendent passer aux aveux, c'est le moment de se méfier, on va maquiller le cadavre.[52]

> [Moreover, I only now like confessions, and authors of confessions write above all in order not to confess, so as to avoid telling us what they know. When they claim to be confessing, that is the time to be suspicious, they are going to put make-up on the corpse.]

In both protagonists, the confessional mode leads them to a psychological impasse, where suspicion and cynicism prevent any possibility of acting with others to find an exit from their dilemmas. The Underground Man is in his 'sous-sol' which he simultaneously praises as the appropriate location of those who are self-aware, 'Vive le sous-sol!' ['Long live the underground!'], and damns as the restrictive walls frustrating his wish for a greater sense of self-possibility, 'Au diable le sous-sol!' ['To hell with the underground!'].[53] Such a sense of confinement and paralysis, whilst being advocated by the Undergound Man as something superior to action based on little self-knowledge, the essence of mediocre people, also leads to despair and a wish to talk to others. Hence the confession and the logorrhoea. Whilst it is true that Clamence hates caves and underground spaces and prefers high and dominating perspectives ('Les soutes, les cales, les souterrains, les grottes, les gouffres me faisaient horreur. . . . Je crois surtout que l'action souterraine ne convenait ni à mon tempérament, ni à mon goût des sommets aérés' ['Bunkers, holds, underground places, caves, chasms horrified me . . . I really believe that underground action did not suit my temperament nor my taste for airy summits']),[54] his 'fall' nonetheless plunges him into the hell/impasse/underground of the concentric circles of Amsterdam where 'Il sera toujours trop tard. Heureusement!' ['It will always be too late. Fortunately!'] and he cries: 'Vivent . . . les enterrements' ['Long live . . . burials'].[55] Both protagonists find themselves talking but are trapped in their own monological worlds.

It should be clear from the above remarks that Dostoevsky's fictional world thoroughly penetrates Camus's writing in La Chute and that one could write a whole book on this subject alone.[56] It is now necessary to address the question of why this should be the case. Kirk does not ask this question, since she is more concerned with a comparative study between La Chute and Le Sous-Sol as a subject of interest in its own right. Sturm asks the question in terms of his assessment of the debt owed by Camus to Dostoevsky and the general influence of the Russian writer on Camus. Dunwoodie asks it and answers it in generic terms, derived from Bakhtin: Camus is reinvigorating and updating the forms and themes of 'la satire Menippée', used by Dostoevsky in Le Sous-Sol and is appropriating and reworking them in a wide-ranging intertextual dialogue which gives prominence not just to Le Sous-Sol but to Crime et châtiment and, less significantly, to Le Double and Le Songe d'un homme ridicule.[57] This is all very well if one sees Camus's interest in Dostoevsky predominantly in terms of 'l'expression d'un jeu d'intertextes' ['the expression of intertextual interplay']. However, following the line of argument advanced in this study, to the effect that Camus's works are frequently designed as replies to some of Dostoevsky's central convictions, the question must be asked: how does *La Chute* work as a reply, when it appears to be so very Dostoevskian in its own right?

It has to be said, from the outset, that some critics, when first reading *La Chute*, immediately suggested that Camus's non-Christian Hellenic humanism was in terminal crisis, that his 'pensée de midi' had been brushed aside historically by events in Korea and Algeria and that he was now haunted by guilt and imperfection and yearning for God.[58] Such an interpretation, if valid (and I am not suggesting that it is) would mean, in our terms, that Camus's whole reply to Dostoevsky had foundered and he was now living in the negative world of Dostoevsky's atheists. Notwithstanding the rather simple-minded autobiographical perspectives evident in such an approach, it is worth stating that Clamence's cynicism and corrosive lucidity, in certain respects, *do* throw down the gauntlet to Camusian humanism by placing duplicitous self-love at the centre of bourgeois if not human reality.[59] Clamence's constant reference to Christ, grace and the Bible might also suggest that Camus has moved closer to Dostoevsky's world of grace as a solution to 'the underground'. It has already been noted how the buffoon Marmeladov's language is close to Clamence's opening words in *La Chute*. Clamence's references to Christ, in one sense, also echo those of Marmeladov who declares, in the *cabaret*, towards the end of his oration:

> Mais nous ne serons pris en pitié que par Celui qui a eu pitié de tous les hommes. Celui qui a tout compris, l'Unique et notre seul Juge . . . Et Il nous tendra Ses bras divins et nous nous y précipiterons . . . et nous fondrons en larmes . . . et nous comprendrons tout . . . et tous comprendront . . .[60]

> [But we shall have pity taken on us by He who pities all men. He who has understood all things, our one and only Judge . . . and He will stretch out His divine arms and we shall rush towards Him . . . and we shall burst into tears . . . and we shall understand everything . . . and all of us shall understand . . .]

These words point to a way out of 'the underground', a rebirth of the spiritually dead and blind through the miracle of Christ, and evidently prefigure the redemption of Raskolnikov, through Christianity, at the end of the novel. The same central conviction is evident in Zosime's final entreaties:

Sur la terre, nous sommes errants et si nous n'avions pas la
précieuse image du Christ pour nous guider, nous succomberions
et nous égarerions tout à fait, comme le genre humain avant le
déluge.[61]

[On Earth, without the precious image of Christ to guide us, we
are rootless wanderers, we would give up and be lost totally, like
humanity before the flood.]

The fact that Dostoevsky will place his vision of Christ into the words
of both a buffoon and a saint is indication enough that Christ's
message has universal appeal.[62] Clamence, in turn, conjures up the
image of Christ in a similar Biblical language:

Il [Christ] parlait doucement à la pécheresse: Moi non plus, je ne
te condamne pas! ça n'empêche rien, ils [people who speak in
Christ's name] condamnent, ils n'absolvent personne . . . Et puis
il [Christ] est parti pour toujours, les laissant juger et condamner,
le pardon à la bouche et la sentence au cœur.[63]

[He spoke gently of sin: I myself do not condemn you! no matter
they (people who speak in Christ's name) condemn alright, they
absolve nobody . . . And then He (Christ) left us for ever, leaving
them to judge and condemn, forgiveness in the mouth but
judgement in the heart.]

Clamence's evocation of Christ, however, does not hold out any
realistic hope of salvation or a Lazarus-like miracle. Christ, for
Clamence, is an impossible yearning to escape from the world of
guilt which is our reality. Although he confesses to a love of Christ
and speaks of: 'l'injustice qu'on lui a faite et qui [lui] serre le
cœur' ['the injustice done to him which makes [his] heart ache'],[64]
ultimately, for Clamence, Christ also is inflicted with guilt, through
the slaughter of the innocents, and knew, by choosing to build his
Chuch on Peter, that his reign would *not* come.[65] *La Chute*, then,
picks up the thematic of general redemption through Christ but only
to declare its impossibility. A similar point could be made about
Clamence's references to the loss of the light, to the fact that we are
too dirty to enter the Greek islands, to the doves which never come
or to the lost peace of the island of Cypango. These all refer to the
inaccessible dream-worlds of pre-lapsarian innocence which haunt
subjectivity. They do not, of course, all have associations with
Dostoevsky and some are related clearly to Camus's own history of
delusions about his period of Algerian 'innocence' and pacifism but

they all converge to underline the impossibility of grace or escape for Clamence, 'la créature solitaire, errant dans les grandes villes . . .' ['the lonely creature, wandering about the big towns . . .'].[66]

If Camus engages Dostoevsky's world of Christian grace in dialogue in *La Chute* only to emphasize its impossibility or to sweep aside what Dunwoodie calls 'la touchante désuétude de la déclaration de foi du minable presonnage dostoïevskien' ['the touchingly outdated declaration of faith from the pitiable Dostoevskian character'] (he means Marmeladov),[67] what solutions *is* Camus offering to the challenge of the underground? Certainly, it has to be said, none is offered in *La Chute* itself where Clamence, as already indicated, falls into a total impasse. Aesthetically, there are good reasons for this, since Camus is not writing an essay about ideas and Clamence's lack of trust and all-pervasive cynicism fully legitimize the solipsistic paralysis which is his final lot in the text. Elsewhere, however, Camus makes the point that there is a solution to Clamence's dilemma:

> Le héros de *La Chute* s'enferme dans une dernière impasse avec sa solution. Mais, j'ai voulu seulement décrire une certaine sorte de phrophète qui sévit dans notre société intellectuelle et je partagerai tout à fait l'avis de Lacroix et de Malebranche sur le remède qui convient: un peu d'estime de soi mélangé à un peu de modestie.[68]

> [The hero of *La Chute* locks himself in a final impasse with his solitude. But I wanted to describe a certain sort of prophet who is rife in today's intellectual circles and I heartily endorse the opinion of Lacroix and Malebranche on the remedy required: a bit of self-respect coupled with a little modesty.]

Such advice would, no doubt, be very acceptable if the text of *La Chute* itself did not powerfully suggest that self-esteem is impossible for the truly conscious man and that the lust for power to be a superman above others is integral to our relationship with ourselves. Camus's opinions on his own text do not, then, help us very much in understanding why he should have thrown away the key which might unlock the door to lead Clamence out of his underground torment.

Placing *La Chute* in context with the rest of Camus's work of the period is equally problematic in identifying Camus's general intentions in creating Clamence. *L'Exil et le royaume*, published one year after *La Chute*, which was originally intended to be part of that collection of short stories, makes it clear, in the most discreet way possible, that a balance between the negative and positive charges of existence is immensely difficult but does promise a kind of happiness: isolation and being with others, the 'solitaire' and the 'solidaire', are both creative and destructive, like silence and loquacity. Clamence's discourse, however, seems to overturn such Cartesian finesse and any kingdom in *La Chute* looks very remote indeed in terms of the delicate balances and double counterpoints of the short stories. The adaptation of *Les Possédés* in 1959, whilst restating the premises of Camus's analysis of radicalism and nihilism in *L'Homme révolté*, and thus, by implication at least, reformulating the relevance of 'la pensée de midi', seems to offer no really adequate answer to the subversive anti-humanist disquisitions of Clamence. *La Chute*, therefore, appears to throw into doubt and confusion just where Camus does stand in relation to his own humanism of 'la pensée de midi'. Undoubtedly, this expands the interpretative possibilities of the text but leaves unsolved the question of what is happening to Camus's philosophical and political evolution.

In terms of our own suggested debate, Camus appears, in *La Chute*, consciously and comprehensively to embrace the despair and tormented rootlessness of Dostoevsky's hapless atheists. He weds Dostoevskian perspectives on life without Christ in the underground to create the fictional space and thematics of his last novel. In so doing, it can be conjectured that Camus, in classic psychoanalytical terms, is introjecting Dostoevsky's world in order to exorcise it, once and for all, from his preoccupations. Camus embraces his demons in order to transcend them. Roger Quilliot has already suggested that Camus uses Clamence to extricate himself, by irony, derision and self-mockery, from the self-doubts and the sense of inadequacy which followed the quarrel with Sartre and Jeanson.[69] Clamence, in this sense, represents the nadir of the Camusian sense of exile and disequilibrium, linked in the author's mind to the subterranean world of Dostoevsky's tormented atheists. Clamence is 'le dernier des derniers' ['the last of the last'][70] but his self-encircled world of guilt and terminal narcissism is already generating, in Camus's own mind, a counterbalance which will mark the beginning of a new emotional cycle in his work, sadly never to be completed: *Le Premier Homme*. Camus's final volume of *Carnets* charts very clearly the personal psychological and moral difficulties experienced by him in the 50s and shows how they underpin the relationship between *La Chute* and *Le Premier Homme*. The following entry for 1959 encapsulates these difficulties:

J'ai voulu vivre pendant des années selon la morale de tous. Je me suis forcé à vivre comme tout le monde, à me ressembler à tout le monde. J'ai dit ce qu'il fallait pour réunir, même quand je me sentais séparé. Et au bout de tout cela ce fut la catastrophe. Maintenant j'erre parmi des débris, je suis sans loi, écartelé, seul et acceptant de l'être, résigné à ma singularité et à mes infirmités. Et je dois reconstruire une vérité—après avoir vécu toute ma vie dans une espèce de mensonge.[71]

[For years I wanted to live according to common values. I forced myself to live as everyone else and to resemble everybody. I said what was needed to unite, even when I felt separate. And at the end of the day it was a disaster. Now I wander about in the ruins, without any laws, apart, alone and accepting my lot, resigned to my singularity and my weaknesses. And I must rebuild a truth— having lived all my life as a kind of lie.]

Le Premier Homme is the beginning of this process of reconstruction and, as we hope to demonstrate, it will also provide Camus with the opportunity to make a break with Dostoevsky and focus much more evidently on Tolstoy.

It was noted in a previous chapter that Camus, in his essay on Roger Martin du Gard, expressed the wish that French novelists would one day produce works which would capture 'l'épaisseur' ['the density'] which, for Camus, is Tolstoy's rule of art, and ally it to Martin du Gard's sobriety. The detail of Camus's argument in this essay is worth examining because it sheds light on his probable intentions in *Le Premier Homme*. Speaking of modern French literature in general, Camus writes:

Notre production pourrait en effet, lorsqu'elle est valable, se réclamer de Dostoïevski plutôt que de Tolstoï. Des ombres passionnées ou inspirées y tracent le commentaire gesticulant d'une réflexion sur la destinée. Sans doute, le relief, l'épaisseur se rencontrent aussi dans les figures de Dostïevski; mais il n'en fait pas, comme Tolstoï, la règle de sa création. Dostoïevski cherche d'abord le mouvement, Tolstoï la forme. Entre les jeunes femmes des *Possédés* et Natacha Rostov, il y a la même différence qu'entre un personnage cinématographique et un héros de théâtre: plus d'animation et moins de chair. Ces faiblesses d'un génie sont du reste compensées (et même justifées), chez Dostoïevski, par l'introduction d'une dimension supplémentaire, spirituelle celle-là, qui prend racine dans le péché ou la sainteté. Mais, à quelques exceptions près, ces notions sont déclarées inactuelles par nos contemporains qui n'ont donc retenu de Dostoïevski qu'un héritage d'ombres.[72]

[When they have value, our literary productions could, in fact, claim to come from Dostoevsky rather than Tolstoy. The gesturing of intense or visionary shadows map out a commentary taking the form of a reflection on destiny. Contrast and density are doubtless to be found in Dostoevsky's characters but they do not constitute the guiding principle of his creative activity as they do for Tolstoy. Dostoevsky seeks movement more than anything else, Tolstoy form. Between the young women of *Les Possédés* and Natasha Rostov, there is the same difference as between a cinema character and a hero of the theatre: more animation and less physical presence. These weaknesses of genius are moreover compensated (and even justified) by the presence in Dostoevsky of an extra dimension, the spiritual one rooted in sin and saintliness. But, with very few exceptions, these ideas are seen as outmoded by our contemporaries who have thus retained only Dostoevsky's legacy of shadows.]

Although Camus is not saying here that he prefers Tolstoy to Dostoevsky or formulating alternatives between which one must choose (à la George Steiner), he does state, later in the essay:

Il y a de grandes chances, en effet, pour que l'ambition réelle de nos écrivains soit, après avoir assimilé *Les Possédés*, d'écrire un jour *La Geurre et la paix*. Au bout d'une longue course à travers les guerres et les négations, ils gardent l'espoir, même s'ils ne l'avouent pas, de retrouver les secrets d'un art universel qui, à force d'humilité et de maîtrise, ressusciterait enfin les personnages dans leur chair et leur durée.[73]

[There is a very good chance, in fact, that the real project of our writers, having assimilated *Les Possédés*, will be one day to write *La Guerre et la paix*. After a long charge through wars and negation, they still hope, even if they don't admit it, to rediscover the secrets of a universal art which, by dint of humility and discipline, will fully recreate characters in flesh and duration.]

Le Premier Homme would appear to represent an attempt by Camus himself to move beyond *Les Possédés* and the 'héritage d'ombres' ['legacy of shadows'] of Dostoevsky and write a Tolstoyan classic. Certainly, the evidence from the *Carnets* suggests that, as Camus sketches out the preliminary designs for his new novel, he is very much immersed in Tolstoy.[74] This does not mean he has forgotten Dostoevsky: he writes, for example, in October 1953, when he is both reading Tolstoy's *Journal* and detailing the first real plan of *Le Premier Homme*:

Ceux qui ont été fécondés à la fois par Dostoïevski et par Tolstoï, qui les comprennent aussi bien l'un que l'autre, avec la même facilité, ceux-là: natures toujours redoutables pour eux-mêmes et pour les autres.[75]

[Those who have been nourished by both Dostoevsky and Tolstoy, who can respond equally readily to both of them, these are people who are redoubtable to themselves and to others.]

However, when it comes to the actual composition of *Le Premier Homme*, the prevailing narrational mood of controlled but emotionally charged and sensitized reconstruction of the past, with its emphasis on the movement of the generations, family births and deaths, is very much in a Tolstoyan vein.

This whole question of the link between *Le Premier Homme*, Tolstoy and Dostoevsky has been discussed in some detail and with much erudition by Jean Sarocchi in the first full-length study of the work.[76] Although he rejects any simplistictic schematization of the Dostoevsky/Tolstoy dialogue which he finds at work in Camus's mind in *Le Premier Homme*, he does come to the following conclusion:

Il serait licite d'avancer que le progrès de Camus romancier consiste à passer de Dostoïevski, l'écrivain à qui le père a manqué, à Tolstoï qui aussitôt l'a trouvé. *Le Premier Homme* serait le moment décisif de ce passage, le texte cardinal qui ouvre une nouvelle travée d'écriture. Mais on se doute qu'une "recherche du père" enterprise vers la cinquantaine est privée de la grâce tolstoïenne, que la forme tolstoïenne de l'autobiographie, pour qui a derrière lui *La Chute* et *La Peste*, exige une rude reconquête de certains points de disponibilité. Tolstoï peut figurer le modèle ultime, une sorte de Dostoïevski plus étendu et détendu, prodigue de paisibles images, mais celui-ci reste, jusqu'au bout, une transition obligée, et plus qu'une transition, un avant- coureur qui a déjà tracé la voie inévitable, car il a lui-même, vers la cinquantaine, écrit à sa façon une "Recherche du père", et si Camus se tourne, dans *Le Premier Homme*, vers la maîtrise de Tolstoï, il est tributaire, pour son dessein herméneutique, des écarts et des incartades de *L'Adolescent*. "Tolstoï ou Gorki (I) le père" désigne (c'est une hypothèse) le milieu idéal où les imagos paternelles soient conjurées, "Dostoïevski (II) le fils" l'énigme d'une filiation qui appareille Jacques Cormery à Arcade Dolgorouki.[77]

[It would be legitimate to argue that Camus's progress as a novelist is to move from Dostoevsky, the writer without a father, to Tolstoy, the one who found the father immediately. *Le Premier Homme* would constitute the decisive moment in this transition, the pivotal text which opens up a new period of writing. But one suspects that a 'quest for the father' undertaken when one is almost fifty will be without Tolstoyan elegance, that Tolstoy's autobiographical mode, for somebody who has written *La Chute* and *La Peste*, will demand a tough reconquest of certain types of detachment. Tolstoy can be seen as the ultimate model, a kind of more relaxed and expansive Dostoevsky, rich in images of peace, but Dostoevsky remains, to the end, the writer who needs to be transcended and it is not just a question of transition, since Dostoevsky is the forerunner who has already mapped out the necessary route himself, for, when approaching fifty, he wrote his own sort of 'quest for the father'; and if Camus, in *Le Premier Homme*, turns towards Tolstoyan mastery, his hermeneutic design still flows from the delinquencies and outbursts of Dostoevsky's *L'Adolescent*. "Tolstoy or Gorki (I) the father" identifies (hypothetically) the ideal space where the paternal imagoes are exorcized, "Dostoevsky (II) the son" the mystery of a relationship linking Jacques Cormery to Arcade Dolgorouki.]

What Sarocchi is claiming here is that, if *Le Premier Homme* does move towards Tolstoy aesthetically (and he concedes that it does), psychologically it does so through ' La Recherche du père' and that this quest is conducted in a Dostoevskian way which takes its emotional patterning from *L'Adolescent*:

> Que la 'Recherche du père', c'est-à-dire la meilleure part du *Premier Homme*, passe par les chemins de Dostoïevski, on s'en convaincra en la comparant à *L'Adolescent*.[78]

> [That the 'Quest for the father', that is to say the greater part of *Le Premier Homme*, follows the pathways of Dostoevsky, is cogently confirmed by comparing it to *L'Adolescent*.]

It is certainly true that Camus had read *L'Adolescent* (although Sarocchi does not appear to have realized this)[79] but the quest for the father in *Le Premier Homme* does not have the tormented, bitter and highly problematic dimensions of *L'Adolescent*, where the father is still alive and eventually rediscovered and reunited with the son and, because of this, Sarocchi's argument does not convince. When Clamence, in *La Chute*, declares : 'Il n'y a plus de père, plus de règle' ['There is no longer any father, any rule'],[80] it serves to remind us that the loss of the father can lead to nihilism and this certainly takes us directly into Dostoevsky's world, where the loss of God the Father creates an existence in which madness, suicide and murder can occur.

Sarocchi is right to suggest that throughout his general work, Camus, in one sense, has to confront the loss of the father and does so in ways which recall Dostoevsky's fiction (we have seen how this is particularly the case with *Caligula*, *Le Malentendu* and *La Chute*).[81] However, there is a degree of serenity, of emotion recollected in tranquillity, in *Le Premier Homme*, which indicates that the quest for the father, despite its familiar paradigms, is not repeating the Œdipal traumas of the earlier works.[82] Of course, there is no reason why the quest for the father should necessarily take a Dostoevskian form. After all, there are fathers in Tolstoy and there are adolescents too but the manner of their representation is very different. Camus was very well aware of this, for he claims that Tolstoy never said anything substantially different from Dostoevsky but did so 'd'une manière différente' ['in a different way'].[83] It is really this 'manière différente' which holds the key to *Le Premier Homme* both in general terms and in terms of the quest for the father. Camus is replying to the Dostoevskian underground of *La Chute* and its fatherless hell with Tolstoyan expanse, a sense of being part of the family and generational history, however tentative that sense of belonging may be. It should certainly be noted that even his reading of *L'Adolescent* draws Camus's attention to the difference between Tolstoy and Dostoevsky, for he writes: 'A la fin de *L'Adolescent* (et dans les trois variantes) Dostoïevski fait ironiquement le procès de Tolstoï' ['At the end of *L'Adolescent* (including the three variants) Dostoevsky ironically puts Tolstoy on trial'].[84] And it is possible that, in these closing pages of *L'Adolescent*, to which Camus is referring, where Versilov, the missing father, now reunited with 'the bastard' Arkadi, talks about Tolstoy to his son, Camus found a directive for *Le Premier Homme*. Versilov here tells his son that he realizes that he is seeking 'la beauté' ['beauty'] and he says that Tolstoy can provide it. Versilov states:

> Ce qui me plaît surtout chez cet historiographe de notre noblesse [Tolstoy], ou chez ses héros, c'est justement cette beauté que [tu cherches ou que] tu cherchais. Il prend le noble depuis son enfance et sa jeunesse, il le peint dans sa famille, il suit ses premiers pas dans la ville, ses premières [idées] joies et ses premières larmes, et ainsi de suite, avec une vérité solide et incontestable.
>
> C'est le psychologue de l'âme noble. Mais surtout cela est donné comme incontestable, et on est forcé d'en convenir . . . d'en convenir et d'être jaloux. Oh! quelle jalousie! Il est des enfants offensés dès l'enfance par la laideur de leur père, de leur père et de leur milieu, et qui commencent dès l'enfance à sentir le caractère désordonné et fortuit des fondements de leur existence, l'absence

de formes établies et de tradition familiale. Ceux-là doivent envier mon auteur et ses personnages, et peut-être même les détester. Oh! ce ne sont pas des héros: ce sont de gentils enfants, qui ont d'excellents et gentils pères qui déjeunent au club et tiennent table ouverte à Moscou; les fils aînés sont hussards ou étudiants, avec leur équipage particulier. Mon auteur les dépeint en toute franchise: pris à part, ils sont souvent ridicules et amusants, parfois même insignifiants, mais dans l'ensemble, comme catégorie sociale, ils forment certainement quelque chose d'achevé. Cette couche supérieure de la population russe a déjà un fondement solide et incontestable. Chaque individu peut avoir ses faiblesses et ses ridicules, mais il est soutenu par un tout bien enraciné depuis deux siècles et davantage. Et malgré le réalisme ou la réalité, le ridicule et le comique, il peut y avoir là du touchant et du pathétique.[85]

[What I like more than anything about this historiographer of our nobility (Tolstoy) and about his heroes, is precisely this beauty which (you are seeking or which) you were seeking. He takes the nobleman from infancy and youth, describes his family life, his first steps in society, his first (ideas) joys and tears, and so on, with solid and undoubted truth. He is the psychologist of the soul of the nobility. But above all, it is all presented as incontrovertible and one is forced to accept it, to accept it and be jealous. Oh! what a jealousy it is! There are children who are damaged, from their earliest years, by the ugliness of their fathers, their fathers and their surroundings, children who in their early infancy are exposed to the chaotic and chance nature of their existences, who have no fixed patterns to their lives and are without family traditions. Such people must envy my author and his characters and perhaps they will even hate them. Oh! they are not real heroes: they are nice children, with nice wonderful fathers who dine in clubs and throw endless dinner parties in Moscow; their eldest sons are officers or university students and have their own carriage and horses. My author describes them quite sincerely: taken individually, they are often ridiculous and amusing, sometimes even insignificant, but taken as a group, as a social category, they certainly constitute something complete in itself. This upper echelon of the Russian people has already acquired a solid and unquestionable base. Each individual might be weak or ridiculous, but each is sustained by a whole whose roots go back two centuries or more. And whatever is the realism or reality of these people, their ridiculous or their comic nature, they can be touching and moving.]

Camus's passage from adolescence to maturity was also haunted by this loss of 'beauté', as he makes clear in 'L'Exil d'Hélène'. He also links the loss of Hélène, as we saw in the earlier part of the chapter, to the colonization of European literature by Dostoevsky's underground. *Le Premier Homme* attempts to bring Hélène back from exile and set Camus on a new course away from the underground of turmoil and polemic. If his dialogue with Dostoevsky is not completely over (and it isn't, because he can refer in the text to the mother as 'un Muichkine ignorant' ['a Muichkin who doesn't know it']),[86] it certainly seems to be heading towards a decreased level of intensity, as Camus launches Jacques Cormery, yet another Christ figure (JC), on his epic voyage to be reunited with his past. That Camus is seeking to recast, in a new synthesis, his former humanism and create an alternative vision to Christianity is clear from his projected ending to the book: twice, Camus refers to the fact that 'le Christ n'a pas attéri en Algérie' ['Christ didn't set foot in Algeria'][87] and sketches out the following conclusion to the text:

Fin.
Rendez la terre, la terre qui n'est à personne. Rendez la terre qui n'est ni à vendre ni à acheter (oui et le Christ n'a jamais débarqué en Algérie puisque même les moines y avaient propriété et concessions).
Et il s'écria, regardant sa mère, et puis les autres:
Rendez la terre. Donnez toute la terre aux pauvres, à ceux qui n'ont rien et qui sont si pauvres qu'ils n'ont même jamais désiré avoir et possédér, à ceux qui sont comme elle dans ce pays, l'immense troupe des misérables, la plupart arabes, et quelques-uns français et qui vivent ou survivent ici par obstination et endurance, dans le seul honneur qui vaille au monde, celui des pauvres, donnez-leur la terre comme on donne ce qui est sacré à ceux qui sont sacrés, et moi alors, pauvre à nouveau et enfin, jeté dans le pire exil à la pointe du monde, je sourirai et mourrai content, sachant que sont enfin réunis sous le soleil de ma naissance la terre que j'ai tant aimée et ceux et celle que j'ai révérés.
Alors le grand anonymat deviendra fécond et il me recouvrira aussi—Je reviendrai dans ce pays.[88]

[Conclusion
Give back the land, the land which belongs to no-one. Give back the land which is not to be bought and sold (yes and Christ never came to Algeria, for even the monks there had property and businesses). And he cried out, looking at his mother, and the others: Give back the land. Give all the land to the poor, to those who have nothing and are so poor that they have never even wanted to have or to possess, to those who are like her in this country, the huge gathering of the wretched, most of them Arabs and a few French who live and survive here by determination and endurance,

with the only worthwhile honour that there is in the world, the honour of the poor, give them the land as one gives sacred things to those who are sacred, then I, poor once more, and exiled to the remotest point in the world, I shall at least smile and die contented, knowing that finally the land that I have loved so much, the people and the woman whom I have adored are joined together again beneath the sun that accompanied my birth. Then the great void will become fertile once more and also engulf me—I shall return to this country.]

Here, Camus creates an answer to the Dostoevskian world of *La Chute* but it is done in a language with a new emotional register, one which is breaking free of the 'héritage d'ombres' ['legacy of shadows'] of Dostoevsky.

Conclusion

Throughout this study, the intention has been to explore and to give substance to the 'ébranlement' to which Camus made reference when first encountering the works of Dostoevsky and to analyse the changing patterns of interest and focus in his responses to the Russian writer. The analytical method used has eschewed a traditional, juxtapositional comparative approach but, at the same time, it cannot be said to have followed the fully-fledged Bakhtinian intertextual approach adopted by Dunwoodie with its emphasis on 'l'expression d'un jeu d'intertextes' ['the expression of intertextual interplay'].[1] Instead, using Camus's own statements about Dostoevsky and about particular works by him as points of departure, we have opted for the thesis of a dialogue between the two writers in terms of which points of convergence and divergence are viewed as attempts, by Camus, both to assimilate Dostoevsky's world to his own and to formulate replies to its central challenges in respect of atheism. The study has not stressed influence but the dynamizing and crystallizing impact of Dostoevsky's work on Camus's intellectual formation and development.

The central objective of the book has been to clarify this notion of dialogue in terms of ideas but part of the method used is to discuss these ideas in terms of Dostoevsky's characters and rebels since Camus found, in Dostoevsky, not abstraction and schematization but a magnetic and haunting world of flesh-and-blood characters, engaged dramatically in all the great spiritual problems of existence.

This dialogue between the two writers can be said to have three major phases. In the first, Dostoevsky is, for Camus, the great novelist/philosopher of the absurd, who proclaimed that love of life without immortality is inconceivable and that suicide, madness and abulia are part of the inexorable logic of consciousness without God. Camus's reply in *Le Mythe de Sisyphe* is to create his positive heroes of the absurd, Tzars of hedonistic freedom who recognize death and this world as the only realities. In this phase of his dialogue with Dostoevsky, Camus, principally through his study of Kirilov, endeavours to hijack Dostoevskian notions of grace and epileptic ecstasy, sever their links with Christian philosophy and reroute them through his own pagan, hedonistic individualism. His dominant aim is to create a new race of men and a new Christ figure, no doubt the only one we deserve, whose Kingdom will be entirely of this world and grounded in awareness of death. Whether it be through the evocation of Algerian youth in *Noces* or through the enigmatic statements of Meursault, Camus is determined to show that lucidity and ecstasy are not only compatible but logically interlinked. His new Christ will combine the intensity of Dostoevsky's *condamné* in *L'Idiot*, the serenity and innocence of Muichkine's experience of epilepsy and the independence and indifference to ethical distinctions of Kirilov's Man-God. Camus's early work assimilates Dostoevsky's world and engages it in dialogue to create a new synthesis in which Sisyphus, although tragic, can be happy because he is without hope. The expression of this new synthesis comes in the spiritually triumphant statement: 'Tout est bien'.

The first phase of this dialogue ends with the demise of Camus's early pacifist response to events in Germany and Europe and the advent of war and Nazism. Historical circumstances fracture his hedonism and the individualist framework of his thought and evidently 'tout n'est pas si bien que ça' ['everything is not as alright as it could be'].[2] Camus feels responsible for Nazism but the ethical nihilism of the quantitive imperative of *Le Mythe de Sisyphe* provides no basis for revolt or resistance. Camus must thus seek to define value in an absurd world. Ivan Karamazov's 'Tout est permis' is the amoral paradigm which now occupies a central place in his preoccupations. Dostoevsky's argument is that values cannot be legitimized in a world without God and that non-religious humanism and socialism outside of Christian parameters are doomed to failure. Camus's dialogue with Dostoevsky, in the second place, is to reply by formulating the principles of a lay humanism derived from his notion of revolt. Ivan's revolt and logic are explored in detail to create a second synthesis, which shifts the paradigms of Dostoevsky's world. *Caligula* and *La Peste* best demonstrate how this new synthesis is taking shape in Camus's mind: Caligula will accept responsibility for the monster within him and Rieux's humanism will have no truck with the divine or attempts to rationalize the plague, but will be the voice of true human love and solidarity. Christian humanism, it will be suggested, is a contradiction in terms for God cannot be on our side if he condemns us to be in a world of suffering and death.

It is during this phase of moral deliberation, as the Cold War intensifies, Stalinism tightens its grip and political choice becomes increasingly expressed in polarized terms, that Dostoevsky becomes, for Camus, the prophet of twentieth-century political nihilism and totalitarianism, displacing Marx as the great predictive thinker of our times. *Les Possédés* and Ivan Karamazov's legend of the Grand Inquisitor combine, in Camus's mind, to haunt and underpin the development of his political thought. He draws a distinction between 'le socialisme de liberté' ['socialism of freedom'] and 'le socialisme mystifié' or 'césarien' ['mystified or Caesarian socialism'] and this distinction defines a limit, in moral terms, which will put a break on the absolutist demands of Ivan's 'tout ou rien' revolt and one which, in political terms, will preclude *Realpolitik*. Camus writes *L'Homme révolté* in a continuing state of dialogue with Dostoevsky. He gives both Ivan Karamazov and the political protagonists of *Les Possédés* (Piotr/Nechaev and Chigalev/Hegel/Rousseau) pivotal positions in the conceptual architecture of both major sections of the book. Whilst basically accepting the overall outlines of Dostoevsky's depiction of revolutionary aspiration and political nihilism, it is Camus's determined project to refute the idea that Ivan's revolt necessarily leads to the 'tout est permis', the Grand Inquisitor's paternalism or the demonic revolutionary politics of *Les Possédés*. Once again, as in *Le Mythe de Sisyphe*, Camus, in *L'Homme révolté*, engages Dostoevsky's world in dialogue both to define areas of convergence and gravitational attraction and to designate an alternative pathway out of its logic. 'La pensée de midi' and the politics of authentic revolt will be Camus's reply to Dostoevsky's challenge that either the reality of Christ and God are accepted or that human beings will become ensnared in moral licence or the nihilistic socialism of *Les Possédés*. If love of life and a godless world are the principal focus of Camus's first dialogue with Dostoevsky, love of the other and non-religious values are at the heart of the second. For Dostoevsky, neither love of life nor love of the other can survive without immortality. For Camus, eventually, love of life and love of the other emerge as complementary and both derive their reality from their transitory as distinct from their eternal state.

With the hindsight of composition and the publication of *Le Premier Homme*, a possible third phase and third synthesis can be identified in Camus's dialogue with Dostoevsky, with *La Chute* at its centre. Our reading of this work, the most Dostoevskian that Camus wrote, rests on the assumption that his 'pensée de midi' and his politics of authentic and inauthentic revolt are, if not in crisis, in some difficulty, as Sartre claimed, in the period 1952 to 1956. This means, in terms of his dialogue with Dostoevsky, that Camus's Hellenic reply to Ivan and *Les Possédés* is foundering and that he is, to some extent, being engulfed by Dostoevsky's 'héritage d'ombres' ['legacy of shadows'].[3] Camus, it is suggested, faces this crisis of confidence in his own humanism by introjecting Dostoevsky's world comprehensively in *La Chute* and, like Gide with his protagonists, through Clamence, sheds a skin to be reborn. In this third phase, Camus is not so much debating intellectually with Dostoevsky but rather initiating, with *Le Premier Homme*, which appears to evolve in a relationship of counter-balance with *La Chute*, a new emotional and creative cycle in his work, drawing the larger part of its in-spiration from Tolstoy.

These three phases of dialogue provide the key simultaneously to Camus's initial and lasting 'ébranlement' and to his statements that he was nourished and formed by *Les Possédés*, a statement that could really refer, as we have seen, to Dostoevsky's work in general. Indeed, when Camus claimed in 'Pour Dostoïevski', in 1955, that 'sans Dostoïevski la littérature française du xxème siècle ne serait pas ce qu'elle est' ['without Dostoevsky French twentieth-century literature would not be what it is'], it is tempting to reformulate the hypothesis in terms of Camus's own writing. Similarly, when he says, in his preface to the works of Roger Martin du Gard, that it should be the aim of French novelists to go beyond Dostoevsky and to move from *Les Possédés* to *La Guerre et la paix*, one feels that this ambition is more Camus's than anybody else's because his own world had become so thoroughly engaged with Dostoevsky's and he needed to go beyond it. Finally, if we have isolated, for the purpose of analysis, Dostoevsky from the complex dialectic of authors at work in Camus's writing, this is not to claim his exclusive or even dominant im-portance but it is to give his work a very prominent and perdurable presence.

Whatever the impact of Dostoevsky on twentieth-century French literature through Proust, Gide, Malraux, Mauriac, Sartre and Sarraute, it must surely be claimed that nowhere is this impact more in evidence than in the work of Camus himself. The dialogue with the Russian writer, engaged when Camus was twenty, is a permanent feature of his work. It is propositionally formulated, as we have seen, in his major philosophical works and finds expression in a variety of modes in his novels, plays, political journalism, speeches and literary essays, adding to their intellectual texture, climate and appeal. It is a great and fascinating dialogue in both its range and relevance and I hope that this study will provide access to it for all those who love and live literature.

Notes

Chapter 1

1. F. W. J. Hemmings, *The Russian Novel in France, 1884–1914* (Oxford: University Press, 1950), p. 2. See also *Dostoïevski et les lettres françaises*, Actes du Colloque de Nice, réunis et présentés par Jean Onimus (Nice: Centre du xxème Siècle, 1981) and M. J. L. Backès, 'Dostoïevski en France', (Doctorat d'état, Paris, 1971).

2. In his study of Dostoevsky, Gide explains that he often found, in the Russian writer's work, a means of susbstantiating many of his own major ideas. See A Gide, *Dostoïevski* (Paris: Plon Nourrit et Cie, 1923), p. 252. Sartre has acknowledged that his own brand of existentialism has, as its point of departure, Ivan Karamazov's famous statement that if God does not exist, all is permitted. See J. P. Sartre, *L'Existentialisme est un humanisme* (Paris: Nagel, 1951), p. 36. See also his reference to *Les Possédés* in his essay on Mauriac, *Situations*, I (Paris: Gallimard, 1947), pp. 36–7. Sarraute considers that Dostoevsky's work contains an embryonic form of the type of character psychology which she tries to employ in her own novels. Cf. N. Sarraute, *L'Ere du soupçon* (Paris: Gallimard, 1956), pp. 15–66, *passim*.

3. N Gourfinkel, *Dostoïevski notre contemporain* (Paris: Calmann Lévy, 1961), p. 8.

4. 'Pour Dostoïevski', Pléiade-Théâtre, p. 1878. Unless otherwise stated, references to Camus are to the two volume *Pléiade* edition of his works. For the sake of simplicity, I refer to these throughout as Pléiade-Théâtre (for the first volume) and Pléiade-Essais (for the second).

5. This information was given to Quilliot by Max Pol-Fouchet, one of Camus's literary acquaintances in Algeria. Cf. 'L'Envers et l'endroit: Commentaires', Pléiade-Essais, p. 1173. J. Grenier, *Albert Camus: Souvenirs* (Paris: Gallimard, 1968), p. 84. Also, the two major biographers of Camus, Lottmann and Todd, provide further confirmation of these details. Cf. H.R. Lottmann, *Albert Camus* (Paris: Editions du Seuil, 1978), p. 71 and O. Todd, *Albert Camus: une vie* (Paris:

Gallimard 1996). p. 78 (references to Dostoevsky in Todd are indexed). Neither biography adds very much to our knowledge of Camus's initial reading of Dostoevsky. We do not know who, if anyone, acted as an intermediary between Camus and Dostoevsky. Gide is a possible figure but it is more likely that Camus read Gide on Dostoevsky because of an existing interest than vice-versa. In any case, Dostoevsky does not need an intermediary, for he was well established in French letters by the 1930s.

6. 'Pour Dostoïevski', Pléiade-Théâtre, p. 1879.

7. 'Interview à Paris Théâtre' (1958), Pléiade-Théâtre, pp. 1715–17. Camus also refers to this production of *Les Frères Karamazov* in an interview with Pierre Mazars. Cf. 'En adaptant *Les Possédés* . . .', *Le Figaro Littéraire* (January 24, 1959), 12 and 14.

8. Admittedly, the Dostoevsky chapter was a late replacement for the Kafka essay which was originally there but Camus was already completing a study of Dostoevsky at the time. Cf. below, Chapter 2, p. 15.

9. First published in *Témoins*, Automne, no. 18–19 (1957–58). It can also be found in Pléiade-Théâtre, pp. 1878–80.

10. 'Pour Dostoïevski', Pléiade-Théâtre, p. 1879.

11. The questionnaire was reprinted in Pléiade-Théâtre, pp. 1882–83.

12. 'Prière d'insérer des *Possédés*', Pléiade-Théâtre, p. 1877.

13. Cf. Pierre Blanchar's statement in *Le Figaro* (January 5, 1960).

14. These references are in *Carnets* I, August and December 1938, 118–19 and 141. The three volumes of Camus's *Carnets* were published by Gallimard in 1962 (Volume I, mai 1935–février 1942), 1964 (Volume II, janvier 1942–mars 1951), and 1989 (Volume III, mars 1951–décembre 1959). Hereafter, I refer to these as *Carnets*, I, II and III.

15. Pléiade-Essais, p. 1073.

16. Ibid., p. 1080.

17. Ibid., p. 336 and p. 403.

18. Ibid., p. 793.

19. Ibid., pp. 1131–155.

20. Ibid., pp. 855–56.

21. Clamence says to his interlocutor: 'Je disais aussi, à qui voulait l'entendre, mon regret qu'il ne fût plus possible d'opérer comme un propriétaire russe dont j'admirais le caractère: il faisait fouetter en même temps ceux de ses paysans qui le saluaient et ceux qui ne le saluaient pas pour punir une audace qu'il jugeait dans les deux cas également éffrontée' ['I also used to say, to anybody willing to listen, how much I regretted that it was no longer possible to behave like a Russian landowner whose character I admired: he arranged to have whipped both those of his peasants who did and those who did not salute him to punish an audacity that he considered equally impudent in both cases']. Cf. *La Chute*, Pléiade-Théâtre, p. 1520. The Russian property owner in question is none other than Dostoevsky's father.

This description of him was not written by Dostoevsky himself (Dostoevsky hardly ever refers to his father) but by one of the peasants who worked on the Dostoevskys' Daroveye estate. It is, naturally, very difficult to state precisely where Camus discovered the description of Dostoevsky's father. A possible source is H. Troyat who refers to this characteristic of the father in the biography published in 1948: *Dostoïevski* (Paris: Librairie Arthème Fayard, 1948), p. 70. However, it is possible that Camus learned about it through friends etc.. The full description is most conveniently consulted in D. Magarshack's *Dostoevsky* (London: Secker and Warburg, 1962), p. 19.

22. *Carnets*, III, 29.
23. Ibid., 108
24. Ibid., 216.
25. G. Brée, A. Camus, (New Brunswick: N. J. Rutgers University Press, 1959), p. 197.
26. It is Camus's analysis of Kirilov and of Stavroguine, in *Les Possédés*, which, as we shall see, is most open to this charge. Cf. below, pp. 64–5, 79–83, 85, 87–94, 157.
27. *Le Mythe de Sisyphe*, Pléiade-Essais, p. 186.
28. 'Prière d'insérer des *Possédés*', Pléiade-Théâtre, p. 1877.
29. 'Pour Dostoïevski', Pléiade-Théâtre, p. 1879.
30. It is worth noting A. Herbert's comment in 'Dostoïevski, Camus et l'immortalité de l'âme', *Revue de Littérature Comparée*, LIV, 3 (juillet 1980), 321–35: 'Il est évident que Camus par sa vision du monde et par la disposition de son esprit offrait un champ fertile à la semence que Dostoïevski allait pouvoir y déposer' ['It is obvious that Camus, through his vision of the world and the cast of his mind, would provide a fertile ground for the seeds which Dostoevsky was going to be able to sow there'].
31. The French critic, Jacques Madaule, also found Camus's attraction to Dostoevsky paradoxical, but for different reasons. He considered it odd that a sun-loving Algerian like Camus should express an interest in a Slav like Dostoevsky. However, Madaule goes on to say that it is not very meaningful to find the attraction strange because of these differing racial characteristics of the two writers. Cf. J. Madaule, 'Camus et Dostoïevski', *La Table Ronde*, numéro spécial, no. 146 (février 1960), 127–36. Madaule's remarks, however, do not invalidate the contrasts made above as they are based on differences of ideas between the two writers.
32. 'Roger Martin du Gard', Pléiade-Essais, p. 1131.
33. *Le Dernier Camus ou Le Premier Homme* (Paris: Nizet, 1995), pp. 108–11.
34. I. Kirk, *Dostoevsky and Camus: The Themes of Consciousness, Isolation, Freedom and Love*, (Munich: Wilhelm Fink Verlag, 1974). This is the published version of her earlier thesis: 'Polemics, Ideology, Structure and Texture in A. Camus's *The Fall* and F. *Dostoevsky's Notes from the Underground*', *Dissertation Abstracts* 29: 570, A (Ind., 1968).

35. Ernest Sturm, *Conscience et Impuissance chez Dostoïevski et Camus,* (Paris: Nizet, 1967).

36. *A Kingdom not of this World: A quest for a Christian Ethics of Revolution with reference to the Thought of Dostoevsky, Berdyaev and Camus.* Stanford Honors Essays in Humanities, no. 8, (California: Stanford Press, 1964).

37. Dunwoodie, op. cit., p. 31.

38. Ibid., p. 29.

Chapter 2

1. *Le Mythe de Sisyphe,* Pléiade-Essais, p. 189.

2. Ibid., p. 180.

3. Ibid., p. 181.

4. Louis Faucon writes in '*Le Mythe de Sisyphe*: Commentaires', Pléiade-Essais, p. 1415: 'On peut penser que les autorités dont dépendaient le visa et le papier n'eussent pas laissé publier l'éloge d'un écrivain tchèque israélite dont les évocations ambiguës d'un univers écrasé par l'arbitraire et la terreur prêtaient à des applications d'actualité. Veto exprès ou précaution de rigueur, la nécessité d'écarter Kafka fut signifiée à Camus' ['It can be assumed that the authorities responsible for granting the visa and the use of the paper would not have allowed the publication of an article praising a Jewish Czech writer whose ambiguous evocations of a world crushed by arbitrary power and terror lent themselves to contemporary applications. Whether by explicit veto or as a necessary precaution, the need to remove the Kafka study was pointed out to Camus'].

5. Pléiade-Essais, pp. 201–11.

6. Faucon argues that Camus, as is clear from the *Carnets,* was preparing himself for a study on Dostoevsky. Camus did not change the arrangement of the texts when evolving circumstances made this possible. (Cf. L. Faucon, Pléiade- Essais p. 1413). Perhaps it is worth noting that Camus's decision to leave the Dostoevsky study in the place intended for Kafka may have been motivated by the fact that Dostoevsky's works provide a better illustration of a betrayal than Kafka's. Dostoevsky's betrayal is easy to establish but Camus seems unable to decide whether *The Castle* does actually constitute a departure from the absurd.

7. *Le Mythe de Sisyphe,* Pléiade-Essais, p. 180.

8. *Journal d'un écrivain,* pp. 371–73. Camus uses Jean Chuzeville's translation of the *Journal.* This was first published in three volumes by Gallimard in 1927. It was republished in a single volume by Gallimard in 1938 and a further edition of the same translation appeared in 1951, again by Gallimard. My references are to the 1951 edition but the translation in all three editions is the same. Hereafter, I shall refer to the edition as the *Journal d'un écrivain.*

9. *Le Mythe de Sisyphe,* Pléiade-Essais, p. 185.

10. Ibid., p. 186.
11. Ibid., p. 186.
12. *Journal d'un écrivain*, p. 416 and p. 419.
13. Ibid., p. 422 and *Le Mythe de Sisyphe*, Pléiade-Essais, p. 186.
14. *Les Frères Karamazov*, III, 299, and *Le Mythe de Sisyphe*, Pléiade-Essais, p. 186. I am using the same edition and translation as Camus of *Les Frères Karamazov*: *Les Frères Karamazov*, 3 vols., Traduit du russe par Henri Mongault et Marc Laval (Paris: Éditions Bossard, 1923).
15. *Le Mythe de Sisyphe*, Pléiade-Essais, p. 187.
16. Ibid., p. 187.
17. The absurd work of art is a fictional account of what was, for Camus, the essential relationship between man and the world—the absurd, born of 'cette confrontation entre l'appel humain et le silence déraisonnable du monde' ['this confrontation between the appeals of humanity and the unreasonable silence of the world'] (ibid., pp. 117–118). It depicts this 'drame de l'intelligence' ['this drama of the intelligence'], as Camus calls it. Ibid., p. 176.
18. Cf. ibid., p. 176: '[L'œuvre absurde] ne peut être la fin, le sens et la consolation d'une vie. Créer ou ne pas créer, cela ne change rien. Le créateur absurde ne tient pas à son œuvre' ['(The absurd work) cannot be the justification and consolation of a life. To create or not to create, this changes nothing at all. The absurd creator does not attach importance to his work'].
19. Cf. ibid., p. 173: 'Créer, c'est vivre deux fois' ['To create is to live twice']. See also P. Thody, *Albert Camus 1913-1960*, p. 152: 'in *Le Mythe de Sisyphe* . . . artistic creation is simply another attempt to get the most out of life.'
20. Camus says, of Kafka's work, in *Le Mythe de Sisyphe*, p. 265: 'Je reconnais donc ici une œuvre absurde dans ses principes. Pour *Le Procès*, par exemple, je peux bien dire que la réussite est totale' ['I thus recognize here an absurd work in all its axioms. As far as *The Trial* is concerned, for example, I can readily say that its success is total']. However, even with Kafka, Camus does not successfully communicate to the reader what he means by the absurd novel, a point made by P. Thody, op. cit., p. 153.
21. For further discussion of the history of *Les Possédés*, see K. Mochulsky, *Dostoevsky*, Translated with an Introduction by M.A. Minihan (Princeton: University Press, 1967), pp. 465–66. Among other things, Mochulsky observes: '*The Devils* was conceived as a vast iron diptych: in opposition to the dark panel was set a light one; in opposition to the demonic personality a "positively beautiful individual". The Christian ideal of beauty is embodied in Bishop Tikhone whose image Dostoevsky had "long ago taken to his heart with enthusiasm". By the deletion of the chapter, "At Tikhone's", this concept was destroyed and only the dark panel of the diptych remained: the picture of hell, of universal ruin, of the raging of the demonic sandstorm.'

22. *Le Mythe de Sisyphe*, Pléiade-Essais, p. 187.
23. Ibid., p. 133.
24. Ibid., p. 187.
25. Ibid., p. 180. It is the fact that this quotation appears just before the Dostoevsky study which makes me think it refers specifically to Dostoevsky and not the other Christian existentialists analysed in *Le Mythe de Sisyphe*. It is also possible that Camus was thinking of himself when making the remark—as though he secretly felt that one day he too would fall victim to illusion of some sort.
26. Miriam T. Sajkovic, *Dostoevsky: his image of man* (Pennsylvania: University Press, 1962), p. 164.
27. *Le Mythe de Sisyphe*, Pléiade-Essais, pp. 186–87. It is because of this basic difference between Camus's response to the rebels and to their creator that I have chosen to devote certain chapters to his relationship with the rebels.
28. Ibid., p. 187.
29. Ibid., p. 177.
30. This remark was made by Dostoevsky in a letter, written in 1870. *Correspondance de Dostoïevski*, IV, 163. I am using the following edition of Dostoevsky's letters: *Correspondance de Dostoïevski*, 4 Vols., Traduction, introduction et notes de Dominique Arban et Nina Gourfinkel (Paris: Calmann- Lévy, 1949-1961). Henceforth, I refer to the letters simply as *Correspondance* I etc..
31. *Le Mythe de Sisyphe*, Pléiade-Essais, p. 187.
32. Ibid., p.187 The article by Boris de Schlœzer, to which Camus makes reference, is in *Mesures* (octobre 15, 1935) and is called 'Les Brouillons des *Frères Karamazov*'.
33. *Correspondance*, I, 157.
34. G. Strem, 'The theme of rebellion in the works of Camus and Dostoevsky', *Revue de Littérature Comparée*, X1, no. 1 (1966), 246–57 (this quotation is 249–50).
35. Dunwoodie, op. cit., pp. 166–67. Dunwoodie's quotations about irrefutable culminating points are taken from the *Pléiade* edition of *Les Frères Karamazov*, pp. xx–xxi. See Bibliography.
36. E.H. Carr, *Dostoevsky, 1821–1881* (London: Unwin Books, 1962), p. 219.
37. *Correspondance*, I, 157.
38. Ibid., III, 178.
39. Ibid., I, 157.
40. The whole problem of Dostoevsky, faith and epilepsy is explored by J. Frank, *Dostoevsky: The Years of Ordeal, 1850–1859*, (Princeton, 1983) pp. 194–96. Frank claims that epilepsy is not at the root of Dostoevsky's faith but that his religious susceptibilities were 'immensely enhanced by his epileptic seizures'. Frank also makes some interesting points about the ecstatic, 'aura' dimensions of Dostoevsky's epilepsy and questions the validity of Zaëhner's belief that it is a 'natural' mystical experience.

41. Dostoevsky describes the sensation fully in *L'Idiot*, when Muichkine, also a victim of the 'holy madness', is on the verge of an attack. Dostoevsky observes: 'Au milieu de l'abattement, du marasme mental, de l'anxiété qu'éprouvait le malade, il y avait des moments où son cerveau s'enflammait tout à coup, pour ainsi dire, et où toutes ses forces vitales atteignaient subitement un degré prodigieux d'intensité. La sensation de la vie, de l'existence consciente, était presque décuplée dans ces instants rapides comme l'éclair. Une clarté extraordinaire illuminait l'esprit et le cœur. Toutes les agitations se calmaient; tous les doutes, toutes les perplexités se résolvaient d'emblée en une harmonie supérieure, en une tranquillité sereine et joyeuse, pleinement rationelle et motivée' ['In the midst of the depression, the mental stagnation and the anxiety experienced by the sick person, there were moments when his mind suddenly burst into flames, so to speak, and when all his vital forces suddenly acquired an extraordinary degree of intensity. The sensation of life itself, of conscious existence was multiplied almost tenfold in these moments which flashed past with lightning rapidity. An extraordinary clarity illuminated mind and heart. All his agitations left him, all doubts and confusions were resolved immediately in a superior harmony, in a serene and joyful tranquility, fully rational and intelligible']. *L'Idiot*, I, 296–7. I am using the following edition: *L'Idiot*, 2 vols., Traduit du russe par Victor Derély et précédé d'une préface par Melchior de Vogüe (Paris: Plon, 1887).
42. Cf. below, Chapter 5.
43. *Le Mythe de Sisyphe*, Pléiade-Essais, p. 188.
44. Ibid., p. 188.
45. Ibid., p. 187.

Chapter 3

1. This was established in Chapter 2: cf. above, pp. 15–16, n. 8 and n. 12. Cf. also *Le Mythe de Sisyphe*, Pléiade-Essais, p. 182 and p. 186. 'Moralité un peu tardive' is divided into two sections, the latter part being entitled 'Assertions mal fondées' ['Ill-founded assertions']. Here, Dostoevsky uses one of his favourite expositional techniques which involves making highly penetrating assertions without substantiating them by argument.
2. M. T. Sajkovic, *Dostoevsky: his image of man*, p. 150.
3. Jean Onimus, *Camus: face au mystère* (Bruges: Desclée de Brouwer, 1965), p. 21, makes the claim that Camus's early 'métaphysique' in significant measure is rooted in Dostoevsky but identifies Kirilov as the major inspirational source, without referring to the *Journal*. G. Strem (loc. cit.) has made the point that Camus's work in general 'seems to have been conceived in a personal, most fertile debate with the Russian novelist'. However, Strem does not develop this idea in any detail, nor does he attempt to show in what respect *Le Mythe de*

Sisyphe is related to the idea of debate. Nevertheless, he does mention the importance of 'The Verdict' ['Jugement'] in *Le Mythe de Sisyphe*, arguing that Camus's ideas on logical suicide 'originate' in this letter and that it 'gave Camus the clue to his theory of the absurd'. Neither point is explored in any depth or detail or given any specific formulation. Dunwoodie has little to say on either 'Jugement' or 'Moralité un peu tardive'. Cf. op. cit., pp. 165–66.

4. 'Moralité un peu tardive', *Journal d'un écrivain*, p. 422.
5. Ibid., p. 138.
6. Ibid., p. 197.
7. Two articles which should be noted concerning this aspect of Camus's early work are: D. H. Walker, 'The Early Camus—a Reconsideration', *The Philosophical Journal*, II, no. 2 (1965), 91–103, and A. Blanchet, 'Pari d'Albert Camus', *Études*, no.5 (mai 1960), 183–99. The latter article is very hostile but the critic's awareness of and sensivity towards anti-Christian themes in Camus is intensified by his own Christian sensibility.
8. Cf. 'Pour Dostoïevski', Pléiade-Théâtre, p. 1879 and *Le Mythe de Sisyphe*, Pléiade-Essais, p. 186.
9. Ibid., p. 187.
10. Cf. above, p. 27, n. 3.
11. Murder occupies Camus more than suicide in the revolt period, although the suicide theme is not entirely absent: a young girl commits suicide in *La Chute*, as does the nihilist, Nada, in *L'État de siège*. For a discussion of this transition from the suicide to the murder theme in the revolt period, see E. Mounier, 'Albert Camus ou l'appel des humiliés', *Esprit*, xviiième année, no. 163 (janvier 1950), 27–66.
12. Both Martha and her mother kill themselves.
13. Camus asserted that Caligula's death was not to be seen so much as an assassination as 'un suicide supérieur'. Cf. 'Préface à l'édition américaine du théâtre', Pléiade-Théâtre, p. 1728.
14. 'La Mort dans l'âme', Pléiade-Essais, p. 35.
15. *Carnets*, I, 25.
16. *Actuelles*, I, Pléiade-Essais, p. 380.
17. R. Quilliot, '*L'Homme révolté*: Commentaires', Pléiade-Essais, p. 1609.
18. P. Thody, op. cit., p. 57. The presence of suicide in Camus's plays could also be viewed as an exploitation of the dramatic potential of the theme, rather than as an expression of a personal preoccupation with the idea.
19. Camus says: 'Je ne dirai pas autre chose que mon amour de vivre. Mais je le dirai à ma façon' ['I shall speak of nothing other than my love of life. But I shall speak of it in my own fashion']. (*Carnets*, I, 25) It could, therefore, be argued that suicide is part of this 'façon' and, as a theme, constitutes a device which enables Camus to emphasize by contrast his desire to live. This, in one sense, is obviously the case in *Le Mythe de Sisyphe*, which declares suicide to be inconsistent with the imperatives of the absurd.

20. L. Faucon, 'Le Mythe de Sisyphe: Commentaires', Pléaide-Essais, p. 1412.
21. Carnets, I, 33–34.
22. When Camus's character says: 'Ma joie n'a pas de prix' ['My joy is priceless'], is it because he realises the revolver gives him the power to end his life at will and thereby escape the laws of nature, or because he discovers Camus's own secret that the inevitability of death makes life more precious? He commits suicide eventually but after more disillusionment (cf. Carnets, I, 34).
23. See R. Quilliot's note in Carnets, I, 33, n. 1.
24. Le Mythe de Sisyphe, Pléiade-Essais, p. 103.
25. Cf. above, p.32, n. 21.
26. 'Le Songe d'un homme ridicule', Journal d'un écrivain, p. 566.
27. Ibid., pp. 512–29.
28. Whilst it is not relevant to the argument developed here, possible confirmation that Camus was familiar with this story is discussed in the next chapter in the context of Camus's claim that Dostoevsky's heroes are modern because they do not fear ridicule. Cf. below, p. 47.
29. 'Jugement', Journal d'un écrivain, p. 371.
30. Le Mythe de Sisyphe, Pléiade-Essais, pp. 106–7.
31. 'Jugement', Journal d'un écrivain, p. 371.
32. Ibid., p. 373.
33. Le Mythe de Sisyphe, Pléiade-Essais, p. 101.
34. 'Jugement', Journal d'un écrivain, p. 371.
35. Ibid., p. 372.
36. Le Mythe de Sisyphe, Pléiade-Essais, pp. 117–18.
37. Ibid., p. 110.
38. 'Jugement', Journal d'un écrivain, p. 372.
39. Le Mythe de Sisyphe, Pléiade-Essais, p. 109.
40. Le Malentendu, Pléiade-Théâtre, p. 179.
41. Ibid., p. 171.
42. 'Jugement', Journal d'un écrivain, p. 371 (Dostoevsky's italics).
43. Ibid., p. 372.
44. Ibid., p. 373.
45. I shall have more to say on Camus's interest in Dostoevsky as a general source of dramatic material in Chapter 8, when the adaptation of Les Possédés is in question. It is worthy of note that one of Camus's most Dostoevskian creations is a woman when Camus himself appears only to be interested in the Russian writer's male characters. It is also interesting that this character resembles Dostoevsky's male atheists and is nothing like any of his female characters.
46. Le Mythe de Sisyphe, Pléiade-Essais, p. 109.

Chapter 4

1. Le Mythe de Sisyphe, Pléiade-Essais, p. 186.
2. Cf. 'Prière d'insérer des Possédés', Pléiade-Théâtre, p. 1877.

3. See 'Non, je ne suis pas existentialiste', Interview with Jeanine Delpech, *Les Nouvelles Littéraires* (novembre 15, 1945), Pléiade-Essais, pp. 1424–27. See also the *Carnets*, II, 129–30, 'Sens de mon œuvre etc'.

4. A. J. Ayer, 'Novelist-Philosophers', *Horizon*, XIII (March 1946), 155–68.

5. *Journal d'un écrivain*, p. 419.

6. Cf. *Correspondance*, I, 157.

7. Ibid., IV, 163.

8. Cf. H. Troyat's remarks in his biography of Dostoevsky: 'Fédor Mikhaïlovitch n'a jamais connu la foi bien assise, l'amour étal qu'il ne cesse d'appeler sur lui. Il veut croire. Mais une lucidité démoniaque le retient au bord de la grâce. Il s'interroge, il interroge les textes. Il discute au lieu d'accepter.' ['Feodor Mikhalovitch never knew very secure faith, the secure love that he increasingly calls for. He wants to believe. But a diabolical lucidity keeps him on the edge of grace. He questions himself, he questions the texts. He debates instead of accepting.'] H. Troyat, *Dostoïevski*, p. 235.

9. Cf. 'Roger Martin du Gard', Pléiade-Essais, p. 1151 and p. 1154. Camus is, of course, discussing du Gard's works from a broadly aesthetic viewpoint in this preface but the comparison between Martin du Gard's heroes and Dostoevsky's rebels is not based on aesthetic considerations.

10. 'Pour Dostoïevski', Pléiade-Théâtre, p. 1879.

11. 'Manifeste du *Théâtre de L'Équipe*', Pléiâde-Théâtre, pp. 1689–90.

12. *Carnets*, I, 118–19.

13. Ibid., 141.

14. Cf. Review of *La Nausée*, Pléiade-Essais, p. 1417, and his statement in *Carnets*, I, 23: 'On ne pense que par images . . .' ['One thinks only by images . . .']

15. See, in particular, *Le Mythe de Sisyphe*, Pléiade-Essais, p. 178, where Camus discusses philosophy and the novel.

16. R. M. Albérès, 'Albert Camus dans son siècle: témoin et étranger', *Table Ronde*, Numéro Spécial, No. 146 (février 1960), 9–15. Dunwoodie, op. cit., p. 160.

17. *Le Mythe de Sisyphe*, Pléiade-Essais, p. 182. Camus refers to 'l'abîme de Dostoïevski' in *Carnets*, II, 35 (an entry for August 1942).

18. Cf. *Les Possédés*, II, 407. I am using the same edition and translation of the work as Camus in *Le Mythe de Sisyphe: Les Possédés*. Traduit du russe par Victor Derély, 2 vols. (Paris: Plon, 1886).

19. 'Le Songe d'un homme ridicule', *Journal d'un écrivain*, pp. 512–29.

20. André Blanchet, 'Pari d'Albert Camus' *Études*, No. 5 (mai 1960), 183–99.

21. A cynical thinker who is believed to have burnt himself to death at the AD 165 Olympic games.

22. A nineteenth-century French philosopher (1814–62) who disappeared mysteriously at sea.

23. *Le Mythe de Sisyphe*, Pléiade-Essais, p. 102.
24. Ibid., p. 102.
25. Ibid., p. 113.
26. Ibid., p. 113.
27. *Les Possédés*, ll, 334, Camus retained this statement in his adaptation of the novel: see *Les Possédés*, Pléiade-Théâtre, p. 1167. For the adaptation, Camus used a different edition and translation of the novel: *Les Démons, Carnets des Démons, Les Pauvres Gens*. Traduction de Boris de Schlœzer (Paris: Gallimard, 1955). *Les Démons* is an alternative and apparently superior translation of the title of *Les Possédés*, but although Camus changed his edition, he kept Derély's translation of the title.
28. Cf. *Le Mythe de Sisyphe*, Pléiade-Essais, p. 121.
29. Mochulsky, *Dostoevsky*, p. 445. Mochulsky's italics.
30. *Les Frères Karamazov*, III, 49.
31. *L'Homme révolté*, Pléiade-Essais, p. 467.
32. *Les Possédés*, I, 28.
33. Ibid., I, 30–31.
34. Ibid., I, 295.
35. Ibid., I, 108, 113.
36. N. Gourfinkel, *Dostoïevski Notre Contemporain*, p. 170.
37. G. Steiner, *Tolstoy or Dostoevsky* (London: Faber & Faber, 1959) p. 154.
38. *Les Frères Karamazov*, II, 60.
39. Cf. *Correspondance*, II, 113, 228. (Lettres à Mme Zagouliaeva et à Wrangel).
40. *Correspondance*, I, 136–9.
41. *L'Idiot*, Traduction de Victor Derély, 2 vols. (Paris: Plon 1887). This reference, l, 76.
42. Ibid., II, 119.
43. *Journal d'un écrivain*, 287.
44. *Carnets*, I, 23.
45. 'La vie est courte et c'est péché que de perdre son temps' ['Life is short and it's a sin to waste one's time']. *Carnets*, I, 22.
46. *Carnets*, II, 276. Camus is evidently referring to Aliocha's statement to Ivan, *Les Frères Karamazov*, I, 348–9.
47. 'Roger Martin du Gard', Pléiade-Essais, p. 1154. As a matter of interest, it is worth recalling that love of life not only provides a key to Camus's attraction to Kirilov and Ivan but helps also to explain his attraction to Martin du Gard's heroes. See n. 9.
48. *Les Frères Karamazov*, I, 347.
49. Ibid., I, 348.
50. Cf. *Les Possédés*, l, 256–8.
51. Cf. *Le Mythe de Sisyphe*, Pléiade-Essais, p. 184 (Kirilov) and *L'Homme révolté*, Ibid p. 467 (Ivan).
52. *Les Possédés*, I, 26.
53. See in particular E. Sellin, 'Meursault and Mychkin on execution: a parallel', *Romance Notes* (Autumn 1968), 11–14, A. Herbert,

'Dostoïevski et l'immortalité de l'âme' *Revue de Littérature Comparée*, No. 215 (juillet–septembre 1980), 321–35 and Eugene Eiche's PhD thesis 'Les personnages dostoïevskiens dans *L'Étranger*', Stansford University 1968. Dunwoodie also deals with the theme of execution at some length in a separate section of his work called 'L'Echafaud' (op. cit., pp. 47–60).

54. *Le Mythe de Sisyphe*, Pléiade-Essais, pp. 138–39.

55. There is a reference to it in *Le Mythe de Sisyphe*, Pléiade-Essais, p. 186. Camus never actually quotes from *L'Idiot* so it is impossible to establish which translation and edition he read of this work. However, I am using the Derély translation, 2 vols. (Paris: Plon, 1887) as I consider this to be the one Camus is most likely to have read (it should be recalled that he read the Derély translation of *Les Possédés*).

56. Cf. above, n. 53.

57. *L'Idiot*, I, 25–6. Dostoevsky's italics.

58. The parallels between Camus and Meursault on capital punishment are conveniently examined in *L'Étranger*, Pléiade-Théâtre, p. 1200.

59. Ibid., p. 1200.

60. Ibid., p. 1204.

61. *L'Idiot*, I, 76.

62. Ibid., I, 26.

63. *L'Étranger*, Pléiade-Théâtre, pp. 1200–01.

64. Ibid., p. 1202.

65. Cf. *Carnets*, I, 24.

66. Ibid., I, 141–2.

67. Camus's preoccupation with and fear of capital punishment have their original psychological roots, or so Camus would have us believe, in the oft-cited account of a public execution given by his father to his mother and later related by her to her son. References to this episode occur repeatedly throughout Camus's work and culminate in *Le Premier Homme* (pp. 78–81). Here Jacques Corméry reveals that, throughout his life, he has been haunted by the idea that he will be taken away and executed and that this 'cauchemar privilégié' ['privileged nightmare'] was caused by the father's account. The development of this haunting into a metaphysical and moral leitmotif in Camus's work passes through the agency of his dialogue with Dostoevsky.

68. Dunwoodie, as stated, also explores the intertextual dialogue between the two writers on the question of capital punishment. Whilst denying the possibility of establishing influence or even 'filiation' as a matter of principle, he states: 'dans la mesure où l'œuvre de Camus évoque inlassablement le monde contemporain—et la condition humaine elle-même—comme "le monde du condamné à mort", on est en effet tenté d'y lire un cas d'appropriation, de réarticulation, de refonte intertextuelles de cette œuvre russe'['to the extent that Camus's work tirelessly evokes the contemporary world—and the human condition itself—as "the world of the man condemned to death", one is indeed

tempted to read it as a case of intertextual appropriation, restatement and reworking of this Russian work']. (op. cit., 50).

69. Loc. cit., 9. In this article, Albérès remarks also: 'Une bonne part du premier Camus naît du passage de *L'Idiot* où Muichkine évoque l'absurde lucidité du condamné à mort' ['A good part of the early Camus originates in that passage of *L'Idiot* where Muichkin discusses the absurd lucidity of the man condemned to death']. He does not, however, develop this or discuss the parallels mentioned above.

70. R. M. Batchelor, 'Dostoevsky and Camus: similarities and contrasts'. *Journal of European Studies*, V, June 1975, 111–51.

71. *Noces*, Pléiade-Essais, p. 75. See also *Carnets*, I, 120: 'Accroître le bonheur d'une vie d'homme, c'est étendre le tragique de son témoignage. L'œuvre d'art (si elle est un témoignage) vraiment tragique doit être celle de l'homme heureux. Parce que cette œuvre d'art sera tout entière soufflée par la mort' ['To augment the happiness of a man's life is to enlarge the tragic dimension of his testimony. The truly tragic work of art (if it is a testimony) must be that of the happy man. Because this work of art will be entirely shot through with death'].

Chapter 5

1. Cf. above, p. 4, n. 7.
2. Camus (Paris, 1963), p. 17 and p. 59.
3. See Bibliography, pp. 229–30.
4. Ervin C. Brody, 'Dostoevsky's Kirilov in Camus's *Le Mythe de Sisyphe*', *Modern Language Review*, Vol. 70, No. 2 (April 1975), 291–305.
5. Julie Vincent, 'Le Mythe de Kirilov', *Comparative Literature Studies*, V. 111, No. 3 (Sept. 1971), 245–53.
6. Dunwoodie, op. cit., p. 161. Dunwoodie does not focus in any great detail on Kirilov and this section of his work is uncharacteristically sketchy.
7. *Le Mythe de Sisyphe*, Pléiade-Essais, p. 185.
8. R. Hingley, *The Undiscovered Dostoevsky* (London: Hamish Hamilton, 1962), pp. 160–61.
9. Ibid., p. 161.
10. Cf. R. Curle, *Characters of Dostoevsky* (London: Heinemann, 1950), p. 166 and p. 169.
11. Cf. above, n. 4.
12. *Le Mythe de Sisyphe*, Pléiade-Essais, p. 197.
13. Ibid., p. 185.
14. Ibid., p. 183.
15. Ibid., p. 183.
16. Ibid., p. 183.
17. Ibid., p. 185 and *Les Possédés*, II, 338–39 (Dostoevsky's italics).
18. Cf. above, n. 13.

19. *Les Possédés*, I, 111.
20. Ibid., I, 111.
21. Ibid., I, 111.
22. Ibid., I, 112.
23. Ibid., II, 336.
24. Ibid., I, 112.
25. Ibid., I, 111.
26. Ibid., II, 338–9.
27. Ibid., I, 257. Camus quotes this: *Le Mythe de Sisyphe*, Pléiade-Essais, p.184.
28. *Les Possédés*, I, 258.
29. *Les Possédés*, II, 305.
30. *Le Mythe de Sisyphe*, Pléiade-Essais, p. 183.
31. Ibid., pp. 139–40.
32. Ibid., pp. 139–42.
33. Ibid., p. 184.
34. Ibid., p. 149.
35. J. C. Marek, 'L'Absence de Dieu et la révolte: Camus et Dostoïevski', *La Revue de l'Université Laval*, X, no.6 (février 1956), 490–510.
36. *Carnets*, I, 141.
37. *Le Mythe de Sisyphe*, Pléiade-Essais, pp. 184–5.
38. R. Quilliot, *La Mer et les Prisons* (Paris: Gallimard, 1956), p. 31.
39. *L'Envers et l'endroit*, Pléiade-Essais, p. 16.
40. In 'Le Vent à Djemila', Camus tells us of 'le grand effort de l'homme qui est de se dérober à la certitude de mourir tout entier' ['the great striving of man which is to escape from the certainty of death as final']. *Noces*, Pléiade-Essais, p. 64.
41. Cf. above, pp. 28–9.
42. *Noces*, Pléiade-Essais, p. 64.
43. Cf. *Noces*, Pléiade-Essais, p. 72.
44. Ibid., p. 76.
45. Ibid., p. 73.
46. There is evidently an element of stoicism in the attitude of Camus and Kirilov here. They are both determined to bear their destiny without giving in to despair or fear. However, they both go beyond stoicism since they do not aim at spiritual tranquillity by detachment, but actually go out and challenge fear with a forceful assertion of self. Some interesting observations on the stoical elements in Camus's philosophy can be found in Antonio Fouton's article: 'Camus entre le Paganisme et le Christianisme', *Table Ronde*, Numéro spécial, no.146 (février 1960), 114–15, and Jean Batt's 'Albert Camus: from *The Myth* to *The Fall*', *Meanjin*, XV1, no.4 (Summer 1957), 411–19. Batt argues that the values of clearsightedness and tenacity praised in *Le Mythe de Sisyphe* represent a revival of the Ancient Stoic ideal of the 'virtuous man'. See also, for a general picture, R. Champigny's *Sur un héros païen* (Paris: Gallimard, 1959).
47. *Caligula*, Pléiade-Théâtre, p. 16.

48. Ibid., p. 16.
49. Ibid., p. 23.
50. Ibid., p. 27.
51. Cf. Caligula's attitude to Mereia and to Le Vieux Patricien. Ibid., p. 68.
52. Cf. 'Préface à L'Edition Américain du Théâtre', Pléiade-Théâtre, p. 1728 and to *Le Mythe de Sisyphe*, Pléiade-Essais, p. 183.
53. Ibid., pp. 16–17 and *Les Possédés*, I, 108.
54. *Le Mythe de Sisyphe*, Pléiade-Essais, p. 197.
55. Ibid., p. 183.
56. *Les Possédés*, I, 258.
57. *Carnets*, I, 59. The words 'porter sa lucidité dans l'extase' are repeated on p. 84, so Camus was obviously much involved with the idea at the time.
58. *Le Mythe de Sisyphe*, Pléiade-Essais, p. 185 and p. 197.
59. Ibid., p. 197, where Camus explicitly links Kirilov's 'tout est bien' to the Greeks.
60. Camus discusses Œdipus's 'tout est bien' on p. 197 and the case of Sisyphus on p. 198.
61. Cf. *La Peste*, Pléiade-Théâtre, p .1445.
62. *Le Mythe de Sisyphe*, Pléiade-Essais, p. 197. The satisfaction achieved by these men springs partly from the awareness that man can morally master his destiny. Approached from this angle of reconciliation, rather than from the idea of will, it is easy to see why Camus was attracted to the Man-God, since Kirilov's attitude embraces the idea that man is capable of a form of victory over his fate. What pleases Camus most about the Greeks and Kirilov is their courage and virile persistence in the face of hardship; they boldly face the reality of their fate and resemble Stendhal's Cardinal Caraffa, whose bravery before his executioner Camus refers to in *Noces*. At the root of Camus's and Kirilov's attitude to destiny lies the previously mentioned question of authenticity, a question to which they frequently return. Both are concerned that their actions should be wedded consistently and honestly to their ideas. Camus mentions Kirilov early on in *Le Mythe de Sisyphe* as one of the few philosophers who act in accordance with their awareness (p. 102), and he included in his adaptation of *Les Possédés* Kirilov's important speech beginning: 'Toute ma vie, j'ai voulu que ce ne fussent pas des mots . . . ['All my life, I have willed that it wouldn't be words']. *Les Possédés*, II, p. 334.
63. Cf. *L'Envers et l'endroit*, Pléiade-Essais, p. 6.
64. Ibid., p. 22.
65. At Djémila, for example, Camus remarks: 'Oui, je suis présent. Et ce qui me frappe à ce moment, c'est que je ne peux aller plus loin. Comme un homme emprisonné à perpétuité—et tout lui est présent' ['Yes, I am present. And what strikes me at this moment is that I cannot go any further. Like a man serving a life-sentence for whom all time is present time']. *Noces*, Pléiade-Essais, p. 63.

66. Ibid., p. 63.
67. *Les Possédés*, II, 303–4.
68. *Le Mythe de Sisyphe*, Pléiade-Essais, p. 183.
69. Ibid., p. 183.
70. *Noces*, Pléiade-Essais, pp. 62–3.
71. It is also possible that Camus was unconsciously echoing Muichkine in *L'Étranger* when Meursault observes that even if he had to spend the rest of his life in a dry tree-trunk, he would not mind. Cf. *L'Étranger*, Pléiade-Théâtre, p. 1178.
72. Cf. C. Gadourek, *Les Innocents et les coupables* (The Hague: Mouton, 1963), p. 30.
73. Cf. Ervin C. Brody, 'The Mask and the Substance', *Neohelicon III*, 3–4 (1975), 121–70.
74. R. Hingley, *The Undiscovered Dostoevsky*, p. 158.
75. J. Marek, loc. cit., 496.
76. G. Steiner, *Tolstoy or Dostoevsky*, p. 213.
77. Chatov constantly castigates Stavroguine for his malevolent influence.
78. Dostoevskian criticism does not dispute that Stavroguine is the centre of the philosophical structure of the novel.
79. K. Molchulsky, *Dostoevsky* (Princeton, 1967), p. 213.
80. *Les Possédés*, II, 334.
81. Camus does notice Kirilov's reference to his fatal dichotomy of mind and heart but loses sight of it completely in his desire to project a positive image of the character. Cf. *Le Mythe de Sisyphe*, Pléiade-Essais, p. 183ff.
82. G. Strem, loc. cit., 249.
83. *Les Possédés*, I, 259. Stavroguine here tells Kirilov that he suspects the engineer will soon believe in God.
84. Cf. ibid., II, 42–3 and particularly Fédka's speech, II, 265–66.
85. A. Herbert, 'Dostoïevski, Camus et l'immortalité de l'âme', *Revue de Littérature Comparée*, LIV, 3 (juillet–septembre 1980), 321–35.
86. Brody, 'Dostoevsky's Kirilov in Camus's *Le Mythe de Sisyphe*', *Modern Language Review*, Vol. 70, No. 2 (April 1975), 291–305.
87. *Les Possédés*, II, 304.
88. *Dostoïevski* (Paris: Plon, 1923), p. 191.
89. *Le Mythe de Sisyphe* pp. 186–7. Camus describes Muichkine's faith as 'ambigu', although he represents for Dostoevsky a Christ-figure.
90. Ibid., p. 188.
91. 'Pari d'Albert Camus', *Etudes*, no.5 (mai 1960), 183–99.
92. *Albert Camus, 1913–60* (London, 1960), p. 37, and p. 45.
93. He noticed that Meursault's calmness was similar to Muichkine's. Cf. *Situations*, I (Paris, 1947), 104, 113.
94. See also on this P. de Boisdeffre, 'Albert Camus ou l'expérience tragique', *Etudes*, no.12 (déc. 1950), 306.
95. For further discussion of these two epileptic states, see Mochulsky, op. cit., pp. 499ff.
96. Dunwoodie sees the ending of *L'Étranger* as a clear intertextual reply

to *L'Idiot* (op. cit., p. 41) ' dans la mesure où la conscience absurde lucide et le bonheur et l'innocence qui en découlent, constituent les valeurs alternatives dont cet autre "christ" est porteur' ['to the extent that lucid absurd awareness and the happiness and innocence which come from it constitute the alternative values which this other "Christ" embodies']. He also argues (p. 36) that in *L'Étranger* generally : 'Le texte camusien s'approprie la problématique dostoïevskienne afin de poser les points de repère d'une réponse radicalement différente' ['The Camusian text appropriates the Dostoevskian problematic in order to put down markers for a radically different reply']. Dunwoodie explores these intertextual resonances in *L'Étranger* in some detail but, from our point of view, it is his conclusion that Camus is replying to Dostoevsky explicitly with a new Christ-figure in *L'Étranger* that we wish to highlight as confirmation of our suggested debate. Camus is really replying to Dostoevsky's entire work and to Dostoevsky himself.

Chapter 6

1. *Le Mythe de Sisyphe*, Pléiade-Essais, p. 185.
2. It is Piotr Stépanovitch who, when conversing with Stavroguine's mother, describes as 'ironique' the life led by her son. Cf. *Les Possédés*, I, 197.
3. *Le Mythe de Sisyphe*, Pléiade-Essais, p. 185.
4. By the time Camus adapts *Les Possédés* for the stage in 1958, he has fully realized the central role of Stavroguine in generating the ideas of Kirilov. Cf. below, Chapter 8, p. 157.
5. See his letter to Dacha, *Les Possédés*, II, 405-9.
6. *Le Mythe de Sisyphe*, Pléiade-Esssais, p. 185. *Les Possédés*, II, p. 407.
7. In his note-books for the novel, Dostoevsky wrote of Stavroguine's attitude: 'Mais l'essentiel, malgré tout—l'incroyance' ['But the essential thing despite all is disbelief']. *Carnets des Démons*, p. 1040.
8. *Les Possédés*, II, 407-8.
9. The Underground Man (the phrase usually used by English critics to designate the protagonist of *Le Sous-Sol*) is, like Stavroguine, unable to act because he considers life futile and he considers active men simplistic: 'Le fruit légal, le fruit naturel de la conscience, c'est, en effet, l'inertie: on se croise sciemment les bras. J'en ai déjà parlé. Je le répète, je le répète: tous les hommes simples et sincères, tous les hommes actifs sont actifs justement parce qu'ils sont obtus et médiocres' ['The legitimate and natural product of awareness is, in fact, inertia: one knowingly downs tools. I have already spoken of it. I repeat, I repeat: all straightforward and sincere people, all people who do things are active precisely because they are limited and mediocre']. *Le Sous-Sol, Le Joueur, L'Eternel Mari*. Introduction par Pierre Pascal, Traduction et Notes par Boris de Schlœzer et Sylvie Luneau (Paris: Gallimard, 1965). See also Mochulsky, *Dostoevsky*,

pp. 245ff. for a discussion of the relationship between paralysis of the will and consciousness in Dostoevsky.

10. I have commented elsewhere on the possible meaning of this key phrase in *L'Étranger*. Cf. *L'Étranger*, ed. Ray Davison (Routledge, 1988). See, in particular, pp. 28–9.

11. *L'Envers et l'endroit*, Pléiade-Essais, p. 8. It is interesting that Camus never shows any interest in Hippolyte of *L'Idiot* although this character was, like Camus, a victim of tuberculosis and considered life futile. However, Hippolyte is a bitter and venomous person and it is perhaps because of this that Camus was not interested in him.

12. Stavroguine indirectly describes himself in this way when he asks Tikhone to recite the Biblical passage beginning 'Écris à l'Ange de l'Église de Laodicée . . .' ['And unto the angel of the church of the Laodiceans write . . .' (Revelation, III 14). See 'La Confession de Stavroguine' (a chapter excluded from the actual novel but of great interest) in *Les Démons, Carnets des Démons, Les Pauvres Gens* etc., p. 715.

13. *Le Mythe de Sisyphe*, Pléiade-Essais, p. 187.

14. Cf. *Les Possédés*, I, 273.

15. Ibid., II, 408.

16. This is a statement which Stavroguine makes to Tikhone in the *Carnets des Démons*, p. 110.

17. *Le Mythe de Sisyphe*, Pléiade-Essais, p. 147.

18. *Les Possédés*, II, 335.

19. Cf. '*Le Mythe de Sisyphe*, Notes et Variantes', Pléiade-Essais, p. 1442, note to p. 147.

20. G. Strem, loc. cit., 248.

21. Cf. *Les Possédés*, II, 277, where Stavroguine tells Chatov that, despite his will to believe, he has not achieved the latter's degree of faith: 'je désirerais vivement confirmer d'un bout à l'autre tout ce que vous venez de dire, mais . . .' ['I would really love to confirm *in toto* everything you have just said but . . .'].

22. *Le Mythe de Sisyphe*, Pléiade-Essais, p. 146.

23. Dunwoodie, op. cit., p. 168.

24. Ibid., p. 168.

25. I am mindful that not everybody shares this view of Stavroguine. Colin Wilson, for example, finds him a half-baked adolescent romantic. See *The Listener*, LXIV (August 4 1960), 195.

26. Dostoevsky aimed high and was usually successful.

27. *Les Possédés*, II, 36.

28. Ibid., II, 407.

29. *Le Mythe de Sisyphe*, Pléiade-Essais, p. 187, n. 2.

30. *La Chute*, Pléiade-Théâtre, p. 1527.

31. This description appears in the 'Foreword' to the 1959 adaptation. Cf. Prière d'Insérer *des Possédés*, Pléiade-Théâtre, p. 1877.

32. Cf. Prière d'Insérer de *La Chute*, Pléiade-Théâtre, p. 2007.

33. Camus ponders on Berdiaiev, Spechniov and Stavroguine as he adapts *Les Possédés* in *Carnets*, III, 108–9.

34. Meursault wants spectators at his execution to greet him with 'des cris de haine' ['cries of hatred'] in the same way that Stavroguine's ironic life is designed, according to Camus, to 'faire lever la haine autour de lui' ['create hatred around him']. *L'Étranger*, Pléiade-Théâtre, p. 1212, *Le Mythe de Sisyphe*, Pléiade-Essais, p. 185.

35. Caligula speaks of 'ce grand vide où le cœur s'apaise' ['this great void where the heart finds peace']. *Caligula*, Pléiade-Théâtre, p. 107.

36. Cf. G. Steiner, *Tolstoi or Dostoevsky*, p. 316.

37. J. Maudale, loc. cit., p. 133.

38. *Le Mythe de Sisyphe*, Pléiade-Essais, p. 183.

39. G. Strem, loc. cit., 250.

40. J. C. Marek, loc. cit., 499.

41. J. Maudale, loc. cit., 131.

42. 'Interview à *Paris-Théâtre* (1958)', Pléiade-Théâtre, pp. 1711–17.

43. *Le Mythe de Sisyphe*, Pléiade-Essais, p. 183. Ivan does not, in fact, say this but his attitude implies that he thinks it. Once again, one sees Camus's implication that the existentialist leap into faith is undignified.

44. *Les Frères Karamazov*, I, 355.

45. *Le Mythe de Sisyphe*, Pléiade-Essais, p. 136. Camus also refers to Ivan's 'esprit terrestre' ['terrestrial mind, mind of this world'] in *L'Homme révolté*, Pléiade-Essais, p. 469. (The context is slightly different, however.)

46. Cf. L. Faucon, '*Le Mythe de Sisyphe*: Commentaires', Pléiade-Essais, p. 1412.

47. *Carnets*, I, 118.

48. Cf. *Remarque sur la révolte*, Pléiade-Essais, p. 1686.

49. Cf. 'Ni Victimes ni bourreaux', Pléiade-Essais, p. 336.

50. *Les Frères Karamazov*, 1, 108–9.

51. Ibid., I, 109.

52. *Le Mythe de Sisyphe*, Pléiade-Essais, p. 109 (Camus's italics).

53. Ibid., 149.

54. 'Retour à Tipasa', *L'Été*, Pléiade-Essais, p. 871.

55. *Le Mythe de Sisyphe*, Pléiade-Essais, p. 149.

56. Generally, Camus's nostalgia for faith which he admits is part of the experience of *l'homme absurde*, as I have already mentioned, is nowhere nearly as strong as that of either Ivan, Stavroguine or Kirilov. Certainly Camus rarely gives the impression that his enjoyment of nature and sensual experience is only a second best after God.

57. *Le Mythe de Sisyphe*, Pléiade-Essais, p. 137. In his study of *Les Frères Karamazov* in *L'Homme révolté*, Camus again argues that Ivan sees man as innocent. *L'Homme révolté*, Pléiade-Essais, p. 465.

58. *Les Frères Karamazov*, I, 359.

59. Ibid., I, 354.

60. Ibid., I, 357–8.

61. Ibid., I, 358–9.

62. *Le Mythe de Sisyphe*, pp. 149–50. In the same passages, Camus argues that the consequences of all actions should be accepted by *l'homme absurde* with 'sérénité'. This could be considered to support the idea, suggested in the chapter on Kirilov, that there is a trace of Kirilov's serenity in the attitude of the early Camus. See also Camus's statement in the essay, p. 186: 'devant ces fins tragiques [the suicides of Kirilov and Stavroguine, Ivan's madness] le mouvement essentiel de l'esprit absurde est de demander: "Qu'est-ce que cela prouve?" ' ['before such tragic ends, the basic movement of the absurd mind is to ask: "So what?" ']

63. J. Cruickshank, *Albert Camus and the Literature of Revolt* (Oxford: University Press, 1960), p. 149.

64. 'Rencontre avec Albert Camus', *Les Nouvelles Littéraires*, (mai 10, 1951). This interview is in the Pléiade-Essais volume pp. 1337–43 (see especially pp. 1342–3). Cf. also 'Lettre à Pierre Bonnel', dated March 18th, 1943, Pléiade-Essais, pp. 1422–4, where Camus wrote: 'mon essai n'aborde pas en réalité le problème de "ce qu'on peut faire" à l'intérieur du cadre. Je me réservais d'y revenir' ['my essay doesn't really deal with the problem of "what can one do" from within the set framework. I was going to come back to that at a later date'].

65. *Le Mythe de Sisyphe*, Pléiade-Essais, p. 150.

66. See the earlier quotation from Mioussov n.50.

67. 'Déjà quand j'écrivais *Le Mythe*, je songeais à l'essai sur la révolte que j'écrirais plus tard' ['Already, when I was writing *Le Mythe*, I was thinking about the essay on revolt that I would write later']. 'Rencontre avec Albert Camus', Pléiade-Essais, p. 1343.

68. Cf. 'Défense de *L'Homme révolté*', Pléiade-Essais, p. 1704: 'Pour moi qui avais longtemps vécu sans morale, comme beaucoup d'hommes de ma génération, professé en somme le nihilisme, quoique sans le savoir toujours, je compris alors que les idées n'étaient pas seulement des jeux pathétiques ou harmonieux, et que, dans certaines occasions, accepter certaines pensées revenait à accepter le meurtre sans limites' ['For myself who had lived a long time without a moral philosophy, like a lot of men of my generation, who had basically professed nihilism albeit without always realizing it, I understood then that ideas are not just emotional or aesthetic games that we play, and that, in certain circumstances, to accept certain thoughts is to accept unrestricted murder']. See also the *Lettres à un ami allemand*, Pléiade-Essais, pp. 239–40.

69. One has only to recall his pre-war political activity in Algeria, an engagement carried out in the name of justice.

70. It seems unlikely that Camus developed his notion of revolt until the last years of the war. Cf. 'Défense de *L'Homme révolté*', Pléiade-Essais, p. 1703. Referring to his experience during the Occupation, Camus writes: 'Pour moi, je ne disposais que d'une révolte sûre d'elle-même mais encore inconsciente de ses raisons etc.' ['As for me, I possessed

only a revolt sure of itself but not yet aware of its rational legitimacy etc.']

71. P. Thody, *Albert Camus 1913–1960*, p. 28. P. Thody is, of course, referring to the Camus before the experience of the Occupation and the Resistance.

72. *Noces*, Pléiade-Essais, p. 72.

73. This is one of the variants quoted by R. Quilliot from a photocopy of a manuscript belonging to Madame Albert Camus. Cf. '*Noces*: Commentaires', Pléiade-Essais, p. 1359, n. 12 to p. 75 of 'L'Été à Alger'. See also Quilliot's reference to the manuscript in the same section, Pléiade-Essais, p. 1353.

74. The schism in Kirilov's personality was analysed in the last chapter and Raskolnikov's conscience prevents him from accepting a crime which he can justify intellectually. Dostoevsky refers to Raskolnikov's schism in a draft letter to Katkov, dated September 1865. Cf. *Correspondance*, II, 247–8.

75. *Les Frères Karamazov*, III, 89–90.

76. Ibid., p. 92.

77. Cf. ' La Défense de *L'Homme révolté*', Pléiade-Essais, p. 1703.

78. In both these works Camus admits to a degree of complicity with nihilism—see the references above in n. 68 for confirmation of this point. Note in particular the remark: 'J'ai décrit un mal dont je ne m'excluais pas' ['I described an evil from which I did not exclude myself']. 'Défense de *L'Homme révolté*', Pléiade-Essais, p. 1705.

79. Cf. *Carnets*, I, 225: 'L'absurde et le pouvoir (cf. Hitler)'.

80. Ibid., II, 304.

81. Cf. *L'Homme révolté*, Pléiade-Essais, p. 469.

82. P. Thody, op. cit., p. 27.

83. *Le Mythe de Sisyphe*, Pléiade-Essais, p. 143.

84. Ibid., p. 143.

85. *Les Frères Karamazov*, I, 347–8. It is worth noting that Clamence too is preoccupied with the possible vulgarity of his excessive love of life: 'j'aime la vie, voilà ma vraie faiblesse. Je l'aime tant que je n'ai aucune imagination pour ce qui n'est pas elle. Une telle avidité a quelque chose de plébéien, vous ne trouvez pas?' ['I love life, that is my real weakness. I love it so much that I cannot imagine anything outside of it. Such hunger is rather plebeian, don't you think?'] *La Chute*, Pléiade-Théâtre, p. 1512.

86. *L'Homme révolté*, Pléiade-Essais, p. 467.

87. *Les Frères Karamazov*, I, 348.

88. Ibid., I, 369.

89. *Carnets*, II, 112.

90. *Le Mythe de Sisyphe*, Pléiade-Essais, p. 140.

91. Cf. *Le Malentendu*, Pléiade-Théâtre, p. 153 and p. 180.

92. Cf. Ibid., p. 179.

93. *Caligula*, Pléiade-Théâtre, p. 179.

94. Caligula is not, however, preoccupied with the innocence of children.

95. G. Strem, loc. cit., 251.
96. *La Peste*, Pléiade-Théâtre, pp. 1394–5.
97. 'L'Incroyant et les Chrétiens' (Fragments d'un exposé fait au couvent des dominicains de la Tour Maubourg en 1948), *Actuelles* I, Pléiade-Essais, pp. 371–75.
98. *Lettres à un ami allemand*, Pléiade-Essais, p. 241.
99. J. Marek, loc. cit., 498.
100. Cf. *La Revue socialiste*, No. 193 (mai 1966), 470.
101. Cf. Dmitri's Dream, *Les Frères Karamazov*, II, 307–9 and *L'Homme révolté*, Pléiade-Essais, p. 706.
102. G. Green, *A Kingdom not of this World: A quest for a Christian Ethic of Revolution with reference to the thought of Dostoevsky, Berdyaev and Camus*, Stanford Honors Essays in Humanities, no. 8, (California: Stanford Press, 1964), p. 8.
103. Cf. *Les Frères Karamazov*, I, 364–7, and *La Peste*, pp. 1312–16.
104. Dunwoodie describes *La Peste* as engaged in a specific intertextual dialogue with *Les Frères Karamazov*. He calls this debate 'un véritable chassé-croisé' (p. 99). The aim of this intertextual dialogue is to appropriate for humanism the values which Dostoevsky grants to Christianity: '*La Peste* propose un début de solution relative, modeste mais *concrète*, qui incorpore à sa propre problématique le traitement dostoïevskien du débat pour laïciser la solution proposée dans *Les Frères Karamazov*, pour se réclamer, au nom de l'action humaniste, des valeurs dont le christianisme se targuait d'avoir le monopole' ['*La Peste* outlines the beginnings of a relative, modest but *concrete* solution which includes in its own problematic Dostoevsky's treatment of the debate, in order to express in lay terms the Christian solution proposed in *Les Frères Karamazov*, to lay claim, in the name of humanist action, to the values which Christianity claimed as its monopoly'].
105. *Les Frères Karamazov*, I, 363.
106. This point is developed more fully in the following chapter.
107. *Les Frères Karamazov*, III, 173.
108. *L'Étranger*, Pléiade-Théâtre, p. 1170.
109. Cf. *Caligula*, Pléiade-Théâtre, p. 78.
110. The relationship between capital punishment in Camus and Dostoevsky as it expresses itself in *L'Étranger* is analysed at length in Eugene Eiche's thesis 'Les Personnages dostoïevskiens dans *L'Étranger*', Stansford, 1968.
111. Dunwoodie explores in some detail the intertextual debates between *L'Étranger*, *L'Idiot and Les Frères Karamazov* (op. cit. pp. 35–47 and pp. 60–73). Using the Bakhtinian notion of 'appropriation', he identifies the parallels between the texts in question to show how Camus: 'oppose un démenti répété à l'intertexte dostoïevskien' ['repeatedly refutes the Dostoevskian intertext'] (p. 73). This 'démenti' is precisely the philosophy of pleasure or what Dunwoodie calls 'la joie', the sheer joy of being alive embodied in Meursault. Whilst Dunwoodie's approach is quite different and does not explore the ideas and

propositions behind the intertexts in dialogue, the conclusions are broadly similar to the ones developed here.

112. Cf. Caligula's question (*Caligula*, Pléiade-Théâtre, p. 116) 'Est-ce donc du bonheur, cette liberté épouvantable?' ['Is this then happiness, this dreadful freedom?']

113. Ibid., p. 78.

114. Ibid., p. 100.

115. Ibid., p. 83.

116. Dunwoodie rates *Caligula* with *La Chute* as 'l'œuvre la plus fortement engagée dans ce dialogue intertextuel [avec Dostoïevski]' ['the work most powerfully engaged in the intertextual dialogue (with Dostoevsky)] (op. cit., p. 200) and describes Caligula's recognition of responsibility at the end of the play as 'un moment exceptionnel dans le dialogue Camus-Dostoïevski: il s'agit en effet du moment où la vision du monde de l'écrivain (pour qui l'absurde est la seule position philosophiquement valable), bascule sous le poids des événements historiques contemporains qui l'éloignent des grands débats métaphysiques véhiculés par les romans polyphoniques dostoïevskiens' ['an exceptional moment in the Camus-Dostoevsky dialogue: indeed it constitutes the moment when the vision of Camus the writer (for whom the absurd is the only valid philosophical position) collapses under the weight of contemporary historical circumstances which distance him from the great metaphysical debates expressed by Dostoevsky's polyphonic novels'] (p. 189). He also argues (pp. 192–6) that the triangle Cherea/Caligula/Scipion represents 'un double du débat triangulaire du roman russe [*Les Frères Karamazov*]' ['a clone of the triangular debate of the Russian novel']. This would mean interpreting Scipion as an Aliocha figure. I find this hard to accept since Aliocha is no advocate of the 'tout est bien' philosophy that underpins Scipion whose views are closer to Kirilov's (see earlier discussion in Chapter 5). It is more plausible, to our way of thinking, to see Scipion as an anti-Aliocha figure or as a pagan alternative to Christian grace. Scipion would thus be seen as part of the new Christ strategy adopted by Camus as a reply to Dostoevsky. Dunwoodie first makes this point in '*Caligula*: L'Univers dostoïevskien et l'évolution de Scipion', *Revue de littérature comparée* (nov 3, 1979), 220–30.

Chapter 7

1. *Journal d'un écrivain*, p. 422.

2. *Carnets*, II, 233.

3. *Les Frères Karamazov*, p. 253. I am still using the translation by Mongault, which Camus used, but I have found it more convenient to refer to the Bibliothèque de la Pléiade Edition, 1965.

4. *L'Homme révolté*, Pléiade-Essais, pp. 469–70.

5. 'Pour Dostoïevski', Pléiade-Théâtre, p. 1875. 'L'homme qui a écrit

"Les questions de Dieu et de l'immortalité sont les mêmes que les questions du socialisme mais sous un autre angle" savait que désormais notre civilisation revendiquerait le salut pour tous ou pour personne'['The man who wrote "The questions of God and immortality are the same as those of socialism but from a different angle" knew that henceforth our civilization would claim salvation for all or nobody'].

6. Cf. 'Prière d'Insérer des *Possédés*', 'Pour Dostoïevski' and the 'Questionnaire pour *Spectacles*', Pléiade-Théâtre, pp.1877–83. In 1945, Camus defined the problem of value as: 'la seule question qui nous paraisse de quelque importance . . . l'homme peut-il, à lui seul et sans le secours de l'éternel, créer ses propres valeurs?' ['the only question which appears to us of any importance . . . can man, by himself and without the help of God, create his own values?'] 'Remarque sur la révolte', Pléiade-Essais, pp. 1695–6.

7. *L'Homme révolté*, p. 465.

8. Ibid., p. 465.

9. Ibid., p. 510.

10. Ibid., p. 466.

11. Ibid., p. 462.

12. Ibid., p. 702. and Dunwoodie, op. cit., p. 175.

13. Ibid., p. 707.

14. Ibid., p. 428.

15. Ibid., p. 467.

16. Ibid., p. 467.

17. Ibid., p. 467.

18. Ibid., p. 467.

19. Ibid., p. 490.

20. Ibid., p. 468.

21. Ibid., p. 468.

22. Ibid., p. 469, n.1. Camus once again, as in *Le Mythe de Sisyphe*, finds it hard to believe that Dostoevsky is not on Ivan's side.

23. Ibid., p. 468.

24. Ibid., p. 469.

25. Ibid., p. 469.

26. Ibid., p. 469.

27. Ibid., p. 469. Camus repeats the point in *Spectacles* in 1958 at the time of the adaptation of *Les Possédés*: 'On a longtemps cru que Marx était le prophète du xxème siècle. On sait maintenant que sa prophétie a fait long feu. Et nous découvrons que le vrai prophète était Dostoïevski. Il a prophétisé le règne des grands Inquisiteurs et le triomphe de la puissance sur la justice' ['For a long time, people believed that Marx was the prophet of the twentieth century. We now know that his prophecy is long in the fulfilment. And we realize that the real prophet was Dostoevsky. He prophesized the reign of the Grand Inquisitor and the triumph of absolute power over justice']. (Pléiade-Théâtre, p. 1882).

28. *Journal d'un écrivain*, pp. 626–33
29. *Carnets*, III, 216.
30. *Journal d'un écrivain*, p. 627.
31. *Carnets*, II, 227 (the references occur between 1947 and 1948).
32. *Journal d'un écrivain*, p. 633.
33. *Les Frères Karamazov*, pp. 177–78.
34. Ibid., p. 342.
35. Ibid., p. 345.
36. Ibid., p. 272.
37. Ibid., p. 274.
38. Ibid., p. 283.
39. *L'Homme révolté*, p. 471.
40. Ibid., p. 470.
41. Ibid., p. 471.
42. Ibid., p. 470.
43. Ibid., p. 470.
44. Ibid., p. 647.
45. *Les Frères Karamzov*, p. 266.
46. 'Le Pain et la liberté', republished in *Actuelles* II, Pléiade-Essais, pp. 791–9.
47. Ibid., p. 797.
48. For further discussion of this point see the very important article by Roger Quilliot, 'Camus et le socialisme' in *Camus et la politique*, Actes du colloque de Nanterre, 5–7 juin 1985, sous la direction de J. Guérin (Paris: 1986), pp. 31–41.
49. 'Le Pain et la liberté', p. 794.
50. *Les Frères Karamazov*, pp. 278–79.
51. 'Épuration des purs', *Actuelles*, II, Pléiade-Essais, pp. 744–5 (my italics).
52. Ibid., pp. 750–3.
53. Ibid., pp. 754–74.
54. Ibid., pp. 777–80.
55. Ibid., pp. 1070–75. This evocation of Helen in exile, together with its allusions to Dostoevsky are also important to my understanding of the Dostoevskian dimensions of *La Chute* (see Chapter 9).
56. 'L'Exil d'Hélène', Pléiade-Essais, pp. 851–7.

Chapter 8

1. 'Pour Dostoïevski', Pléiade-Théâtre, p. 1879.
2. Ibid., p. 1879.
3. 'Prière d'insérer des *Possédés*', Pléiade-Théâtre, p. 1877.
4. 'Questionnaire pour *Spectacles*,' Ibid., p. 1882.
5. Ibid., p. 1882.
6. Pléiade-Essais, pp. 560–70.
7. Ibid., pp. 579–82.

8. For further discussion of the link between Raskolnikov and Pisarev, see J. Frank, op. cit., Vol. 1V, *The Miraculous Years*, p. 435. Camus was well aware that Raskolnikov explores the depths of Pisarev's ethical relativism and refers to it in *L'Homme révolté*, Pléiade-Essais, p. 561. It is also interesting to note that the relationship between radical politics and the mother figures in Camus's dilemmas over Algeria.

9. *Le Sous-Sol* in *Dostoïevski*, V, Pléiade, pp. 714–16.

10. A very detailed analysis is provided in Frank, *The Miraculous Years*, pp. 435–52 (a chapter entitled 'History and Myth in *The Devils*').

11. I am grateful to Dr Roger Cockerel of the Exeter Russian Department for providing me with the Russian equivalent phrase.

12. Cf. *Crime et châtiment*, 'Indications chronologiques', in *Dostoïevski*, I, Pléiade. p. 28.

13. Dostoevsky discusses the whole question of Herzen, Belinski and liberal idealism in *Journal d'un écrivain*, pp. 105–9.

14. *Les Démons*, in *Dostoïevski*, III, Pléiade, p. 392.

15. Dostoevsky refers to 'le droit au déshonneur' in the *Diary of a Writer*, translated and annotated by Boris Brasol, Salt Lake City, 1979, pp. 271ff. (March 1876, chapter II, section 4, 'Isolated phenomena'). Unfortunately, this section is not included in the French edition. The phrase used by Dostoevsky in the original Russian version of the Diary, 'pravo na beschest'e' (see n.11 above) is identical to the one used by Karmazinov. The most likely source of the original phrase is Nechaev's journal, *People's Revenge*.

16. *Les Démons*, pp. 1267–8.

17. Ibid., p. 258.

18. Ibid., p. 426.

19. Ibid., p. 425.

20. Ibid., pp. 426–7.

21. Ibid., p. 442 and p. 444.

22. Frank, *The Miraculous Years*, p. 450.

23. The hostility displayed by Marx and Engels to Bakunin and the anarchist radicals and the determined attempt by the former to distance revolutionary endeavour from the latter's moral nihilism does not prevent Camus from arguing that nihilism entered Marxism to create the totalitarian state.

24. Dunwoodie, op. cit., p. 176.

25. *L'Homme révolté*, Pléiade-Essais, p. 517.

26. Ibid., p. 568.

27. Ibid., p. 566.

28. Ibid., p. 566.

29. Ibid., p. 567.

30. Ibid., p. 567.

31. Ibid., p. 567.

32. Ibid., p. 569. See also *Actuelles*, I ('Réponses à d'Astier') Ibid., p. 361.

33. Ibid., p. 569.

34. Ibid., p. 569.

35. *Dostoïevski notre contemporain*, p. 227.
36. *L'Homme révolté*, Pléiade-Essais, p. 579.
37. Ibid., p. 580.
38. Ibid., p. 580.
39. Ibid., p. 581.
40. Ibid., p. 580.
41. Camus is at pains, in the section of the essay called 'Les Déicides', to link Hegel with Rousseau, calling *La Phénoménologie de l'esprit* 'un *Émile* métaphysique'. He also argues that Rousseau's notion of the general will is present in Hegel's thought. Generally, Camus seems to come close to Talmon's view that all totalitarian thought emanates from Rousseau, whatever Rousseau's own claims to being a democrat may be.
42. *Les Démons*, p. 392.
43. 'C'est Kaliayev et ses frères russes ou allemands qui dans l'histoire du monde s'opposent vraiment à Hegel . . .' ['It is Kaliayev and his Russian or German brothers who in world history really oppose Hegel . . .'] *L'Homme révolté*, Pléiade–Essais, p. 578.
44. Ibid., p. 579.
45. Ibid., p. 578.
46. *Les Justes*, Pléiade-Théâtre, p. 337.
47. Ibid., p. 336.
48. Ibid., p. 336.
49. Ibid., p. 338.
50. Ibid., p. 356.
51. Dunwoodie is right to argue (op. cit. p. 181) that Stepan's rejection of love echoes the Grand Inquisitor's rejection of Christ's love in *Les Frères Karamazov* (p. 278). Both are sombre characters fighting for dominion over the Earth.
52. *Journal d'un écrivain*, p. 1000.
53. Gide, op. cit. p. 58.
54. 'Prière d'insérer des *Possédés*', Pléiade-Théâtre, p. 131.
55. This has been done elsewhere and, most recently, by Dunwoodie, op. cit. pp. 202–233.
56. Cf. above, pp. 38–9, 74–5.
57. 'Questionnaire pour *Spectacles*', Pléiade-Théâtre p. 1882.
58. C. Cézar, 'Albert Camus adapte Dostoïevski', Les *Nouvelles Littéraires* (janvier 29, 1959).
59. Quoted by Olivier Todd, op. cit. p. 728.
60. *Les Possédés*, Pléiade-Théâtre, p. 926.
61. Ibid., p. 1111.
62. Ibid., p. 1108.
63. Ibid., p. 1102.
64. Ibid., p. 984.
65. Ibid., p. 995.
66. Ibid., p. 995.
67. Cf. above, p.85, p. 93

68. Olivier Todd summarizes the general reaction of the Parisian press to *Les Possédés* on pp. 727–36 of his biography.
69. R. Poulet, 'Pourquoi adapte-t-il au lieu d'écrire' *Carrefour*, XVI, no.754 (février 25, 1959).
70. Guy Leclerc, 'Au Théâtre Antoine. *Les Possédés* de Dostoïevski (adaptation d'Albert Camus). Un long spectacle'. *L'Humanité* (janvier 31, 1959).
71. P Morelle, '*Les Possédés* au Théâtre Antoine', *Libération*, (janvier 31, 1959).
72. Renée Saurel, '*Les Possédés*', *Les Temps Modernes*', XIV (février/mars 1959), 1508–9.
73. Op. cit. p.733.
74. 'Actualité de la politique Camusienne', in *Albert Camus, Les Extrêmes et L'Equilibre*, pp. 103–4.
75. 'Prière d'insérer des *Possédés*', Pléiade–Théâtre, p. 1877.
76. 'Roger Martin du Gard', Pléiade–Essais, p. 1131.

Chapter 9

1. Clamence, *La Chute*, Pléiade-Théâtre, p. 1545.
2. A possible title of *La Chute* was the re-use of Lermontov's *Un Héros de notre temps*.
3. *L'Été*, Pléiade-Essais, p. 854.
4. Ibid., pp. 854–5.
5. Ibid., p. 856.
6. This theme is explained in R.L. Jackson's *Dostoevsky's Underground Man in Russian Literature* (The Hague: Mouton, 1958).
7. *L'Été*, Pléiade-Essais, p. 856.
8. It is worth noting that both Brée and Peyre are quick to pick up these indications of the link between Clamence and Dostoevsky's 'buffoons'. Brée describes Clamence as 'this prodigious buffoon' ("A Grain of Salt", *Yale French Studies*, no. 25 (Spring 1960), 43). Peyre suggests that *La Chute* should be read as 'a satire of the self-indictment practised by Christians and atheistic existentialists alike, by Dostoevsky's 'buffoons', [Peyre refers here to *L'Été*], and by advocates of universal and unlimited responsibility'. ('Camus, The Pagan', Ibid., 23).
9. 'Clamence and Marmeladov: a parallel' *Roman Notes* (1972) 226–30.
10. *Crime et châtiment*, Pléiade, p. 49. It is not possible to determine when Camus read *Crime et châtiment* but the first explicit reference to it is in *L'Homme révolté*, Pléiade- Essais, p. 561. Camus does not quote from the work, however, so it is difficult to know which edition and translation he used. The Ergaz translation which I am using; is perhaps the most likely. It was published by Gallimard in the Pléiade collection (1950). It is true that Camus used the Dérely translation of *Les Possédés* and I have suggested that he used Dérely's translation of *L'Idiot*. Dérely also translated *Crime et châtiment*, but Marmeladov's speech is perhaps

not so strikingly similar here to the opening of *La Chute*. Cf. *Crime et châtiment*, traduit du Russe par V. Dérely, 2 vols. (Paris: Plon, 1884), I, 14.

11. Ibid., 49.
12. *La Chute*, Pléiade-Théâtre, p. 1475. In both scenes, the barman plays a part in the description. In Dostoevsky's novel, he interrupts Marmeladov's speech to make sarcastic points against him. In *La Chute*, it is Clamence who constantly refers sarcastically to the barman and calls him 'l'estimable gorille qui préside aux destinées de cet établissement' ['The worthy gorilla who is in charge of destinies in this establishment'].
13. *Carnets*, II, 252 contains three quotations from *Le Sous-Sol*.
14. Jacques Madaule, loc. cit., 132, says of *La Chute*: 'Nul n'est plus Dostoïevskien' ['None is more Dostoevskian']. The already cited works of Kirk, Sturm and Dunwoodie are the most detailed explorations of Dostoevsky's presence in *La Chute*.
15. Cf. Myrna Magnan-Shardt, '*La Chute* comme *skaz*, une hypothèse génétique', in *Revue des lettres modernes*, série Albert Camus 6, 1973 J. Ominus (ed.), *Dostoïevski et les lettres françaises*' and E. Sturm's *Préface* to Dunwoodie's book.
16. Dunwoodie, op. cit., p. 141.
17. Ibid., p. 139.
18. The Underground Man does not believe that people live their lives by reason and, therefore, they will not accept utilitarian notions of rational self-interest. For this reason, he also believes the 'crystal palace' cannot be built.
19. Dunwoodie, op. cit., pp. 139–40.
20. Cf. above. Chapter 3, Dunwoodie, op. cit., pp. 134–5, E. Trahan, loc. cit., 338–43 and J. Bloch-Michel, 'Une Littérature de l'ennui', *Preuves* (janvier/juin 1962) 14–23. Bloch-Michel is totally convinced that the key to the structure of *La Chute* is to be found in *Le Sous-Sol* and the story 'Krotkaïa', the November 1876 entry for the *Journal d'un écrivain*. The latter hypothesis seems unconvincing.
21 *Journal d'un écrivain*, pp. 572–73.
22. Pléiade-Essais, p. 182.
23. Dunwoodie explores these parallels in order to demonstrate how Camus's discourse appropriates that of Dostoevsky in *Crime et châtiment* in particular, in order to extend and rework them. Cf. Dunwoodie, op. cit., pp. 118–26.
24. *La Chute*, Pléiade-Théâtre, pp. 1535–6. *Crime et châtiment*, p. 128.
25. Dunwoodie, op. cit., pp. 119–22.
26. *La Chute*, Pléiade-Théâtre, p. 1509.
27. Ibid., p. 1493. For further discussion of 'dédoublement', see Yvette Louria, 'Dédoublement in Dostoevsky and Camus', *Modern Language Review*, LVI, 1 (January1961), 82–83 and Dunwoodie. op. cit., pp. 152–3. Dunwoodie links 'la fissuration de la conscience' to 'le moment essentiel de la détronisation' ['the fracturing of consciousness' to 'the

essential moment of dethroning'], that moment when Clamence and the Underground Man lose their ascendancy.

28. *La Chute*, Pléiade-Théâtre, pp. 1495–6. As with *Le Double*, it is not yet possible to establish if and when Camus read the work. It is interesting to note that *Les Nuits blanches* is informed by a similar dialectic to the one referred to by Camus in 'L'Exil d'Hélène'. The protagonist throws into opposition the beauty of St Petersburg in the spring and the St Petersburg of 'd'assez étranges coins' ['fairly weird places'], where the sun doesn't penetrate and where 'on mène une vie tout autre' ['strange lives are lived']. *Les Nuits blanches*, p. 628, and p. 641.

29. *La Chute*, Pléiade-Théâtre, p. 1513.

30. Ibid., p. 1533.

31. Ibid., p. 1533 and p. 1531.

32. *Carnets*, II, 227.

33. *Les Frères Karamazov*, p. 310 and p. 346. Zosime first hears these words from his dying brother but he later adapts them as the basis of Christian solidarity and love when he pardons his enemy in a duel and refuses to fight. 'Coupable' is sometimes translated as 'responsable' but this doesn't invalidate the points made.

34. Ibid., p. 30.

35. Ibid., p. 29.

36. *La Chute*, Pléiade-Théâtre, p. 1533.

37. *Les Frères Karamazov*, pp. 346–7.

38. *La Chute*, Pléiade-Théâtre, p. 1543.

39. *Les Frères Karamazov*, p. 44.

40. *La Chute*, Pléiade-Théâtre, p. 1535.

41. Ibid., p. 1542.

42. *Les Frères Karamazov*, pp. 273–6.

43. *La Chute*, Pléiade-Théâtre, p. 1544.

44. *Le Sous-Sol*, p. 684.

45. Ibid., p. 696.

46. *Carnets*, II, 252.

47. *Le Sous-Sol*, p. 709.

48. *La Chute*, Pléiade-Théâtre, p. 1477.

49. *Le Sous-Sol*, p. 704.

50. Ibid., p. 690, *La Chute*, Pléiade-Théâtre, p. 1503.

51. *Le Sous-Sol*, p. 689. *La Chute*, Pléiade-Théâtre, p. 1547: 'Alors, planant par la pensée au-dessus de tout ce continent qui m'est soumis sans le savoir, buvant le jour d'absinthe qui se lève, ivre enfin de mauvaises paroles, je suis heureux, je suis heureux, vous dis-je, je vous interdis de ne pas croire que je suis heureux, je suis heureux à mourir!' ['Then hovering in thought above the circle of the continent which is under my authority without anyone knowing it, drinking the absinthe of the dawn, drunk with bad language, I am happy, I am happy, I tell you, and I forbid you to think that I am not happy, I could die of happiness!']

52. *Le Sous-Sol*, p. 718, *La Chute*, Pléiade-Théâtre, p. 1536.
53. *Le Sous-Sol*, p. 716.
54. *La Chute*, Pléiade-Théâtre, p. 1485 and p. 1537. Such is Clamence's dislike of underground places that he refuses to join the Resistance!
55. Ibid., p. 1549 and p. 1492.
56. The range of parallels between *La Chute* and Dostoevsky's world can be gauged from the following critical comments: Madaule links Stavroguine's wait for Matriocha to Clamence's neglect of the girl committing suicide (loc. cit., 133). René Micha feels that there are 'marked similarities between *La Chute* and the Confession de Stavroguine' ('L'Agneau dans le placard', *La Nouvelle Revue Française*, no. 87 (mars 1, 1960), 503, whilst Strem argues that Clamence is Ivan 'on the social level' (loc. cit., 254) although it is none too clear what he means. Carina Gadourek compares Clamence to Stavroguine, saying they are both believers who do not believe and non-believers who believe (*Les Innocents et les coupables*, p. 192). André Blanchet makes the important point that Clamence's Christ is very different from Dostoevsky's 'Pari d'Albert Camus (suite)', *Études* no. 6 (juin 1960), 343. See also C.A. Viggiani, 'Camus and the Fall from Innocence', *Yale French Studies*, no. 25 (Spring 1960), 65–71, Trahan, loc. cit., 348 and Hartman, loc. cit., 107.
57. Dunwoodie, op. cit., pp. 117–55 and p. 161.
58. Olivier Todd discusses the reception of *La Chute*, op. cit., pp. 636–53, Lottmann, op. cit., pp. 570–4.
59. Clamence refers to the concentric canals of Amsterdam as 'l'enfer bourgeois' ['bourgeois hell'] and targets 'l'homme moderne' ['modern man'] for his satire (p. 1477 and p. 1481). Camus obviously doesn't want to catch the whole of human reality in Clamence's nets of duplicity, although it sometimes feels like that.
60. *Crime et châtiment*, p. 61.
61. *Les Frères Karamazov*, p. 345.
62. Dunwoodie (op. cit., p. 133) tries to devalue Marmeladov's declaration of faith by describing him as '[un] minable personnage dostoïevskien' ['(a) pitiable Dostoevskian character']. However, the same idea is articulated through Zosime.
63. *La Chute*, Pléiade-Théâtre, pp. 1552–3.
64. Ibid., p. 1532.
65. Ibid., pp. 1531–32.
66. Ibid., p 1534.
67. Dunwoodie, op. cit., p. 133. Cf. above, n. 62.
68. Quoted by I. Kirk, op. cit., p. 217. This quotation is taken from a letter from Camus to Quilliot.
69. 'Présentation de *La Chute*', Pléiade-Théatre, p. 2002.
70. Cf. above, n. 1.
71. *Carnets* III, 266. The first explicit reference to *Le Premier Homme* is in *Carnets*, III, 100 (1953), although there are earlier ones without the title which clearly refer to the same novel (96–97). At the same time,

Camus is working on *La Chute* under its earlier title *Le Pilori* (101). The two works thus evolve simultaneously in his mind.

72. 'Roger Martin du Gard', Pléiade-Essais, p. 1131.

73. Ibid., p.1132.

74. References to Tolstoy outnumber those to Dostoevsky (although there are several) in *Carnets*, III. Camus is reading Tolstoy's *Diary* and *Letters* as well as a number of other texts, including *Childhood, Boyhood and Youth*. These references are all clearly indexed in *Carnets*, III.

75. *Carnets*, III, 103. See also 100 and 102. We should also recall that portraits of both Tolstoy and Dostoevsky hung in Camus's study.

76. Sarocchi, op. cit., pp. 89–111.

77. Ibid., p. 107.

78. Ibid., p. 108.

79. *Carnets*, III, 206 (July 1957). No references to *Carnets*, III appear in Sarocchi for some reason.

80. *La Chute*, Pléiade-Théâtre, p. 1543.

81. It is particularly in the domain of the theatre that Camus's works appear to be strongly marked by Dostoevsky. Of course, we know from his observations when adapting *Les Possédés* that Camus felt that Dostoevsky's novels readily lend themselves to theatre. Clamence, in *La Chute*, is a tragi-comic character with a great sense of drama and it is perhaps partly for this reason that *La Chute* has more in common, both in terms of technique and content, with Camus's early theatre than with *L'Étranger* or *La Peste*.

82. Sarocchi is right to point out that the mother ceases to be silent and actually talks to the son in *Le Premier Homme*. The *Oedipal* triangle is developing beyond the silent mother/lost father configuration of earlier works. Cf., *Le Premier Homme*, pp. 62–5.

83. 'Pour Dostoïevski', Pléiade-Théâtre, p. 1879.

84. *Carnets*, III, 206.

85. *L'Adolescent*, p. 623.

86. *Le Premier Homme*, p. 295. See also p. 287 where Camus refers to: 'D:[Fréquentation et séparation dans *Les Possédés*]'.

87. Ibid., p. 292 and p. 320.

88. Ibid., pp. 320–1.

Conclusion

1. Dunwoodie, op. cit., p. 161.

2. Author's gloss on Camus's original statement.

3. In emphasizing the 'dark' side of Dostoevsky at this point in our study, as Camus does in his study of Martin du Gard, we do not wish to understate the many positive features which attracted Camus to Dostoevsky's world. We have already rejected Albérès's thesis, supported by Batchelor, that Dostoevsky represented, for Camus, 'la méditation de la mort' ['the meditation of death'] etc. Cf. above, Chapter 4, p. 61.

Bibliography

Editions used:

Camus, Albert
Théâtre, Récits, Nouvelles. Préface de Jean Grenier. Textes établis et annotés par Roger Quilliot (Paris: Gallimard, 1965).
Essais. Introduction par Roger Quilliot. Textes établis et annotés par Roger Quilliot et Louis Faucon (Paris: Gallimard, 1967).
Carnets. Notes de Roger Quilliot, 3 vols. (Paris: Gallimard, 1962, 1964 and 1989).
La Mort heureuse, Cahiers Albert Camus, 1 (Paris: Gallimard, 1971).
Le Premier Homme, Cahiers Albert Camus, 7 (Paris: Gallimard, 1994).
Albert Camus, Jean Grenier, Correspondance 1932–60. Avertissement et notes de Marguerite Dobrenn (Paris: Gallimard, 1981).

Dostoïevski, Fedor
Les Frères Karamazov. Traduit du russe par Henri Mongault et Marc Laval, 3 vols. (Paris: Editions Bossard, 1923).
Les Possédés. Traduit du russe par Victor Derély, 2 vols. (Paris: Plon, 1886).
L'Idiot, Traduit du russe par Victor Derély. Préface de Melchior de Vogüé, 2 vols. (Paris: Plon, 1887).
Le Crime et le châtiment. Traduit du russe par Victor Derély, 2 vols. (Paris: Plon, 1884).
Journal d'un écrivain. Traduction de Jean Chuzeville (Paris: Gallimard, 1951).
La Correspondance de Dostoïevski. 4 vols. (Paris: Calmann-Levy, 1949–1961).
(i) Introduction et notes de Dominique Arban (1949).
(ii) Traduction et notes de Nina Gourfinkel (1959).
(iii) Traduction et notes de Nina Gourfinkel (1960).
(iv) Traduction et notes de Nina Gourfinkel (1961).
Œuvres de Dostoïevski. Introduction de Pierre Pascal. Traductions et notes de D. Ergaz, V. Pozner, B. de Schlœzer, H. Mongault, L. Desormonts,

A. Mousset, S. Luneau et Pierre Pascal. Bibliographies de S. Luneau: (Paris: Gallimard).

(i) *Crime et châtiment, Journal de Raskolnikov, Carnets de Crime et châtiment, Souvenirs de la maison des morts* (1950).

(ii) *Les Frères Karamazov, Carnets des Frères Karamazov, Niétotchka Niezanov* (1965).

(iii) *L'Idiot, Carnets de L'Idiot, Humiliés et offensés* (1957).

(iv) *Les Démons, Carnets des Démons, Les Pauvres Gens* (1966).

(v) *L'Adolescent, Nuits blanches, Le Sous-Sol, Le Joueur, L'Eternel mari* (1965).

(vi) *Récits, Chroniques et Polémiques* (1969).

The Novels of Feodor Dostoevsky. Trans. by Constance Garnett, 12 vols. (London: W. Heinemann, 1912–20).

The Diary of a Writer. Translated and annotated by Boris Brasol (Santa Barbara: Peregrine Smith, 1979).

Books, theses and articles on Camus's response to Dostoevsky:

(i) *Books and theses:*

Dunwoodie, P., *Une Histoire ambivalente: le dialogue Camus–Dostoïevski* (Paris: Nizet, 1996).

Green, Garrett, *A Kingdom not of this World: A Quest for a Christian Ethic of Revolution with Reference to the Thought of Dostoevsky, Berdyaev and Camus*, Stanford Honors Essays in Humanities, no. 8 (California: Stanford Press, 1964).

Eiche, Eugene, 'Les Personnages dostoïevskiens dans *L'Étranger*' (unpublished doctoral thesis, University of Stafford, 1968; abstract in *DA*, 29 (1969), 2251–58).

Kirk, Irina, *Dostoevskij and Camus: The Themes of Consciousness, Isolation, Freedom and Love* (Munich: Wilhelm Fink Verlag, 1974).

—'Polemics, Ideology, Structure, and Texture in A. Camus's *The Fall* and F. Dostoevsky's *Notes From Underground*' (unpublished doctoral thesis, Indiana University, 1968: in *DA* 29 (1969), 570A).

Natov, N., 'Camus and Dostoevsky: a comparative study' (unpublished doctoral thesis, Michigan University, 1969).

Onimus, Jean (ed.), *Dostoïevski et les lettres françaises* (Actes du colloque de Nice: Centre du xxème siècle, 1981).

Ries, Joachim S., 'Camus the Adaptor: An Analysis of Camus's dramatization of Dostoevsky's novel *The Possessed*' (unpublished doctoral thesis, University of Washington, 1965; in *DA*, 26 (1966), 4673.

Sturm, Ernest, *Conscience et impuissance chez Dostoïevski et Camus* (Paris: Nizet, 1967).

(ii) *Articles:*
(a) Articles of general interest:

Albérès, René M., 'Albert Camus dans son siècle: témoin et étranger', *Table Ronde*, Numéro spécial, no. 146 (février 1960), pp. 9–15.

Batchelor, R., 'Dostoevsky and Camus: Similarities and Contrasts', *Journal of European Studies*, V (June 1975) pp. 1–51.

Bloch-Michel, Jean, Une littérature de l'ennui', *Preuves*, 131 (janvier–juin 1962), pp. 14–23.

Brenner, Jacques, 'L'Homme du souterrain', *Table Ronde*, Numéro spécial, no. 146 (fevrier 1960), pp 99–102.

Brody, E.C., 'Dostoevsky's Kirilov in Camus's *Le Mythe de Sisyphe*', *Modern Language Review*, LXX, 2 (April 1975), pp. 291–305.

—'The Mask and the Substance: The Kirilov theme in Dostoevsky's *The Possessed* and Camus's *Les Possédés*', in M. Szabolsci et G.M. Vajda (eds), *Neohelicon*, III—*Acta comparationis litterarum universarum* (The Hague: Mouton, 1975), pp. 121–70.

—'Dostoevsky's Presence in Camus's Early Works', *Neohelicon*, VIII, (1981), pp. 77–118.

Daniel, J., 'Innocence in Camus and Dostoievsky', in *Camus's L'Étranger: 50 years on*, ed. by A. King pp. 24–35. (New York: St Martin's, 1992), pp. 24–35.

Davison, Ray, 'Clamence et Marmeladov: A Parallel', *Romance Notes*, XIV, 2, (Spring 1972), pp. 226–30.

—'Camus's Attitude to Dostoevsky's Kirilov and the Impact of the Engineer's Ideas on Camus's Early Work', *Orbis Litterarum*, XXX, 3 (1975), pp. 225–40.

Dunwoodie, P., '*La Mort heureuse* et *Crime et châtiment*: une étude comparée', *Revue de littérature comparée*, XLVI, 4 (oct.–déc. 1972), pp. 498–504.

—'*Caligula*: l'univers dostoïevskien et l'évolution de Scipion', *Revue de littérature comparée*, LIII, 2 (avril–juin 1979), pp. 220–30.

Hackel, S., 'Raskolnikov Through the Looking-glass: Dostoevsky and Camus's *L'Étranger*', *Contemporary Literature*, IX (Spring 1968), pp. 208–19.

Haig, S., 'The Epilogue of *Crime and Punishment* and Camus's "La Femme adultère"', *Comparative Literature Studies*, III, 4 (1966), pp. 445–9.

Hassine, J., 'Camus et Dostoïevski ou l'écriture de l'exil et de la culpabilité', *La Revue des lettres modernes*, série Albert Camus, 13 (1989) pp. 65–93.

Herbert, A., 'Dostoïevski, Camus et l'immortalité de l'âme', *Revue de littérature comparée*, LIV, 3 (juillet 1980), pp. 321–35.

Horvath, K., 'Dostoïevski et Camus: introduction à une analyse comparée', *Acta Litteraria Academiae Scientiarum Hungaricae*, XXX, 3–4, (1988), pp. 211–28.

Kirk, Irina, 'Dramatization of Consciousness in Camus and Dostoevsky', *Bucknell Review*, XVI, no. 1 (March 1968), pp. 96–104.

Louria, Yvette, 'Dédoublement in Dostoevsky and Camus', *The Modern Language Review*, LVI, 1 (January 1961), pp. 82–3.

Madaule, Jacques, 'Camus et Dostoïevski', *Table Ronde*, Numéro spécial, no. 146 (février 1960), pp. 127–36.

Magnan-Shardt, M., '*La Chute* comme skaz, une hypothèse génétique', in *La Revue des lettres modernes*, série Albert Camus, 6 (1973).

Marek, Joseph C., 'L'Absence de Dieu et la révolte: Camus et Dostoïevski', *La Revue de L'Université Laval*, X, no. 6 (février 1956), pp. 490–510.

Meszaros, V.B., '*Crime et châtiment* dans l'œuvre de Camus', in *Littérature et réalité* (Budapest: Akademiai Kiado, 1966).

Micha, R., 'L'Agneau dans le placard', *La Nouvelle Revue Française*, Numéro Special, no. 87 (mars 1960), pp. 501–5.

Natov, N., 'Albert Camus's Attitude towards Dostoevsky', *Revue de littérature comparée*, LV, 3–4 (juillet 1981), pp. 439–64.

Perrot, J., 'Le Descartes dostoïevskien de *La Chute* de Camus', *La Revue des lettres modernes*, série Albert Camus 5 (1972), pp. 129–53.

Peyre, H., 'Existentialism: A Literature of Despair', *Yale French Studies*, 1, (1948), pp. 21–41.

Rawa, T., 'Camus et Dostoïevski: quelques analogies textuelles', *La Revue des langues vivantes*, XXXVIII, 5 (1972), pp. 452–66.

Roberts, C.H., 'Camus et Dostoïevski: comparaison structurale et thématique de *La Chute* de Camus et du *Sous-Sol* de Dostoïevski', *La Revue des lettres modernes*, série Albert Camus, 4 (1971), pp. 52–70.

Sellin, E., 'Meursault et Myshkin on Executions: A Parallel', *Romance Notes*, X, 1 (autumn 1968), pp. 11–14.

Sperber, M.A., 'Symptoms and Structure of Borderline Personality Organization: Camus's *The Fall* and Dostoevsky's *Notes from Underground*', *Literature and Psychology*, XXIII, 3 (1973) pp. 102–13.

Strem, George, 'The Theme of Rebellion in the Works of Camus and Dostoevsky', *Revue de littérature comparée*, XI, no. 1 (1966), pp. 246–57.

Trahan, Elizabeth, 'Clamence vs. Dostoevsky: An Approach to *La Chute*', *Comparative Literature*, XVIII, no. 4 (Fall 1966), pp. 337–50.

Vincent, J., 'Le Mythe de Kirilov: Camus, Dostoïevski et les traducteurs', *Comparative Literature Studies*, VIII, 3 (September 1971), pp. 245–53.

Wasiolek, E., 'Dostoevsky, Camus and Faulkner: Transcendance and Mutilation', *Philosophy and Literature*, 1, 2 (Spring 1977), pp. 131–46.

(b) Articles on the adaptation of *Les Possédés*:

The following articles from the *Fonds Rondel* discuss Camus's dramatization of *Les Possédés*. As already explained, this collection is in the *Bibliothèque de L'Arsenal* in Paris. Unfortunately, page references to the newspapers from which the articles are taken are not given in the collection.

Anon., '20 Millions, 33 Acteurs, 180 répétitions, 26 changements de décors en 3h. 30 de spectacle pour *Les Possédés* au Théâtre Antoine', *France-Soir* (janvier 28, 1959).

—'Pour adapter *Les Possédés* au Théâtre Antoine, Camus a battu le record des répétitions', *Aurore* (janvier 25, 1959).

—'*Les Possédés*', *Journal de Genève* (février 21, 1959).

—'*Les Possédés*', *Le Figaro* (janvier 16, 1959).

Berger, Pierre, '*Les Possédés*: une aventure de la fidélité', *Paris-Journal* (janvier 31, 1959).

—'*Les Possédés* vont à Vénise', *Paris-Journal* (mai 26, 1959).

Blanchar, Pierre, *Le Figaro* (janvier 5, 1960).

Cézar, Claude, 'Albert Camus adapte Dostoïevski', *Les Nouvelles Littéraires* (janvier 29, 1959).

Favalelli, Max, '*Les Possédés* d'Albert Camus d'après Dostoïevski', *Paris-Presse* (janvier 31, 1959).

Fayard, Jean, 'Soirée Dostoïevski-Camus au Théâtre Antoine', *Le Figaro* (janvier 30, 1959).

Gordeaux, Paul, '*Les Possédés*, pièce en trois parties d'Albert Camus, d'après le roman de Dostoïevski', *France-Soir* (janvier 31, 1959).

Jotterand, Franck, '*Les Possédés* de Dostoïevski adaptés par Camus', *La Gazette de Lausanne* (février 7, 1959).

July, G., 'Albert Camus présente les *Possédés* au Théâtre Antoine . . . c'est une éclatante réussite', *Aurore* (janvier 31, 1959).

Kanters, Robert, '*Les Possédés*', *L'Express* (février 5, 1959).

Kemp, Robert, '*Les Possédés* au Théâtre Antoine', *Le Monde* (janvier 31, 1959).

Leclerc, Guy, 'Au Théâtre Antoine. Les *Possédés* de Dostoïevski (adaptation d'Albert Camus). Un long spectacle'. *L'Humanité* (janvier 31, 1959).

Lerminier, Georges, '*Les Possédés* d'Albert Camus d'après le roman de Dostoïevski', *Parisien Libéré* (janvier 31, 1959).

M[arcabru], P[ierre], 'Après l'échec de Copeau et de Baty, Camus réussira-t-il?', *Arts* (janvier 28, 1959).

—'Ni Camus ni Dostoïevski', *Arts* (février 4, 1959).

Marcel, Gabriel, '*Les Possédés*: un roman fleuve endigué par Albert Camus', *Les Nouvelles Littéraires* (février 5, 1959).

Morelle, Paul, '*Les Possédés* au Théâtre Antoine', *Libération* (janvier 31, 1959).

Pascal, Jacques, 'Albert Camus a adapté et mis en scène les *Possédés* de Dostoïevski', *Réforme* (février 4, 1959).

Robin, Jean-François, 'Mayo est passé du réalisme à l'impressionnisme'. *Combat* (janvier 22, 1959).

Sarraute, Claude, 'Albert Camus présente les *Possédés* de Dostoïevski', *Le Monde* (janvier 22, 1959).

Spiraux, Alain, 'Le 29 Janvier au Théâtre Antoine les *Possédés* débutent à 20 hrs', *Combat* (janvier 17, 1959).

—'La Presse parisienne partagée au sujet des *Possédés* d'Albert Camus au Théâtre Antoine', *Combat* (février 3, 1959).

Trevenon, Patrick, 'A. Camus oblige ses 23 acteurs à boire le vodka et écouter le folklore russe', *Paris-Presse* (janvier 17, 1959).

Vallacri, Stephane, '*Les Possédés* de Camus' *Lettres Françaises* (février 5, 1959).

Vigneron, Jean, 'Les *Possédés* d'Albert Camus, d'après Dostoïevski', *Le Ciné* (février 5, 1959).

The authorship of the following articles from the *Fonds Rondel* is uncertain.

T. (?), 'Les *Possédés* de Dostoïevski et Camus', *Le Canard Enchaîné* (février 4, 1959).

J.A. (?), 'Camus: les *Possédés* voués au triomphe', *Paris-Journal* (janvier 17, 1959).

Other articles on *Les Possédés:*

Alter, André, 'Une Union prophétique et réaliste', *Témoignage Chrétien* (février 6, 1959), p. 15.

—'Les *Possédés*', *Revue de la Société d'Histoire du Théâtre*, XII, no. 4 (1960), pp. 321–36.

Chiaromonte, Nicola, 'Camus e Stavroguine', *Il Mondo*, XI, no. 8 (febb. 24, 1959), p. 15.

Gouhier, Henri, 'A. Camus et le théâtre', *Table Ronde*, Numéro spécial, no. 146 (fevrier 1960), pp. 62–66.

Gourfinkel, Nina, 'Les *Possédés*', *Revue de la Société d'Histoire du Théâtre*, XII, no. 4 (1960), pp. 337–42.

Gutierrez, Felix, 'Pastiche', *Mainstream*, XIII, no. 5 (May 1960), pp. 62–3.

Hope–Wallace, P., '*The Possessed* at the Mermaid', *The Guardian* (25 October 1963).

Lebesque, Morvan, 'Bilan Positif', *Carrefour*, XVI, no. 751 (février 4, 1959) p. 11.

Lemarchand, Jacques, 'Les *Possédés* d'Albert Camus d'après Dostoïevski au Théâtre Antoine', *Le Figaro Littéraire* (février 7, 1959) p. 12.

Mazars, Pierre, 'En adaptant les *Possédés* . . .', *Le Figaro Littéraire* (janvier 24, 1959), p. 12 and p. 14.

Onimus, Jean, 'Camus adapte à la scène Faulkner et Dostoïevski', *Revue des Sciences Humaines*, N. 5, fasc. 104 (octobre–décembre 1961), pp. 607–21.

Poulet, Robert, 'Pourquoi adapte-t-il au lieu d'écrire? Voici le secret d'Albert Camus', *Carrefour*, XVI no. 754 (février 25, 1959), p. 12.

Ramsay, W., 'Albert Camus on Capital Punishment: His Adaptation of *The Possessed*', *Yale Review*, LXVIII (June 4, 1959).

Rousseau, A.M., 'L'Adaptation scénique des *Possédés* de Dostoïevski par Albert Camus', in Actes du Ve Congrès international de littérature comparée [Belgrade 1976] (Amsterdam: Swets & Zeitlinger, 1969).

Saurel, Renée, 'Les Possédés', Les *Temps Modernes*, XIV (février–mars 1959), pp. 1508–9.

Vascaux, Gabriel, 'Dostoïevski chez Antoine', *Cahiers des Saisons*, no. 16 (Printemps 1959), pp. 75–6.

Wilson, Colin, '*The Possessed*, a Play by Albert Camus', *The Listener*, LXIV, no. 1636 (August 4, 1960), p. 195.

Critical works and articles used or found useful:

Albérès, René M., 'Ambiguïtés de la révolte', *La Revue de Paris*, LX (juin 1953), pp. 57–66.

—*Les Hommes traqués* (Paris, 1953).

Arban, Dominique, *Dostoïevski le coupable* (Paris: Julliard, 1953).

—*Dostoïevski par lui-même* (Paris: Éditions du Seuil, 1962).

—'Entretien avec Albert Camus', *Opéra* (octobre 17, 1945), p. 2.

Ayer, A.J., *Novelist-Philosophers, Horizon*, XIII (March 1946), pp. 155–68.

Backès, M.J.L., '*Dostoïevski en France*, 1884–1930,' (Thèse de doctorat d'état, Paris, Sorbonne (1971)).

Bakhtine, M., *La Poétique de Dostoïevski*, trans. by I. Kolitcheff, Introduction J. Kristeva (Paris: Seuil, 1970).

Batt, Jean, 'Albert Camus: from *The Myth* to *The Fall*', *Meanjin*, XVI, no. 4 (Summer 1957), pp. 411–19.

—'Albert Camus: a Tribute', *Meanjin*, XIX, no. 1 (Spring 1960), pp. 55–8.

Béguin, Albert, 'Albert Camus, la révolte et le bonheur', *Esprit*, XX, no. 4 (avril 1952), pp. 736–46.

Beigbeder, Marc, 'Le Monde n'est pas absurde', *Esprit*, XIII, no. 3 (février 1945), pp. 415–19.

Bespaloff, Rachel, 'Réflexions sur l'esprit de la tragédie', *Deucalion*, II (1947), pp. 171–93.

Blanchet, André, '*L'Homme révolté* d'Albert Camus', *Etudes*, I (janvier 1952), pp. 48–60.

—'La Vie littéraire: la querelle Sartre-Camus', *Etudes*, II (novembre 1952), pp. 238–46.

—'Pari d'Albert Camus', *Etudes*, V (mai 1960), pp. 183–99.

—'Pari d'Albert Camus (suite)', *Etudes*, VI (juin 1960), pp. 330–44.

Bloch, Haskell, M., 'Albert Camus: Towards a Definition of Tragedy', *University of Toronto Quarterly*, CXIX, no. 4 (July 1950), pp. 354–60.

Bloch-Michell, Jean, 'A. Camus et la tentation de l'innocence', *Preuves*, no. 110 (avril 1964), pp. 3–9.

—'Les Intermittences de la mémoire', *Preuves*, 155 (janvier 1964), pp. 66–70.

Bonnier, Henri, *Albert Camus ou la force d'être* (Paris: Vitte, 1959).

Brée, Germaine, *Albert Camus* (New Brunswick: Rutgers University Press, 1959).

Brisville, Jean-Claude, *Camus* (Paris: Gallimard, 1959).

Brombert, Victor, 'Camus and the Novel of the "Absurd"', *Yale French Studies*, I, no. 1 (Spring–Summer 1948), pp. 119–23.

Carr, Edward H., *Dostoevsky 1821–1881* (London: Unwin Books, 1962).

Catteau, J., *La Création littéraire chez Dostoïevski* (Paris: 1978).

—(ed.), '*Dostoïevski*', Cahiers de l'Herne, 1983.

Champigny, Robert, 'Existentialism in the Modern French Novel', *Thought*, XXXI, no. 122 (Autumn 1956), pp. 365–84.

—'Camus's Fictional Works: the Plight of Innocence', *The American Society Legion of Honor Magazine*, XXVIII, no. 2 (Summer 1957), pp. 173–82.

—'The Comedy of Ethics', *Yale French Studies*, XXV (Spring 1960), pp. 72–4.

—*Sur un Héros païen* (Paris: Gallimard, 1959).

Chapple, R., *A Dostoevsky Dictionary* (Michigan: Ardis, 1944).

Clive, Geoffrey, 'The Sickness unto Death in the Underworld: a Study of Nihilism', *Harvard Theological Review*, I, no. 3 (July 1958), pp. 135–67.

Coombs, I., *Camus homme de théâtre* (Paris: Nizet, 1968).

Couch, John Philip, 'Albert Camus: Dramatic Adaptations and Translations', *French Review*, XXXIII, no. 1 (October 1959), pp. 27–36.

—'Camus and Faulkner: The Search for the Language of Modern Tragedy', *Yale French Studies*, XXV (Spring 1960), pp. 120–25.

Cruickshank, John, *Albert Camus and the Literature of Revolt* (Oxford: University Press, 1960).

—(ed.), *The Novelist as Philosopher: Studies in French Fiction, 1935–1960* (Oxford: University Press, 1962).

Curle, Richard, *Characters of Dostoevsky* (London: Heinemann, 1950).

Davison, Ray, (ed.), *L'Étranger*. (London: Routledge, 1988).

Devismes, Le Président, *La Justice selon Albert Camus* (Melun: Imprimerie Administrative, 1960).

Durand, Anne, *Le Cas Albert Camus* (Paris: Hachette, 1961).

Du Rostu, 'Un Pascal sans Christ: Albert Camus I', *Etudes*, CCLXVII (octobre 1945), pp. 48–65.

—'Un Pascal sans Christ: Albert Camus II', *Etudes*, CCLXVII (novembre 1945), pp. 165–77.

Fouton, Antonio, 'Camus entre le Paganisme et le Christianisme', *Table Ronde*, Numéro spécial, no. 146 (février 1960), pp. 114–15.

Frank, J., *The Years of Revolt, 1821–49* (Princeton: 1976).

—*The Years of Ordeal, 1850–59* (Princeton: 1983).

—*The Stir of Liberation, 1860–65* (Princeton: 1986).

—*The Miraculous Years, 1865–71* (Princeton: 1995).

Gadourek, Carina, *Les Innocents et les coupables* (The Hague: Mouton, 1963).

Gagnebin Laurent, *Albert Camus dans sa lumière* (Lausanne: Cahiers de la Renaissance Vaudoise, 46, 1964).

Gay-Crosier, R., (ed.), *Albert Camus, textes, intertextes, contextes autour de 'La Chute'*, série Albert Camus, 15 (Paris: Lettres Modernes, 1993).

—*Les Envers d'un échec: étude sur le théâtre d'Albert Camus* (Paris: Minard, 1967).

Gélinas, Germain-Paul, *La Liberté dans la pensée d'Albert Camus* (Fribourg: Éditions Universitaires, 1965).

Gide, André, *Dostoïevski* (Paris: Plon, 1923).

Ginestier, Paul, *La Pensée de Camus* (Paris: Bordas, 1964),

Gouhier, Henri, 'Sens du Tragique', *La Revue Théâtrale*, no. 1 (mai-juin 1946), pp. 26–34.

Gourfinkel, Nina, *Dostoïevski notre contemporain* (Paris: Calmann Levy, 1961).

Grenier, Jean, *Albert Camus (Souvenirs)* (Paris: Gallimard, 1968).

—'Un Oui, un non, une ligne droite', *Le Figaro littéraire* (octobre 26, 1957), p. 1 and p.5.

Guardini, R., *L'Univers religieux de Dostoïevski*, trans. by H. Romano, H. Engelmann et R. Givord (Paris: Éditions du Seuil, 1948).

Guérard, A.J., 'Albert Camus et le refus de l'éternel', *L'Arche*, no. VI (octobre–novembre 1944), pp. 158–163.

Guérin, Jeanyves, *Camus et la politique*, Actes du colloque de Nanterre, 5–7 juin, 1985.(Paris: Editions L'Harmattau, 1986).

Hemmings, Frederick W.J., *The Russian Novel in France 1884–1914* (Oxford: University Press, 1950).

Hingley, Ronald, *The Undiscovered Dostoevsky* (London: Hamish Hamilton, 1962).

Ivanov, Vyacheslav, *Freedom and the Tragic Life: A Study on Dostoevsky*, trans. by Norman Cameron (New York: Noonday, 1957).

Jackson, Robert, L., *Dostoevsky's Underground Man in Russian Literature* (The Hague: Mouton, 1958).

Jones, M.V., *Dostoevsky after Bakhtin* (London: C.U.P., 1990).

Katkov, G., 'Steerforth and Stavrogin: On The Sources of *The Possessed*', *The Slavonic Review*, XXVII, no. 69 (May, 1949), pp. 469–88.

Kauffmann, Walter A. (ed.), *Existentialism from Dostoevsky to Sartre* (New York: Meridian Books, 1956).

—*Religion from Tolstoy to Camus* (New York: Harper, 1961).

—'Existentialism and Death', *Chicago Review*, XIII, no. 2 (Summer 1959), pp. 75–93.

Lafon, Noël, 'Albert Camus à *Combat*: de la résistance à la révolution', *La Revue Socialiste*, no. 191 (mars 1966), pp. 235–55, and no. 193 (mai 1966), pp. 449–70.

Lirondelle, A., 'Le Roman russe en France à la fin du XIXe siècle', *Revue des Cours et Conférences* (juillet 30, 1925), pp. 723–4.

Loose, John, 'The Christian as Camus's Absurd Man', *Journal of Religion*, XLII, no. 3 (July 1962), pp. 203–14.

Lottman, Herbert R., *Albert Camus* (Paris: Seuil, 1978).

Magarshack, David, *Dostoevsky* (London: Secker and Warburg, 1962).

Maquet, Albert, *Albert Camus ou l'invincible été* (Paris: Debresse, 1955).

Molnar, Thomas, 'On Camus and Capital Punishment', *Modern Age*, II, no. 3 (Summer 1958), pp. 298–306.

Mounier, Emmanuel, 'Albert Camus ou l'appel des humiliés', *Esprit*, XVIII, no. 163 (janvier 1950), pp. 27–66.

Muchulsky, Konstantin, *Dostoevsky*, trans. with an introduction by M.A. Minihan (Princeton: University Press, 1967).

Nelson, Brian (ed.), *Forms of Commitment: Intellectuals in Contemporary France*, Monash Romance Studies, I (Melbourne: Aristoc Press, 1995).

Nicholas, André, *Une Philosophie de l'existence: Albert Camus* (Paris: Presses Universitaires de France, 1964).

Nguyen-Van-Huy, Pierre, *La Métaphysique du bonheur chez Albert Camus* (Neuchâtel: La Baconnière, 1962).

Onimus, Jean, *Camus: face au mystère* (Bruges: Desclée de Brouwer, 1965).

Papamalamis, Dmitris, *Albert Camus et la pensée grecque* (Nancy-Saint-Nicholas du Port: Imprimerie V. Idrux, 1965).

Peyre, Henri, 'Albert Camus, an Anti-Christian Moralist', *American Philosophical Society*, CII, no. 5 (October 20, 1958), pp. 477–82.

—'The Ideas Men Lived by Wouldn't Do', *The New York Times Book Review* (October 4, 1959), p. 4.

—'An Algerian Sun Lights Europe's Fog', *The New York Times Book Review* (April 5, 1959), p. 1 and p. 30.

—'Camus the Pagan', *Yale French Studies*, XXV (Spring 1960), pp. 20–25.

—'Pascal and our Contemporaries', *The American Society Legion of Honor Magazine*, XXXV, no. 2 (1964), pp. 75–85.

Quilliot, Roger, *La Mer et les prisons* (Paris: Gallimard, 1956).

—'Un monde ambigu', *Preuves*, CX (avril 1960), pp. 28–38.

—'Albert Camus et L'Étranger', *La Revue Socialiste*, no. 154 (juin 1962), pp. 32–9.

Ramsey, Warren, 'Albert Camus on Capital Punishment', *Yale Review*, XLVIII, no. 4 (June 1959), p. 12.

Revue d'histoire du théâtre, 'Albert Camus, homme de théâtre', numéro spécial, XII, no. 4 (octobre–décembre, 1960), pp. 317–59.

Sajkovic, Miriam T., *Dostoevsky: His Image of Man* (Pennsylvania: University Press, 1962).

Sarocchi, J., *Le Dernier Camus ou le premier homme* (Paris: Nizet, 1995).

Sarraute, Nathalie, *L'Ere du soupçon* (Paris: Gallimard, 1956).

Sartre, Jean-Paul, *Situations*, I (Paris: Gallimard, 1947).

—*L'Existentialisme est un humanisme* (Paris: Nagel, 1951).

Schlœzer, Boris de, 'Les Brouillons des *Frères Karamazov*' Mesures (octobre 15, 1935).

Scott, Nathan A., *Albert Camus* (New York: Hillary House, 1962).

Simmons, Ernest J., *Dostoevsky: The Making of a Novelist* (London: John Lehman, 1950).

Simon, Pierre-Henri, *Présence de Camus* (Bruxelles: Renaissance du Livre, 1961).

St Aubyn, F.C. 'Albert Camus and the Death of the Other: An Existentialist Interpretation', *French Studies*, XVI, no. 2 (April 1962), pp. 124–41.

Steiner, George, *Tolstoi or Dostoevsky* (London: Faber and Faber, 1959).

Thody, Philip, *Albert Camus: A Study of his Work* (London: Hamish Hamilton, 1957).

—*Albert Camus 1913–1960* (London, Hamish Hamilton, 1960).

—*Twentieth-Century Literature: Critical Issues and Themes* (London: Macmillan, 1996).

Thoorens, Léon, *Albert Camus* (Paris: La Sixaine, 1946).

Todd, Olivier, *Albert Camus: une vie* (Paris: Gallimard, 1996).

Troyat, Henri, *Dostoïevski* (Paris: Fayard, 1948).

Viggiani, Carl A., 'Albert Camus and the Fall from Innocence', *Yale French Studies*, XXV (Spring 1960), pp. 65–71.

—'Albert Camus's First Publications', *Modern Languages Notes*, LXXV, no. 7 (November 1960), pp. 589–96.

Walker, David H. (ed.), *Albert Camus: les extrêmes et l'équilibre*. Actes du colloque de Keele, 25–29 mars 1993 (Amsterdam-Atlanta: Rodopi, 1994).

—'Camus at the Crossroads', *Twentieth Century*, CLXVI, no. 990 (August 1950), pp. 73–7.

—'The Early Camus—a Reconsideration', *The Philosophical Journal*, II, no. 2 (1965), pp. 91–103.

Weber, Robert W., 'Raskolnikov, Addie Bundren, Meursault: sur la continuité d'un mythe', *Archiv für das Studium der Neueren Sprachen* (August 1965), pp. 81–92.

Wellek, René, *Dostoevsky: A Collection of Critical Essays* (Englewood Cliffs: Prentice Hall, 1962).

Yalom, Marilyn E., '*La Chute* and a *Hero of our Time*', *French Review*, XXXVI, no. 2 (December 1962), pp. 138–45.

—'Albert Camus and the Myth of the Trial', *Modern Languages Quarterly*, XXV, no. 4 (December 1964), pp. 434–50.

Index